Michael Faulkner
March 2006

Walking in America

Walking in America

Edited by
DONALD ZOCHERT

Illustrated by
LASZLO KUBINYI

Alfred A. Knopf   New York   1975

THIS IS A BORZOI BOOK
PUBLISHED BY ALFRED A. KNOPF, INC.

Library of Congress Cataloging in Publication Data

Zochert, Donald, comp.   Walking in America.

    CONTENTS: Thoreau, H. D. The fluvial walk.—Muir, J. A thousand-mile walk to the Gulf.—Derleth, A. Quiet streets, empty roads. [etc.]
    1. American prose literature.   2. Walking—Addresses, essays, lectures.
3. United States—Description and travel.   I. Title.
PS648.W3Z6   814'.008'03   74–7750
ISBN 0–394–48711–7

Manufactured in the United States of America

Published November 29, 1974
Second Printing, May 1975

Acknowledgments

"A Thousand-Mile Walk to the Gulf" is abridged from A *Thousand-Mile Walk to the Gulf*, by John Muir, edited by William Frederick Bade. Copyright © 1916 by Houghton Mifflin Co. Reprinted by permission of Houghton Mifflin Co.

"Quiet Streets, Empty Roads" is a selected collection from *Countryman's Journal*, by August Derleth, copyright © 1963 by August Derleth; and *Wisconsin Country: A Sac Prairie Journal*, by August Derleth, copyright © 1965 by August Derleth. Reprinted by permission of the August Derleth Estate.

"The Lure of Doonerak" is from *Arctic Wilderness*, by Robert Marshall, edited by George Marshall. It was originally published by the University of California Press in 1956. Reprinted by permission of The Regents of the University of California.

"Hobnobbing" is from *The American Notebooks*, by Nathaniel Hawthorne, edited by Claude M. Simpson (pp. 340–3, 394–7). Volume III of the Centenary Edition of the Works of Nathaniel Hawthorne, edited by William Charvat (1905–1966), Roy Harvey Pearce, and Claude M. Simpson; Fredson Bowers, textual editor. Copyright © 1932, 1960, and 1972 by the Ohio State University Press. Reprinted by permission of the editors and the Ohio State University Press.

"The Hounds of Darkness" is from *The Night Country*, by Loren Eiseley. Copyright © 1971 by Loren Eiseley. Reprinted by permission of Charles Scribner's Sons.

"Brahmin in the Wilderness" is from *The Journals of Francis Parkman*, Volume I, by Francis Parkman, edited by Mason Wade. Copyright © 1947 by the Massachusetts Historical Society. Reprinted by permission of Harper & Row, Inc.

"The Peaceable Kingdom" is from *The Harvest of a Quiet Eye*, by Odell Shepard. Copyright © 1927 and 1955 by Odell Shepard. Reprinted by permission of Houghton Mifflin Co.

"Leaving the Surface" is from *The Man Who Walked Through Time*, by Colin Fletcher. Copyright © 1967 by Colin Fletcher. Reprinted by permission of Alfred A. Knopf, Inc.

"Why Not Go Home Tonight?" is from *Of Men and Mountains*, by William O. Douglas. Copyright © 1950, by William Douglas. Reprinted by permission of Harper & Row, Inc.

"The Cedar Chopper" is from *Adventures with a Texas Naturalist*, New (Revised) Edition. Copyright © 1961 by Lillian G. Bedichek. Reprinted by permission of the University of Texas Press.

"An Inland Stroll" is from *The Outermost House*, by Henry Beston. Copyright © 1928, 1949, and 1956 by Henry Beston. Reprinted by permission of Holt, Rinehart and Winston, Inc.

For Nancy

*"Not that I have already obtained,
but I press on"*

—ST. PAUL

Contents

Preface

Sometimes it is easier to say what a thing is not than what it is. This is not a book about how to walk, where to walk, or why to walk. It is not an apologia for feet, a condemnation of the wheel, or a geography of anything but the spirit. This is a book of experience, by men who went out singly or together—sometimes with their blood up, sometimes at a saunter—to see what lay beyond the hill, or within themselves. It is a record of men who marched upon discoveries in America.

The walking papers collected here are written by various hands. They tell of endless trails that led beyond the paths of men; of women tucked away in lonely cabins believing the world was soon to end; of a man who danced like the light and made a sound like swarming bees, and another who talked to himself behind the screen of a summer night. They tell of places where everything may be seen, and nothing recognized; and places where nothing may be seen. They tell of small towns, back roads, wilderness—real and imagined; of freedom, of terrors, of mystery and beauty; and not a little of that sufficient spirit known only to those who are on their own. They tell of an America to be found only on foot.

There is a considerable amount of literature on walking in America, from which these accounts are drawn. Little of this literature has survived its original publication. That by professional pedestrians is often dull and plodding. Some claims distinction only through an intriguing title—*Fast and Loose in Dixie*, for example—and then disappoints. Much is devoted more to nature than to walking. These have been avoided, not out of prejudice to what they represent but from a desire to concentrate on the experience of walking in America well-told. For the same reason, many fine essays *about* walking—Thoreau's classic essay, for one—have also been excluded. What remains are the accounts of men who walked out upon America with a clear and eager eye, and put down their actual experience with honesty and without artifice. What remains, hopefully, is the spirit of walking in America.

In this regard, Henry Beston, in a letter to the poet David McCord, passed on a strange story which had been related to him second- or third-hand. It seems a certain scholar was awakened in the middle of the night with a verse "ringing through his head." He jotted it down, as a scholar is likely to do, and fell back to sleep—certain, in that half-awake moment, that he had recorded something of the utmost importance. In the morning he felt otherwise, for this is what he had written:

> *Walker with one eye,*
> *Walker with two.*
> *Something to live for*
> *And nothing to do.*

Yet perhaps this would-be poet underestimated the power of his mind at rest, for his compelling dactyls have the rhythm of walking, and his final lines carry the edge of expectancy held by all who would march upon discoveries in America. This book is for such as these: for walkers with one eye and walkers with two, with something to live for, and nothing to do.

DONALD ZOCHERT

HENRY DAVID THOREAU

The Fluvial Walk

"Here is a road where no dust was ever known . . ."

Henry David Thoreau hardly needs an introduction; he traveled a great deal in Concord. Few of his walks, however, were as refreshing—or as novel—as the one which he took down the middle of the Assabet River on a sweltering summer day in 1852, clad only in a shirt and hat "to protect your exposed parts from the sun." Genius in this case was composed equally of inspiration and perspiration. Thoreau was 35 years old at the time—in fact, the second passage below occurred on his birthday. We shall meet him again on higher ground.

This account is taken from Thoreau's journal entries of July 10 and July 12, 1852, in The Writings of Henry David Thoreau. Journal, *edited by Bradford Torrey.*

Another day, if possible still hotter than the last. We have already had three or four such, and still no rain. The soil under the sward in the yard is dusty as an ash-heap for a foot in depth, and young trees are suffering and dying. . . . It is with a suffocating sensation and a slight pain in the head that I walk the Union Turnpike where the heat is reflected from the road. The leaves of the elms on the dry highways begin to roll up. I have to lift my hat to let the air cool my head. But I find a refreshing breeze from over the river and meadow. . . .

The long, narrow open intervals in the woods near the Assabet are quite dry now, in some parts yellow with the upright loosestrife. One of these meadows, a quarter of a mile long by a few rods wide, narrow and winding and bounded on all sides by maples, showing the undersides of their leaves, swamp white oaks with their glossy dark-green leaves, and birches, etc., and full of meadow-sweet just coming into bloom and cranberry vines and a dry kind of grass, is a very attractive place to walk in.

We undressed on this side, carried our clothes down in the stream a considerable distance, and finally bathed in earnest from the opposite side. The heat tempted us to prolong this luxury. . . . The river has here a sandy bottom and is for the most part quite shallow. I made quite an excursion up and down it in the water, a fluvial, a water walk. It seemed the properest highway for this weather. Now in water a foot or two deep, now suddenly descending through valleys up to my neck, but all alike agreeable. . . . When I had left the river and walked in the woods for some time, and jumped into the river again, I was surprised to find for the first time how warm it was,—as it seemed to me, almost warm enough to boil eggs,—like water that has stood a considerable while in a kettle over a fire.

There are many interesting objects of study as you walk up and down a clear river like this in the water, where you can see every inequality in the bottom and every object on it. The breams' nests are interesting and even handsome, and the shallow water in them over the sand is so warm to my hand that I think their ova will soon be hatched. Also the numerous heaps of stones, made I know not certainly by what fish, many of them rising above the surface. There are weeds on the bottom which remind you of the sea. . . . The bottom is also scored with furrows made by the clams moving about, sometimes a rod long; and always the clam lies at one end. So this fish can change its position and get into deeper and cooler water. I was in doubt before whether the clam made these furrows, for one apparently fresh that I examined had a "mud clam" at the end; but these, which were very numerous, had living clams.

There are but few fishes to be seen. They have, no doubt, retreated to the deepest water. In one somewhat muddier place, close to the shore, I came upon an old pout cruising with her young. She dashed away at my approach, but the fry remained. They were of various sizes from a third of an inch to an inch and a half long, quite black and pout-shaped, except that the head was most developed in the smallest. They were constantly moving about in a somewhat circular, or rather lenticular, school, about fifteen or eighteen inches in diameter, and I estimated that there were at least a thousand of them. Presently the old pout came back and took the lead of her brood, which followed her, or rather gathered about her, like chickens about a hen; but this mother had so many children she didn't know what to do. Her maternal yearnings must be on a great scale. When one half of the divided school found her out, they came down upon her and completely invested her like a small cloud. She was soon joined by another smaller pout, apparently her mate, and all, both old and young, began to be very familiar with me; they came round my legs and felt them with their feelers, and the old pouts nibbled my toes, while the fry half concealed my feet. Probably if I had been standing on the bank with my clothes on they would have been more

shy. Ever and anon the old pouts dashed aside to drive away a passing bream or perch. The larger one kept circling about her charge, as if to keep them together within a certain compass. If any of her flock were lost or devoured she could hardly have missed them. I wondered if there was any calling of the roll at night,—whether she, like a faithful shepherdess, ever told her tale under some hawthorn in the river's dales. Ever ready to do battle with the wolves that might break into her fold. The young pouts are protected then for a season by the old. Some had evidently been hatched before the others. One of these large pouts had a large velvet-black spot which included the right pectoral fin, a kind of disease which I have often observed on them.

I wonder if any Roman emperor ever indulged in such luxury as this,—of walking up and down a river in torrid weather with only a hat to shade the head. What were the baths of Caracalla to this? Now we traverse a long water plain some two feet deep; now we descend into a darker river valley, where the bottom is lost sight of and the water rises to our armpits; now we go over a hard iron pan; now we stoop and go under a low bough of the *Salix nigra*; now we slump into soft mud amid the pads of the *Nymphaea odorata*, at this hour shut. On this road there is no other traveller to turn out for.

When I first came out of the water, the short, dry grass was burning hot to my bare feet, and my skin was soon parched and dry in the sun.

We finally return to the dry land, and recline in the shade of an apple tree on a bank overlooking the meadow. I still hear the bobo-link. (There are comparatively few clams in the sandy Assabet, but methinks there are more than usual everywhere this year.) The stones lying in the sun on this hillside where the grass has been cut are as hot to the hand as an egg just boiled, and very uncomfortable to hold, so do they absorb the heat. Every hour we expect a thundershower to cool the air, but none comes.

Now for another fluvial walk. There is always a current of air above the water, blowing up or down the course of the river, so that this is the coolest highway. Divesting yourself of all clothing but your shirt and hat, which are to protect your exposed parts from the sun, you are prepared for the fluvial excursion. You choose what depths you like, tucking your toga higher or lower, as you take the deep middle of the road or the shallow sidewalks. Here is a road where no dust was ever known, no intolerable drouth.

Now your feet expand on a smooth sandy bottom, now contract timidly on pebbles, now slump in genial fatty mud—greasy, saponaceous—amid the pads. You scare out whole schools of small breams and perch, and sometimes a pickerel, which have taken shelter from the sun under the pads. This river is so clear compared with the South Branch, or main stream, that all their secrets are betrayed to you. Or you meet with and interrupt a turtle taking a more leisurely walk up the stream. Ever and anon you cross some furrow in the sand, made by a muskrat, leading off to right or left to their galleries in the bank, and you thrust your foot into the entrance, which is just below the surface of the water and is strewn with grass and rushes, of which they make their nests. In shallow water near the shore, your feet at once detect the presence of springs in the bank emptying in, by the sudden coolness of the water, and there, if you are thirsty, you dig a little well in the sand with your hands, and when you return, after it has settled and clarified itself, get a draught of pure cold water there. . . .

I hear the toads still at night, together with bullfrogs, but not so universally nor loud as formerly. I go to walk at twilight,—at the same time that toads go to their walks, and are seen hopping about the sidewalks or the pump. Now, a quarter after nine, as I walk along the river-bank, long after starlight, and perhaps an hour or more after sunset, I see some of those high-pillared clouds of the day, in the southwest, still reflecting a downy light from the regions of day, they are so high. It is a pleasing reminiscence of the day in the midst of the deepening shadows of the night. The dor-bugs hum around me, as I sit on the river-bank beyond the ash tree. Warm as is the night,— one of the warmest in the whole year,—there is an aurora, a low arc of a circle, in the north. The twilight ends to-night apparently about a quarter before ten. There is no moon.

JOHN MUIR

A Thousand-Mile Walk to the Gulf

"My plan was simply to push on . . . by the wildest, leafiest, and least trodden way I could find."

Late in the summer of 1867—the clouds of civil war had yet to settle—a solitary figure made his way quickly through the streets of Louisville and stepped off on a thousand-mile walk to the Gulf of Mexico. Lean and blue-eyed, John Muir was 29 years old. Born in Scotland and raised in the lake country of central Wisconsin, he had quit his job at an Indianapolis wagon factory to make this grand adventure to what he called "the Florida of my dreams." One day his name would be given to a wilderness far to the west in California; he would lose his heart to the mountains, and establish the Sierra Club. But in 1867 he was still anonymous: a tinkerer, an inventor, a farmboy whose passion was botany. He was an innocent abroad in search of flowers, walking an America which grew more mysterious with every step. And he found more than flowers.

This account is taken from John Muir's A Thousand-Mile Walk to the Gulf, *edited by William Frederick Bade. Most of the strictly botanical observations have been omitted.*

I had long been looking from the wild woods and gardens of the Northern States to those of the warm South, and at last, all drawbacks overcome, I set forth on the first day of September, 1867, joyful and free, on a thousand-mile walk to the Gulf of Mexico. Crossing the Ohio at Louisville, I steered through the big city by compass without speaking a word to anyone. Beyond the city I found a road running southward, and after passing a scatterment of suburban cabins and cottages I reached the green woods and spread out my pocket map to rough-hew a plan for my journey.

My plan was simply to push on in a general southward direction by the wildest, leafiest, and least trodden way I could find, promising the greatest extent of virgin forest. Folding my map, I shouldered my little bag and plant press and strode away among the old Kentucky oaks, rejoicing in splendid visions of pines and palms and tropic flowers in glorious array, not, however, without a few cold shadows of loneliness, although the great oaks seemed to spread their arms in welcome. Walked twenty miles, mostly on river bottom, and found shelter in a rickety tavern.

September 3. Escaped from the dust and squalor of my garret bedroom to the glorious forest. For a few hours I followed the farmers' paths, but soon wandered away from the roads and encountered many a tribe of twisted vines difficult to pass. Emerging about noon from a grove of giant sunflowers, I found myself on the brink of a tumbling rocky stream. I did not expect to find bridges on my wild ways, and at once started to ford, when a negro woman on the opposite bank earnestly called on me to wait until she could tell the "men folks" to bring me a horse—that the river was too deep and rapid to wade and that I would "sartain be drowned" if I attempted to cross. I replied that my bag and plants would ballast me; that the water did not appear to be deep, and that if I were carried away, I was a good swimmer and would soon dry in the sunshine. But the cautious old soul replied that no one ever waded that river and set off for a horse, saying that it was no trouble at all.

In a few minutes the ferry horse came gingerly down the bank through vines and weeds. His long stilt legs proved him a natural wader. He was white and the little sable negro boy that rode him looked like a bug on his back. After many a tottering halt the outward voyage was safely made, and I mounted behind little Nig. He was a queer specimen, puffy and jet as an India rubber doll and his hair was matted in sections like the wool of a merino sheep. The old horse, overladen with his black and white burden, rocked and stumbled on his stilt legs with fair promises of a fall. But all ducking signs failed and we arrived in safety among the weeds and vines of the rugged bank. A salt bath would have done us no harm. I could swim and little Afric looked as if he might float like a bladder.

Passed gangs of woodmen engaged in felling and hewing the grand oaks for market. Fruit very abundant. Magnificent flowing hill scenery all afternoon. Walked southeast from Elizabethtown till wearied and lay down in the bushes by guess.

September 4. The sun was gilding the hilltops when I was awakened by the alarm notes of birds whose dwelling in a hazel thicket I had disturbed. They flitted excitedly close to my head, as if scolding or asking angry questions, while several beautiful plants, strangers to me, were looking me full in the face. The first botanical discovery in bed! This was one of the most delightful camp grounds, though groped for in the dark, and I lingered about it enjoying its trees and soft lights and music.

Walked ten miles of forest. The farmers hereabouts are tall, stout, happy fellows, fond of guns and horses. Enjoyed friendly chats with them. Arrived at dark in a village that seemed to be drawing its last breath. Was guided to the "tavern" by a negro who was extremely accommodating. "No trouble at all," he said.

September 5. No bird or flower or friendly tree above me this morning; only squalid garret rubbish and dust. Escaped to the woods. Arrived about noon at Munfordville; was soon discovered and examined by Mr. Munford himself, a pioneer and father of the village. He is a surveyor—has held all county offices, and every seeker of roads and lands applies to him for information. He regards all the villagers as his children, and all strangers who enter Munfordville as his own visitors. He informed me that all scientific men applied to him for information, and as I was a botanist, he either possessed, or ought to possess, the knowledge I was seeking, and so I received long lessons concerning roots and herbs for every mortal ill. Thanking my benefactor for his kindness, I escaped to the fields and followed a railroad along the base of a grand hill ridge. Took refuge in a log schoolhouse that stood on a hillside beneath stately oaks and slept on the softest looking of the benches.

September 6. Started at the earliest bird song. Overtook an old negro driving an ox team. Rode with him a few miles and had some interesting chat concerning war, wild fruits of the woods, et cetera. "Right heah," said he, "is where the Rebs was a-tearin' up the track, and they all a sudden thought they seed the Yankees a-comin', obah dem big hills dar, and Lo'd, how dey run." I asked him if he would like a renewal of these sad war times, when his flexible face suddenly calmed, and he said with intense earnestness, "Oh, Lo'd, want no mo wa, Lo'd no."

Got belated in the hill woods. Inquired my way at a farmhouse and was invited to stay overnight in a rare, hearty, hospitable manner. Engaged in familiar running talk on politics, war times, and theology.

September 7. Left the hospitable Kentuckians with their sincere good wishes and bore away southward again through the deep green woods. In noble forests all day.

September 8. Deep, green, bossy sea of waving, flowing hilltops. This evening I could find none willing to take me in, and so lay down on a hillside and fell asleep.

September 9. Another day in the most favored province of bird and flower. Passed the Kentucky line towards evening and obtained food and shelter from a thrifty Tennessee farmer, after he had made use of all the ordinary, anti-hospitable arguments of cautious comfortable families.

September 10. Escaped from a heap of uncordial kindness to the generous bosom of the woods. After a few miles of level ground in luxuriant tangles of brooding vines, I began the ascent of the Cumberland Mountains. I had climbed but a short distance when I was overtaken by a young man on horseback, who soon showed that he intended to rob me if he should find the job worth while. After he had inquired where I came from, and where I was going, he offered to carry my bag. I told him that it was so light that I did not feel it at all a burden; but he insisted and coaxed until I allowed him to carry it.

As soon as he had gained possession I noticed that he gradually increased his speed, evidently trying to get far enough ahead of me to examine the contents without being observed. But I was too good a walker and runner for him to get far. At a turn of the road, after trotting his horse for about half an hour, and when he thought he was out of sight, I caught him rummaging my poor bag. Finding there only a comb, brush, towel, soap, a change of underclothing, a copy of Burns' poems, Milton's *Paradise Lost*, and a small *New Testament*, he waited for me, handed back my bag, and returned down the hill, saying that he had forgotten something.

Passed the poor, rickety, thrice-dead village of Jamestown, an incredibly dreary place. Toward the top of the Cumberland grade, about two hours before sundown I came to a log house, and as I had been warned that all the broad plateau of the range for forty or fifty miles was desolate, I began thus early to seek a lodging for the night.

Arriving at the last house, my knock at the door was answered by a bright, good-natured, good-looking woman, who in reply to my request for a night's lodging and food, said, "Oh, I guess so. I think you can stay. Come in and I'll call my husband." She then called her husband, a blacksmith, who was at work at his forge. He came out, hammer in hand, bare-breasted, sweaty, begrimed, and covered with shaggy black hair. In reply to his wife's statement, that this young man wished to stop over night, he quickly replied, "That's all right; tell him to go into the house." When he came in after his hard day's work and sat down to dinner, he solemnly asked a blessing on the frugal meal, consisting solely of corn bread and bacon. Then, looking across the table at me, he said, "Young man, what are you doing down here?" I replied that I was looking at plants. "Plants? What kind of plants?" I said, "Oh, all kinds; grass, weeds, flowers, trees, mosses, ferns,—almost everything that grows is interesting to me."

"Well, young man," he queried, "you mean to say that you are not employed by the Government on some private business?" "No," I said, "I am not employed by any one except myself. I love all kinds of plants, and I came down here to these Southern States to get acquainted with as many of them as possible."

"You look like a strong-minded man," he replied, "and surely you are able to do something better than wander over the country and look at weeds and blossoms. These are hard times, and real work is required of every man that is able. Picking up blossoms doesn't seem to be a man's work at all in any kind of times."

To this I replied, "You are a believer in the *Bible*, are you not?" "Oh, yes." "Well, you know Solomon was a strong-minded man, and he is generally believed to have been the very wisest man the world ever saw, and yet he considered it was worth while to study plants; not only to go and pick them up as I am doing, but to study them; and you know we are told that he wrote a book about plants, not only of the great cedars of Lebanon, but of little bits of things growing in the cracks of the walls."

This evidently satisfied him, and he acknowledged that he had never thought of blossoms in that way before. He repeated again and again that I must be a very strong-minded man, and admitted that no doubt I was fully justified in picking up blossoms. He then told me that although the war was over, walking across the Cumberland Mountains still was far from safe on account of small bands of guerrillas who were in hiding along the roads, and earnestly entreated me to turn back and not to think of walking so far as the Gulf of Mexico until the country became quiet once more. In the morning he repeated the warning and entreated me to turn back, which never for a moment interfered with my resolution to pursue my glorious walk.

September 11. Long stretch of level sandstone plateau, lightly furrowed and dimpled with shallow groove-like valleys and hills. Large areas beneath the trees are covered with formidable green briers and brambles, armed with hooked claws, and almost impenetrable. Houses are far apart and uninhabited, orchards and fences in ruins— sad marks of war. About noon my road became dim and at last vanished among desolate fields. Lost and hungry, I knew my direction but could not keep it on account of the briers. After a great deal of defensive fighting and struggling I escaped to a road and a house, but failed to find food or shelter.

Towards sundown, as I was walking rapidly along a straight stretch in the road, I suddenly came in sight of ten mounted men riding abreast. They undoubtedly had seen me before I discovered them, for they had stopped their horses and were evidently watching me. I saw at once that it was useless to attempt to avoid them, for the ground thereabout was quite open. I knew that there was nothing for it but to face them fearlessly, without showing the slightest suspicion of foul play. Therefore, without halting even for a moment, I advanced rapidly with long strides as though I intended to walk through the midst of them. When I got within a rod or so I looked up in their faces and smilingly bade them "Howdy." Stopping never an instant, I turned to one side and walked around them to get on the road again, and kept on without venturing to look back or to betray the slightest fear of being robbed.

After I had gone about one hundred or one hundred and fifty yards, I ventured a quick glance back, without stopping, and saw in this flash of an eye that all the ten had turned their horses toward me and were evidently talking about me; supposedly, with reference to what my object was, where I was going, and whether it would be worth while to rob me. They all were mounted on rather scrawny horses, and all wore long hair hanging down on their shoulders. Evidently they belonged to the most irreclaimable of the guerrilla bands who, long accustomed to plunder, deplored the coming of peace. I was not followed, however, probably because the plants projecting from my plant press made them believe that I was a poor herb doctor, a common occupation in these mountain regions.

After dark I discovered, a little off the road, another house, inhabited by negroes, where I succeeded in obtaining a much needed meal of string beans, buttermilk, and corn bread. At the table I was seated in a bottomless chair, and as I became sore and heavy, I sank deeper and deeper, pressing my knees to my breast, and my mouth settled to the level of my plate. But wild hunger cares for none of these things, and my curiously compressed position prevented the too free indulgence of boisterous appetite. Of course, I was compelled to sleep with the trees in the one great bedroom of the open night.

September 12. Awoke drenched with mountain mist, which made a grand show, as it moved away before the hot sun. Passed Montgomery, a shabby village at the head of the east slope of the Cumberland Mountains. Obtained breakfast in a clean house and began the descent of the mountains. Reached Kingston before dark.

September 13. Walked all day across small parallel valleys that flute the surface of the one wide valley. The roads never seem to proceed with any fixed purpose, but wander as if lost. At last, consulting my map and compass, I neglected all directions and finally reached the house of a negro driver, with whom I put up for the night. Received a good deal of knowledge which may be of use should I ever be a negro teamster.

September 14. Walked through many a leafy valley, shady grove, and cool brooklet. Reached Madisonville, a brisk village. Stayed overnight with a pleasant young farmer.

September 15. Most glorious billowy mountain scenery. Reached a house before night, and asked leave to stop. "Well, you're welcome to stop," said the mountaineer, "if you think you can live till morning on what I have to live on all the time." Found the old gentleman very communicative. Was favored with long "bar" stories, deer hunts, etc., and in the morning was pressed to stay for a day or two.

September 19. Bidding farewell to my worthy mountaineer, I pursued my way to the South. As I was leaving, he repeated the warnings of danger ahead, saying that there were a good many people living like wild beasts on whatever they could steal, and that murders were sometimes committed for four or five dollars, and even less.

My path to-day led me along the leafy banks of the Hiwassee, a most impressive mountain river. In Murphy [North Carolina] I was hailed by the sheriff who could not determine by my colors and rigging to what country or craft I belonged. Since the war, every other stranger in these lonely parts is supposed to be a criminal, and all are objects of curiosity or apprehensive concern. After a few minutes' conversation with this chief man of Murphy I was pronounced harmless, and invited to his house.

September 20. All day among the groves and gorges of Murphy with Mr. Beale.

September 21. Most luxuriant forest. Many brooks running across the road. At night I was cordially received by a farmer whose wife, though smart and neat in her appearance, was an inveterate smoker.

September 22. About noon I reached the last mountain summit on my way to the sea. It is called the Blue Ridge and before it lies a prospect very different from any I had passed, namely, a vast uniform expanse of dark pine woods, extending to the sea; an impressive view at any time and under any circumstances, but particularly so to one emerging from the mountains.

Traveled in the wake of three poor but merry mountaineers—an old woman, a young woman, and a young man—who sat, leaned, and lay in the box of a shackly wagon that seemed to be held together by spiritualism, and was kept in agitation by a very large and a very small mule. In going downhill the looseness of the harness and the joints of the wagon allowed the mules to back nearly out of sight beneath the box, and the three who occupied it were slid against the front boards in a heap over the mules' ears. Before they could unravel their limbs from this unmannerly and impolite disorder, a new ridge in the road frequently tilted them with a swish and a bump against the back boards in a mixing that was still more grotesque.

I expected to see man, woman, and mules mingled in piebald ruin at the bottom of some rocky hollow, but they seemed to have full confidence in the back board and front board of the wagon box. So they continued to slide comfortably up and down, from end to end, in slippery obedience to the law of gravitation, as the grades demanded. Where the jolting was moderate, they engaged in conversation on love, marriage, and camp-meeting, according to the custom of the country. The old lady, through all the vicissitudes of the transportation, held a bouquet of French marigolds.

September 23. Am now fairly out of the mountains. Passed the comfortable, finely shaded little town of Gainesville. At night I reached the home of a young man with whom I had worked in Indiana, Mr. Prater. He was down here on a visit to his father and mother. This was a plain backwoods family, living out of sight among knobby timbered hillocks not far from the river. The evening was passed in mixed conversation on southern and northern generalities.

September 24. Spent this day with Mr. Prater sailing on the Chattahoochee, feasting on grapes that had dropped from the overhanging vines.

September 25. Bade good-bye to this friendly family. Mr. Prater accompanied me a short distance from the house and warned me over and over again to be on the outlook for rattlesnakes. They are now leaving the damp lowlands, he told me, so that the danger is much greater because they are on their travels. Thus warned, I set out for Savannah, but got lost in the vine-fenced hills and hollows of the river bottom. After repeated failures I succeeded in finding a place on the river bank where I could force my way into the stream through the vine-tangles. I succeeded in crossing the river by wading and swimming, careless of wetting, knowing that I would soon dry in the hot sunshine.

Debated with myself whether to proceed down the river valley until I could buy a boat, or lumber to make one, for a sail instead of a march through Georgia. I was intoxicated with the beauty of these glorious river banks, which I fancied might increase in grandeur as I approached the sea. But I finally concluded that such a pleasure sail would be less profitable than a walk, and so sauntered on southward as soon as I was dry. Rattlesnakes abundant. Lodged at a farmhouse.

September 26. Reached Athens in the afternoon, a remarkably beautiful and aristocratic town, containing many classic and magnificent mansions of wealthy planters.

September 27. Long zigzag walk amid the old plantations, a few of which are still cultivated in the old way by the same negroes who worked them before the war. Witnessed the most gorgeous sunset I ever enjoyed in this bright world of light. Was directed by a very civil negro to lodgings for the night. Daily bread hereabouts means sweet potatoes and rusty bacon.

September 28. The water oak is abundant on stream banks and in damp hollows. Grasses are becoming tall and cane-like and do not cover the ground with their leaves as at the North. Strange plants are crowding about me now. Scarce a familiar face appears among all the flowers of the day's walk.

September 29. . . . .

September 30. Traveled to-day more than forty miles without dinner or supper. No family would receive me, so I had to push on to Augusta. Went hungry to bed and awoke with a sore stomach—sore, I suppose, from its walls rubbing on each other without anything to grind. A negro kindly directed me to the best hotel, called, I think, the Planter's. Got a good bed for a dollar.

October 1. Found a cheap breakfast in a market-place; then set off along the Savannah River to Savannah. Am made to feel that I am now in a strange land. I know hardly any of the plants, but few of the birds, and I am unable to see the country for the solemn, dark, mysterious cypress woods which cover everything.

The winds are full of strange sounds, making one feel far from the people and plants and fruitful fields of home. Night is coming on and I am filled with an indescribable loneliness. Felt feverish; bathed in a black, silent stream; nervously watchful for alligators. Obtained lodging in a planter's house among cotton fields. Although the family seemed to be pretty well-off, the only light in the house was bits of pitch-pine burned in the fireplace.

October 2. In the low bottom forest of the Savannah River. Met a young African with whom I had a long talk. Was amused by his eloquent narrative of coon hunting, alligators, and many superstitions. He showed me a place where a railroad train had run off the track, and assured me that the ghosts of the killed may be seen every dark night.

October 3. In "pine barrens" most of the day. Here I sauntered in delightful freedom, meeting none of the cat-clawed vines, or shrubs, of the alluvial bottoms.

Toward evening I arrived at the home of Mr. Cameron, a wealthy planter, who had large bands of slaves at work in his cotton fields. They still call him "Massa." When I arrived I found him busily engaged in scouring the rust off some cotton-gin saws which had been lying for months at the bottom of his mill-pond to prevent Sherman's "bummers" from destroying them. The most valuable parts of the grist-mill were hidden in the same way. "If Bill Sherman," he said, "should ever come down now without his army, he would never go back."

After supper, as we sat by the fire talking on my favorite subject of botany, I described the country I had passed through, its botanical character, etc. "Young man," he said, after hearing my talks on botany, "I see that your hobby is botany. My hobby is e-lec-tricity. I believe that the time is coming, though we may not live to see it, when that mysterious power or force, used now only for telegraphy, will eventually supply the power for running railroad trains and steamships, for lighting, and, in a word, electricity will do all the work of the world."

October 4. New plants constantly appearing. All day in dense, wet, dark, mysterious forest of flat-topped taxodiums.

October 5. Saw the stately banana for the first time, growing luxuriantly in wayside gardens. At night with a very pleasant, intelligent family, but as usual was admitted only after I had undergone a severe course of questioning.

October 6. Immense swamps, still more completely fenced and darkened, that are never ruffled with winds or scorched with drought.

October 7. Impenetrable taxodium swamp, seemingly boundless. Passed the night with a very pleasant family of Georgians, after the usual questions and cross questions.

October 8. Reached Savannah, but find no word from home, and the money that I had ordered to be sent by express from Portage [Wisconsin] by my brother had not yet arrived. Feel dreadfully lonesome and poor. Went to the meanest looking lodging-house that I could find, on account of its cheapness.

October 9. After going again to the express office and post office, and wandering about the streets, I found a road which led me to the Bonaventure graveyard. It is only three or four miles from Savannah. There is but little to be seen on the way in land, water, or sky, that would lead one to hope for the glories of Bonaventure. The ragged desolate fields, on both sides of the road, are overrun with coarse rank weeds, and show scarce a trace of cultivation.

The sun was set ere I was past the negroes' huts and rice fields, and I arrived near the graves in the silent hour of the gloaming. All of the avenue where I walked was in shadow, but an exposed tombstone frequently shone out in startling whiteness on either hand, and thickets of sparkleberry bushes gleamed like heaps of crystal. Not a breath of air moved the gray moss, and the great black arms of the trees met overhead and covered the avenue. Though tired, I sauntered a while enchanted, then lay down under one of the great oaks. I found a little mound that served for a pillow, placed my plant press and bag beside me and rested fairly well, though somewhat disturbed by large prickly-footed beetles creeping across my hands and face, and by a lot of stinging hungry mosquitoes.

When I awoke, the sun was up and all Nature was rejoicing. I heard the screaming of the bald eagles, and of some strange waders in the rushes. I heard the hum of Savannah with the long jarring halloos of negroes far away. On rising I found that my head had been resting on a grave, and though my sleep had not been quite so sound as that of the person below, I arose refreshed, and looking about me, the morning sunbeams pouring through the oaks and gardens dripping with dew, the beauty displayed was so glorious and exhilarating that hunger and care seemed only a dream.

Muir dwelt among the tombs at Bonaventure for several days, walking each day into Savannah, returning by devious routes to his unconventional retreat, so as not to be discovered. Finally the promised funds arrived from his family in Wisconsin, and he shipped aboard the steamship Sylvan Shore *for Fernandina, Florida.*

October 15. To-day, at last, I reached Florida, the so-called "Land of Flowers," that I had so long waited for.

In visiting Florida in my dreams, I always came suddenly on a

close forest of trees, every one in flower, and bent down and en-
tangled to network by luxuriant, bright-blooming vines, and over all a
flood of bright sunlight. But such was not the gate by which I entered
the promised land. Salt marshes, belonging more to the sea than to the
land; with groves here and there, green and unflowered, sunk to the
shoulders in sedges and rushes; with trees farther back, ill defined
in their boundary, and instead of rising in hilly waves and swellings,
stretching inland in low water-like levels.

Florida is so watery and vine-tied that pathless wanderings are
not easily possible in any direction. I started to cross the State by a
gap hewn for the locomotive, walking sometimes between the rails,
stepping from tie to tie, or walking on the strip of sand at the sides,
gazing into the mysterious forest.

October 16. Last evening when I was in the trackless woods, the
great mysterious night becoming more mysterious in the thickening
darkness, I gave up hope of finding food or a house. All manner of
night sounds came from strange insects and beasts, one by one, or
crowded together.

When I came to an open place where pines grew, it was about
ten o'clock, and I thought that now at last I would find dry ground.
But even the sandy barren was wet, and I had to grope in the dark a
long time, feeling the ground with my hands when my feet ceased to
plash, before I at last discovered a little hillock dry enough to lie down
on. In the morning I was cold and wet with dew, and I set out
breakfastless. Flowers and beauty I had in abundance, but no bread.

Near the middle of the forenoon I came to a shanty where a
party of loggers were getting out long pines for ship spars. They were
the wildest of all the white savages I have met. The long-haired ex-
guerrillas of the mountains of Tennessee and North Carolina are
uncivilized fellows; but for downright barbarism these Florida loggers
excel. Nevertheless, they gave me a portion of their yellow pork and
hominy without either apparent hospitality or a grudge, and I was
glad to escape to the forest again.

A few hours later I dined with three men and three dogs. I was
viciously attacked by the latter, who undertook to undress me with
their teeth. I was nearly dragged down backward, but escaped un-
bitten. Liver pie, mixed with sweet potatoes and fat duff, was set
before me, and after I had finished a moderate portion, one of the
men, turning to his companion, remarked: "Wall, I guess that man
quit eatin' 'cause he had nothin' more to eat. I'll get him more
potato."

October 17. Passed through a good many miles of open level pine barrens.

October 18. Reached Gainesville late in the night. When within three or four miles of the town I noticed a light off in the pine woods. As I was very thirsty, I thought I would venture toward it with the hope of obtaining water. In creeping cautiously and noiselessly through the grass to discover whether or no it was a camp of robber negroes, I came suddenly in full view of the best-lighted and most primitive of all the domestic establishments I have yet seen in town or grove.

There was, first of all, a big, glowing log fire, illuminating the overleaning bushes and trees, bringing out leaf and spray with more than noonday distinctness, and making still darker the surrounding wood. In the center of this globe of light sat two negroes. I could see their ivory gleaming from the great lips, and their smooth cheeks flashing off light as if made of glass. I ventured forward to the radiant presence of the black pair, and, after being stared at with that desperate fixedness which is said to subdue the lion, I was handed water in a gourd from somewhere out of the darkness.

I was standing for a moment beside the big fire, looking at the unsurpassable simplicity of the establishment, and asking questions about the road to Gainesville, when my attention was called to a black lump of something lying in the ashes of the fire. It seemed to be made of rubber; but ere I had time for much speculation, the woman bent wooingly over the black object and said with motherly kindness, "Come, honey, eat yo' hominy." At the sound of "hominy," the rubber gave strong manifestations of vitality and proved to be a burly little negro boy, rising from the earth naked as to the earth he came. Had he emerged from the black muck of a marsh, we might easily have believed that the Lord had manufactured him like Adam direct from the earth.

Gainesville is rather attractive—an oasis in the desert, compared with other villages. Obtained food and lodging at a sort of tavern.

October 19. Dry land nearly all day. Passed several thrifty cotton plantations with comfortable residences, contrasting sharply with the squalid hovels of my first days in Florida. Slept in the barrens at the side of a log. Suffered from cold and was drenched with dew. What a comfort a companion would be in the dark loneliness of such nights! Did not dare to make a fire for fear of discovery by robber negroes, who, I was warned, would kill a man for a dollar or two. Had a long walk after nightfall, hoping to discover a house. Became very thirsty and often was compelled to drink from slimy pools groped for in the grass, with the fear of alligators before my eyes.

October 20. Swamp very dense during this day's journey. No stream that I crossed to-day appeared to have the least idea where it was going. Saw an alligator splash into the sedgy brown water by the roadside from a log.

Arrived at night at the house of Captain Simmons, one of the very few scholarly, intelligent men that I have met in Florida. He had been an officer in the Confederate army in the war and was, of course, prejudiced against the North, but polite and kind to me, nevertheless. Our conversation, as we sat by the light of the fire, was on the one great question, slavery and its concomitants. I managed, however, to switch off to something more congenial occasionally—the birds of the neighborhood, the animals, the climate, and what spring, summer, and winter are like in these parts.

About the climate, I could not get much information, as he had always lived in the South and, of course, saw nothing extraordinary in weather to which he had always been accustomed. But in speaking of animals, he at once became enthusiastic and told many stories of hairbreadth escapes, in the woods about his house, from bears, hungry alligators, wounded deer, etc.

"And now," said he, forgetting in his kindness that I was from the hated North, "you must stay with me a few days. Deer are abundant. I will lend you a rifle and we'll go hunting. And perhaps we will see a bear, for they are far from scarce here, and there are some big gray wolves, too."

I concluded to stop. I was weary and the prospect of getting a little rest was a tempting consideration after so many restless nights and long, hard walks by day.

Refreshed after two days' rest, Muir resumed his walk, and his hard journey came to an abrupt end which belied the effort he had put into it and yet redeemed it with an epiphany which carried him back to a world he had left far behind.

October 23. To-day I reached the sea.

While I was yet many miles back in the palmy woods, I caught the scent of the salt sea breeze which, although I had so many years lived far from sea breezes, suddenly conjured up Dunbar, its rocky coast, winds and waves; and my whole childhood, that seemed to have utterly vanished in the New World, was now restored amid the Florida woods by that one breath from the sea.

Forgotten were the palms and magnolias and the thousand flowers that enclosed me. I could see only dulse and tangle, long-winged gulls, the Bass Rock in the Firth of Forth, and the old castle, schools, churches, and long country rambles in search of birds' nests. For nineteen years my vision was bounded by forests, but to-day, emerging from a multitude of tropical plants, I beheld the Gulf of Mexico stretching away unbounded, except by the sky. What dreams and speculative matter for thought arose as I stood on the strand, gazing out on the burnished, treeless plain!

AUGUST DERLETH

Quiet Streets, Empty Roads

"Memories and meditations filled the darkness all around . . ."

August Derleth walked a different America than John Muir. He walked only on home ground, within the circumference of the small Midwestern town where he was born, where he grew up, and where he chose to remain. A prolific writer and literary entrepreneur—he led the resurgence of interest in H. P. Lovecraft, for instance—August Derleth put much of his most charming work into his journals and daybooks. He wrote without illusion about the people he knew best— about Flem Prouty, and how he was cured of bugs by a blue light; about Ellen Gundlach, who smoked a cigarette for the sake of her house plants, and Mr. Elky, who made himself a new set of false teeth when he started hissing through the old ones ("They fit like a glove."); about Circ, who claimed mosquitoes go to roost at 10 o'clock. And he wrote about his walks. Certainly no one more easily captured the air of strolling through the streets and roads of the small town in America. August Derleth died on the Fourth of July, 1971.

These selections are from Countryman's Journal *and* Wisconsin Country: A Sac Prairie Journal, *by August Derleth—written in the 1940s.*

With Hugo Schwenker to walk down the railroad tracks through the marshes tonight. At the Spring Slough Rusty Crosby was fishing with Frank and Toby Schmitz. "We're bullheading," they said, when I asked what they were after. "But I guess they won't bite till after dark," added Rusty. "We'll build a fire and wait." We stood for a while making small talk; they had elected to fish from the bank southeast of the trestle, where great old maple and birch trees towered over. We went on down the tracks, walking in silence, listening to peepers, cricket frogs, and the first leopard frogs, the calls of which made a background for the vespers of the birds, walking as far as Heiney's Crossing, and turning there to see Arcturus and Spica lighting up the eastern heaven, and all the constellations of winter brilliant across the western sky, together with Jupiter, Saturn, and Mars. Darkness had come down when we reached the Spring Slough again, but the boys' fire made a bright orange glow among the black tree trunks, lit on the side nearest the fire with the dancing flames.

One of the boys stood against a tree; the other two sat at the bank, the firelight in their faces, their eyes shining. The fire itself was reflected in the water just off the bank. The little scene made a pocket of pleasant warmth, and the wood smoke filled the air with its sweetness. None of the boys was aware of us, so intent were they on their fishing; so we went silently on across the trestle, listening to jacksnipe booming overhead and all the rising sounds of the April night.

When I came up out of the woods at the east end of the back river bridge this evening, I found old Bob sitting at the bridge with a bottle of wine beside him and a gun across his knees. He looked a sheet or two in the wind. I asked him what he was doing there. "I aim t' git me a woodchuck," he said. "See," he went on, pointing waveringly, "there's his hole. I'm gonna have roast woodchuck." Recalling that Thoreau had tried woodchuck and decided against making it stable fare, I inquired whether he had eaten it before. "Sure," he said enthusiastically. "A woodchuck makes real good soup." I left him in the gathering dusk, somewhat dubious about his ability to hit his quarry if the woodchuck did show himself.

Approaching the Schluckabier house unseen, I could not help overhearing a violent and somewhat irrational argument between two of the middle-aged sisters and the husband of one of them. This ceased abruptly as they caught sight of me from where they sat in the shade of a catalpa tree in the lawn, and they put on their most ingratiating air, hailing me and beginning to talk about the weather and of how bad the mosquitoes were—"They bite you without a license even!"—and then, after I had gone sufficiently far, in their estimation—though I was not yet out of earshot—they began their argument once more.

Sac Prairie had the air of a typical early spring evening tonight. The pungence and fragrance of diffused grass-fire smoke lay along the streets, and the twilight rang with the cries of children playing frantically against being called in for bed. I walked up the familiar streets in the neighborhood of the high school and the Park Hall, savoring the evening—hearing a baby crying through the partly open door of the Lampertius house, shut after I had gone by—seeing Mrs. Oscar Becker come apprehensively out from the shadow of her porch to the sidewalk and stand under the street light calling Johnny, her youngest, who came out of the next street on his bicycle, whereupon she went, reassured, into the house once more—experiencing the nostalgia of the arc lights in a line against the faint afterglow still lingering, as always, and the starred heavens seen among the thickening branches. I left the evening . . . with reluctance.

Old Mrs. Block hailed me as I passed her house on the edge of town today. She was at work in the ditch, though half-blind, and called out, in German, "Is that somebody I know?" I shouted back that it was, and told her who. She came up in sturdy if labored fashion and explained that she could neither see nor hear well, and thought I was a Keller boy, but which Keller would that be? I raised my voice a little more and finally brought her to understand that I was not a Keller boy, and ultimately persuaded her to settle upon my identity. She explained that she was on her way over to Mrs. Weber's—two blocks into town—to return a plate on which Mrs. Weber had brought her a piece of pie; so I must perforce walk with her to Webers'.

She had put down the plate at the edge of her tree-bank. I walked over and picked it up, and then walked with her toward Webers'. She immediately launched upon a recital of her woes—she was ninety-six years old, she said, and still going, though the Lord only knew for how long; her boy—that is, her grandson Valentine—worked all day at Stoffel's now; formerly he had worked there only part of the time, but now it was all the time. She wandered to the subject of war; we were all being punished, she held; it was the Lord's work; it was the same as in the days of Babel and Babylon, we were all talking different languages—by which I assumed that she meant we held to distorted and conflicting values—and we were being punished for it; indeed, she said ominously, the worst was yet to come, saying this with that comfortable assurance of the very old who know full well they will not be here long enough to suffer it. Three of her chickens, which had the run of the house with her, tried to follow her, but she chased them back. "I have three hens, that's enough—but my neighbor has a hundred and three, and my three are all the time over there, and theirs over here." At Webers' we parted, she saying with a heavy sigh, "Oh, it's a hard life—and a long one—too long. If only my father had sold me that time he had the chance! How different it would have been!"—harking back to that irrational dream which had obsessed her all her life, stemming from a time when, on shipboard crossing to America, she, then a beautiful child, had so drawn the attention of a fellow traveler that he had offered to buy her; her father had refused the offer, and now, looking back over an arduous life, she dreamed of how different her life could have been—as all men dream. . . .

Walking down from Upper Sac Prairie tonight, I was struck, as always, by the strange iridescence of the hills under the bright, now almost full moon—Sugar Loaf, Juniper Bluff and the adjoining slopes —an iridescence that glows forth from the snow-held slopes with their ridge trees dark on the sky. The hills shine as with some inner light of their own, giving off a sheen which seems richer than the light of the moon, and seems to have a tangibility great enough to lie over the lights shining yellowly in the houses along the base of the hills there, lending them a kind of spectral unreality. It is as if the entire earth were luminous, and the hills in that light have a special kind of beauty which every countryman must know very well. I stood for a while looking over at the hills, which were all the more bright for the contrast afforded by the dark river flowing by between the hills and the place where I stood; and I thought of the lives lived out in the shadow of those hills, the lives whose symbols in a manner of speaking were the little squares of yellow window lights now paled almost to invisibility by the singular glowing of the snow-clad hills rising up beyond them.

Passing George Marzolf's house in mid-evening, I heard the sound of his piano vying with the susurration of wind in the cottonwood before the house, and I knew the old man sat in the dark playing again, as he often does. There was a dim light in the kitchen; presumably his wife sat there; but there was no light in any other part of the house, and none where he was. Nevertheless, the pleasant sound of his playing drifted out into the fragrant night; it was muted, as if he feared to disturb passers-by, but he need not have feared this, for his music was old, familiar music, surely melodic enough to please any ear, simple instrumental pieces, contemplatively played, as if he were about soothing himself, as so many people turn to music or books or painting to take refuge against the tribulations of living. The music and the wind's sound in the leaves were one, muted and still, almost like the May speaking voicelessly into the star-bright night, or like a kind of portrait of that aging man sitting there alone in the darkness of his room with all the spring pressing in upon that little house, and his memories and meditations filling the darkness all around.

Late tonight I walked out along a country road, going for some distance down a little-traveled road under the stars, listening to jacksnipes and whippoorwills, to crickets and cicadas and katydids, to killdeers calling desultorily over along the river, and, walking along, I was conscious of the character and atmosphere of houses, derived not only from their setting, but from the lives which have been lived or are being lived there.

I passed the old Frailey farm, now housing a young couple and their two children, settled in a kind of hollow of the hills just off the road, with the gaunt old barn thrust forth and dominating the small house with its aura of old Frailey who, despairing of ever making ends meet, had at last hanged himself from a rafter in the hay-loft. Something of that violence lingered still in that place; something almost visible there in that shadowed hollow, as if something remained of that melancholy and despair which had impelled the old man to take his own life.

Only a little farther along, the Culson farm hugged the ground, in a low place off the road, with the meadows stretching out toward the river behind it, and across the road, the hills rising up. The aura of quiet peace which rose from it was deceptive, for the neighbor, going by, knew that the young Culsons were divided by an unresolvable conflict—he being held close to the land by his affection for it, she wearing away at him to sell his land, his buildings, his woods, and get away, into town, to the city, each pulling his own way, so that day after day he worked his land, and she sped away in the car to visit the towns and the cities nearby, coming home every evening only to complain bitterly of his stolidity, to wear down his resistance little by little, to destroy him, if need be, to escape into the superficial glitter of urban life.

And, not far away, in a dense grove of trees, the dark, silent Wolden farm, the barn on one side of the road, the house on the other, seldom showing a light, save only, early in the evening, a pale yellow from the lamplight at one window to show that someone lived there still, in a kind of pocket of time, Bill Wolden, middle-aged, single, alone, letting his farm decay while he, too, decayed, walking into town at any hour of day or night to seek escape in the bottle. The

neglected house and barn, the close-pressing trees, limbs thrust forth
at the house, untrimmed, unhampered, the numberless cats flourish-
ing there, the ramshackle outlying buildings, the collapsed wood-
pile—all gave mute testimony of Bill Wolden's submission to this
decline.

It was as if the houses themselves in their character and atmosphere spoke of the tragedy of the little lives which were associated
with them . . . all the more visible in the hours of darkness.

Walking from Ganzlins' house to the harness shop tonight, I was
keenly aware of the aspect of a summer evening in the village—of
people sitting on the porches, many reading, some just sitting. The air
was still, the sky overcast, and rain imminent; it was as if people,
trees, houses, all alike awaited rain. There was, moreover, an atmosphere of quiet peace, the calmness of a village at rest for the night,
though the evening was not yet far advanced, a kind of brooding calm
in this cloud-premature dusk. And yet, scarcely half an hour later,
after a sudden squall, the streets were alive with people—children
wading in mud puddles under the street lights, and their parents out
at every corner, discussing the storm, and trying to help the gutter
water escape down clogged sewers.

Late tonight, as I was on the way home, I heard the murmur of voices
from Circ's open door, and stopped there beside the door, where I
could plainly see that Circ was quite alone. He was entertaining
himself, sitting at his table with a paper or magazine before him,
ostensibly reading, with his cap on. His words and sentences came at
rather long intervals, and were spoken for the most part in a gutteral
tone of voice.

"He's here."
"Yes."
A long pause.
"Yes."
Again a long pause.
"Yes, I know it."
"What do you say?"
"I say—*yes!*"
I could not understand his pretense, save that it rose out of that

loneliness common to all men, and, rather than interrupt him, I took my leave noiselessly.

Carl Lachmund told me this evening in the harness shop that Circ had once again startled the family; he had been asked by Emmy Marquardt to run some trifling errand and had begged off on the excuse that he could not walk easily, "because I walked so much in the war back in 1918."

ROBERT MARSHALL

The Lure of Doonerak

"Is it possible to reconcile oneself to the second best?"

Robert Marshall was a "bureaucrat" who couldn't stay behind a desk.
He belonged in boots. And when he laced them on, they took him
time and again to Alaska's Upper Koyukuk country, reaching north
toward the Brooks Range and "a vast lonely expanse where men are
so rare and exceptional that the most ordinary individual takes on an
importance impossible to conceive in the outside world." Marshall
had gone from college into the United States Forest Service. This is
where his career was spent; he later was a founder of The Wilderness
Society. He was not a polished literary stylist, but by any measure of
manhood he was as rare and exceptional as the men he found on the
Upper Koyukuk. He had less than a year to live when he made this
last trek into the arctic wilderness of Alaska, where distance and
direction were uncertain, and hardship was assured. He died in 1939,
at the age of 38.

This account is taken from Robert Marshall's Arctic Wilderness,
edited by George Marshall.

In June, 1939, nine months after our unsuccessful attempt to climb
Mount Doonerak, I was fortunate enough to be able to return, for the
fourth time, to Alaska. I could not resist the lure of unconquered
Doonerak.

As the plane circled the Wiseman landing field it was exciting to
recognize each cabin, to observe which of the women had their
laundry on the line, to pick out the individual Eskimo children
running to the field. We landed at one o'clock in the afternoon on
what should have been the longest day of the year, except that for all
practical purposes every day for three months was equally long, with
twenty-four hours of daylight.

As soon as the welcomes were over and my baggage carried the
quarter mile to the roadhouse, Jesse Allen and I retired to his cabin to
discuss plans for our next trip. Our foremost objective would be
Mount Doonerak. We decided on five days hard back packing overland for another attempt at a first ascent. Afterward we would explore
the unknown Arctic Divide at the heads of the North Fork of the
Koyukuk and the Hammond River. We would be out for twenty-four
days.

We had planned the autumn before, when the previous expedition was not yet completed, that Jesse Allen, Kenneth Harvey, and I would be partners in another attempt at Doonerak. Ernie Johnson was busy with mining and could not come. In his place, Nutirwik, a Kobuk Eskimo, who had the reputation of being the best hunter in the Koyukuk, joined us. Unlike most other Eskimos in the region, he lived alone. This small man—he was scarcely more than five feet tall—with his thin face, high cheekbones, and little gnarled hands more than held his own with his sturdier-looking companions. His prominent eyebrows were in sharp contrast with his thin eyes. He had a strong, sensitive face and remarkably few wrinkles for a man close to sixty who had lived out of doors all his life. His name literally means blizzard. When he had come to live among the whites about 1903 he changed it to Harry Snowden, but we continued to use his Eskimo name on these wilderness adventures. He brought with him his dogs, Coffee and White-eye, while Harvey brought his dog, Moose; they aided materially in dispersing the load.

This load consisted of 285 pounds, of which approximately one-third was photographic and scientific equipment, which would not get lighter; one-third tent, bedding, dishes, packsacks, rifle, ammunition, ax, extra socks and shoes, first aid material, and the like, which likewise would not diminish; and only one-third food, which would gradually decrease until we obtained fresh meat. A few weeks before my arrival, Jesse had packed out staples to a cache on upper Hammond River.

Most of Wiseman was at the roadhouse when we hoisted our packs to our shoulders on the evening of June 23. Harvey, Nutirwik, and I each carried about 55 pounds; one-armed Jesse, who was sixty years old, took 40 pounds; and the three dogs who were soft from months of inaction, 25-30 pounds each. But if dogs get soft from just sitting around and getting fed, so does a bureaucrat, and it was pleasant that for our first day's journey we were taking only the six-mile climb on the road to Nolan Creek. Pleasant also was the chatter of Verne Watts who accompanied us from town with a pack of his own. Pointing to Harvey's advancing baldness, he said: "You'll have to tie a string around your head pretty soon to tell how high to wash your face in the morning." But most pleasant of all was a cold rain which struck us fiercely for a few minutes when we were halfway to Nolan; it put an end to the heat of the evening and to the mosquitoes which had been swarming in great masses around us.

At Nolan Creek we scattered to the cabins of different genial hosts who had invited us to spend the night. I went for nine hours of luxurious sleep to the cabin of George Eaton, now seventy-eight, with whom I had stopped in 1929, 1930, and 1931. Then, although about seventy, he had still been a powerful man, boasting that he could outshovel any man in the Koyukuk, and apparently expecting to be active until he was a hundred years old. Now he was old and unhappy in the realization that active life was over, but still unbroken. He said: "It's terrible to me, Bob, to think my legs is so bad I can't go on a trip like you fellows is going on, but it doesn't bother me a bit that I'm going to die some day soon. I've got to go, and I don't know when, and I'm glad I don't."

We spent the sunny next day on Nolan Creek while I went up and down the valley, chatting with old friends. Almost everyone on the creek dropped in afterward to say good-bye as we headed out at eight in the evening.

We planned to travel during the night hours in these days of twenty-four hour daylight, because the temperature was cooler then and the mosquitoes a little less thick. But on the steep ascent to Snowshoe Pass perspiration and mosquitoes were both profuse until the low sun was temporarily hidden behind the mountainside we were climbing. When we crossed the height of land at ten in the evening we stepped back into sunlight. Just to the right of the sun, forty miles to the north, black and massive and immense, was old Mount Doonerak, looking utterly unscalable from this angle. But we were not discouraged, knowing a mountain has many angles.

Besides, a person could not be discouraged with bright evening sunshine making flowers and moss fairly glow all around. There was the yellow green of sphagnum, the creamy yellow of reindeer moss, the pure gold of arctic cinquefoil and poppy, the rich purple of lupine, and the white, cottony tassels of millions of sedge plants waving everywhere.

But these white tassels, for all their beauty, were flags of warning to tell us they waved over sedge tussocks. We avoided them wherever we possibly could as we lugged our packs over the side hills of Glacier River. We made travel as easy as possible by resting at fifty-minute intervals for ten minutes and by stopping for over an hour in the middle of the journey to eat a midnight supper of canned ham and tea. At four o'clock in the morning we made camp near the remains of an old igloo built many years before by arctic Eskimos, over here for a hunt.

Camp consisted of a 10 by 11 foot rectangular canvas, sloping backward from a horizontal front ridgepole, held taut by other poles and ropes, and covering a patch of level ground where we laid spruce boughs. On the boughs we spread our sleeping bags. There was also ample space under the fly to place supplies we wanted to keep dry. Directly in front of the fly we built a fire of dry spruce and cotton-wood. After a supper of macaroni and cheese, canned ham, bread and butter, and green tea, we retired for the "night" at the odd hour of seven in the morning and did not stir until four in the afternoon.

With this upside-down schedule the evening meal became break-fast, hence we had oatmeal, bacon, and coffee. It was shortly before eight when we started again. We followed the right bank of the Glacier River for mile after mile of slow, plodding travel. It is hard to describe how slow and plodding it really seems when you are out of practice and there is no trail and you have a 55-pound pack tugging on your headstrap and shoulders. You have hardly gone five minutes when the muscles in your neck are so sore that you know every step for the next six or seven hours will be pain. You throw off the head-strap to rest the neck and the pack pulls so violently on your shoulders you imagine it is turning them inside out. You go back to the headstrap again, pushing against it for all you are worth, perspir-ing freely in spite of the hour of evening, swatting at fifty mosquitoes which have lighted on your forehead and your cheeks and your neck, letting down your black mosquito net which instantly makes the whole world dark, pulling it up again when you almost stifle in the sultry evening, noticing suddenly that your ankle is sore where the boot has rubbed off the skin, stumbling over sedge tussocks, forcing your way through thick willow brush, sliding along on uncertain side hills ankle deep with sphagnum moss, neck aching, shoulders aching, ankle aching, on, on, on.

But surprising things happen in the midst of such travel. Unex-pectedly you notice a clump of lovely *Pyrola* you almost stepped on, with round, shiny leaves and with stalks topped by almost bell-shaped five-petaled white flowers. Now, under a clump of spruce, you dis-cover those gayest of white flowers, the *Dryas*, fairly sparkling with their eight bright petals set off against the light green of the sphag-num moss. Now your attention is drawn to fresh sheep or bear tracks on the mud of the river bar or, on occasion, to tracks of wolves traveling together.

Then, as you get into the swing of it, the pack seems to bother less the farther you go. You no longer look at your watch every ten minutes to see how soon the end of the fifty-minute shift will come. You enjoy more and more the freshness and the freedom from trails and human signs in this remote country, and you realize that one incentive for setting out to climb Mount Doonerak is the satisfaction in conquering the seventy-five miles of back packing across untamed country, which is necessary to reach its base.

Around eleven at theoretical night it started to rain steadily, though not hard. This did not deter us from thirty-eight hearty back slaps at midnight as Harvey moved into his thirty-eighth birthday. A short time later, as we were starting up after midnight supper, something in Moose's swagger seemed to irritate White-eye, who was still virtually a stranger to him, and amid frightful snarls we had the one and only dog fight of the expedition.

We pitched camp at three in the morning directly under the great limestone tower of Chimney Mountain. It rose sheer on three sides for three to four-hundred feet, but on the fourth it sloped at an angle that could be climbed. The chimney was perched on top of a 1,500-foot mountain, and it was a stirring feeling to be camped directly underneath it. Weird and amazing, too, when I woke after hours of unbroken slumber, expecting to see the familiar alley back of an old stable converted into a garage which had greeted my eyes upon awaking all of a Washington winter, to find this wild chimney overhanging me. It took a while to connect with reality and convince myself that I was not dreaming.

The next night we traveled across the low pass between Glacier and Clear rivers with no adventures, but with the pleasing sight of a moose feeding along the marshy edge of a small lake in the middle of the pass. We made what proved to be an exceptionally comfortable three-day camp in the willows at the junction of Holmes Creek and Clear River.

Next evening it was overcast, but the clouds were high, so Harvey and I decided to seek out the never-visited source of Pinnyanaktuk Creek, one of ten large creeks flowing into that super-Yosemite of the North, the eight-mile glacial valley of upper Clear River. On the winter trip of March, 1931, I had named this creek with the Eskimo word meaning "superlatively rugged." Looking up into it was like looking into a great basin which instead of being hollow, was filled with sharply pointed peaks packed closely together.

We pushed our way across two and a half miles of sedge tussocks and soft moss and Labrador tea in full white blossom, to the point

where Pinnyanaktuk flows into Clear River at the foot of the mountains. Within the first three miles of its boulder-filled course, two
large forks plunged in from the right, and the view up each revealed
many unknown crags. Shortly after passing the second fork, Harvey
spied four sheep on the hillside to the left. As we needed fresh meat
badly, he decided to go after them.

Meanwhile I continued up the valley. The main Pinnyanaktuk
climbed rapidly, sometimes cutting through steep dirt banks, sometimes splashing over bedrock, often tearing its way through yet
unmelted snowbanks. The bluish white of the anemone profusely
speckled the sphagnum. Wherever I looked was the deep purple of
phlox and shooting star. The heather was thick; its delicate white
bells were lovely and filled the atmosphere with a delightful scent.
The creek roaring in the rocky gorge below made stirring music, and
every sense seemed satisfied except the sense of touch, which to my
unpleasant surprise was just as much abused by mosquitoes above
3,000 feet, with the ground all excellently drained, as it had been in
the boggy lowlands.

When I reached a bench along the uppermost forks of Pinnyanaktuk I could see the final divide between Clear River and North
Fork less than two miles away. Shortly before, I had heard a shot
echoing in the steep valley and felt confident that Harvey had got his
sheep. Although it was midnight, I snapped several pictures. In the
middle of this occupation I was startled by small rocks bounding
down the hillside above me. I looked up in time to see four sheep
beating a retreat across the slide rock.

When I rejoined Harvey he had a fine 90-pound ram. We cut
him up and divided the load among ourselves and Moose. At the
mouth of Pinnyanaktuk we left the meat on a gravel bar, and hiked
briskly along the river bottom five miles up to the source branches of
Clear River valley. The clouds had all vanished during the night and
the air was crisp and clear. We enjoyed exciting views up St. Patrick's
Creek (which runs parallel to Pinnyanaktuk) on our side of the Clear
River and up a couple of deep, nameless creeks on the other. On the
return journey the sun over the mountains kept lighting more and
more of the valley and the great precipice walls which bounded it.

Back at the mouth of the Pinnyanaktuk we picked up the sheep
and strode into camp among the willows of the Holmes Creek–Clear
River junction at four in the morning. Jesse and Nutirwik had caught
a nice mess of grayling, so we were now plentifully supplied. That

morning we enjoyed the first sheep meal, which as usual consisted of those choice morsels, heart, tongue, and liver.

When I awoke at two in the afternoon the sun was still shining so brightly that I rushed up on the hill back of camp to photograph everything in sight. The whole gay valley seemed to be white and green with millions of flowers and plants. Not the white and green of lifeless paintings, but living, vivid colors sparkling from miles of hillside in the crystal-clear atmosphere. So they had sparkled for many millenniums since the last ice sheet receded, without any purpose of being looked upon by man, but as just a part of great objective nature.

The fresh sheep plus my journey to upper Pinnyanaktuk Creek somewhat changed our plans. I got the notion that instead of reconnoitering Mount Doonerak from the mountains of upper Pyramid Creek, as we had originally planned, we could climb the wall at the head of Pinnyanaktuk Creek and see the south side of Mount Doonerak just as well from there. At the same time we could eat another day's worth of meat and the eby save packing that much extra load over Holmes Pass.

So Harvey and I set out again for Pinnyanaktuk Creek. The first miles to the upper forks were a repetition of the previous night's gay blossoms and jagged pinnacles. Above the upper forks we climbed over slide rock and snowbanks to the very source of Pinnyanaktuk, and then by easy grade to the 5,000-foot divide.

There, just ahead of us, was the great black bulk of Mount Doonerak, rising gigantically into the sky, directly in front of the sun. To our left was one of the steep mountains at the head of Pinnyanaktuk, and this peak we decided to climb in order to get a better picture of the lay of the land. The best possible picture was certainly needed, because the land, as seen from the top, did not look as we expected. We at first had thought that the deep creek behind which Mount Doonerak rose was Pyramid Creek; then, after checking the known topography, we realized this could not be right. Suddenly I discovered that Bombardment Creek, which we always supposed had its source only a few miles south of the North Fork (on the north side of Doonerak and Hanging Glacier Mountain), actually cut a deep gorge between the two peaks. Pyramid came nowhere near Mount Doonerak, and the fog-covered mountain at its head which Ernie and I had assumed was Mount Doonerak the previous summer, in reality was part of Hanging Glacier Mountain. Worst of all, while that mountain could be climbed from the south side, just as we reported, Mount

Doonerak's south side was almost sheer for 6,000 feet and appeared utterly unscalable. The only possibility in the half of its circumference which we could see was a very steep ridge running toward lower Bombardment Creek. Even this possibility seemed highly remote, but at least we knew that Bombardment Creek and not Pyramid Creek, as we had thought, was the best site for our first base camp.

We spent more than an hour, equally distributed around midnight, on the summit, and called our peak Midnight Mountain. As if to celebrate the christening, at exactly midnight the sun suddenly illuminated the finger of Chimney Mountain, jutting into the sky a dozen miles southward. Twenty minutes after midnight the sun shot out from behind Mount Doonerak. Even the sun, however, did not make us warm and we had to pound each other frequently to stop shivering. Yet we savored the intimate view of hundreds of nearby, never-scaled pinnacles, blackly puncturing the midnight arctic sky.

Next evening we broke our comfortable three-day camp at the Holmes Creek junction and started the long uphill drag toward Holmes Pass, eight and a half miles to the northeast and 1,300 feet above us. First we stumbled over sedge tussock- and moss-covered hillsides for a couple of hours, scrambling through the dense brush of the dwarf birch, pushing for all we were worth against headstraps as we gained steep grades. A heavy rainstorm broke shortly after we started and soon had us soaked to the skin. We stopped for a lunch of tea and cold mutton chops at the last dry willows big enough to make a fire. Then we splashed along up Holmes Creek, sometimes on gravel bars, sometimes through willow brush, often right through the water. At one place the creek narrowed into a canyon not more than ten feet wide and half barricaded by a huge wall of yet unmelted ice. In order to get around this we had to climb a steep bank for several hundred feet and then descend again to the creek.

We reached the broad pass just before midnight. It was completely barren of woody growth, but profusely covered by many-colored flowers and the lovely greens and yellows of mosses and lichens. To the west, was the familiar North Fork.

The steep descent into Pyramid Creek was almost as hard as the ascent to Holmes Pass had been. We had to be constantly on edge to keep from falling as we stepped over water-splashed boulders. Lower down, the creek became too deep to be forded comfortably, so we took to the side-hill moss. This was slippery, but not hard going except at half a dozen steep, brushy gulches. At one place the brush tore into the breeching on the pack of White-eye, and we had to repair it on the hillside.

It was nearly four in the morning when we made camp in ankle-deep sphagnum moss under a thrifty young spruce stand near the mouth of Pyramid Creek. The scene of last autumn's shipwreck was only four miles to the south, but none of us had any inclination to visit it. We had, however, a great desire to sleep, and after a huge supper of pea soup, sheep steak, and boiled dried apples, we retired at seven-thirty in the morning for ten hours of slumber.

Another night's hard scrambling through thick brush and along soft, slippery moss-covered hillsides, with 65-pound packs tearing at our neck and shoulder muscles, brought us the nine and a half miles to our destination at the junction of Bombardment Creek and the upper North Fork. Here we set up base camp for our assault on Mount Doonerak.

It was a lovely location on a spruce flat between the two streams. The sphagnum moss covered the ground in great, dry mats, fifteen inches thick, which beat a feather bed for softness. The early morning sun, rising upriver, gave a sparkling brightness to a 200-foot waterfall tumbling off the side of Hanging Glacier Mountain which loomed high over our camp.

When we awoke next evening, the bright sunlight had given away to an ominous sky. Just as we finished our oatmeal and mutton it started to rain hard. Nevertheless, we decided to spend an active night. Jesse and Nutirwik walked back eight miles to our cache of last year where we had left 44 pounds of food, and picked up some sugar, rice, butter, and dried apples. Harvey and I set out to explore the intriguing recesses of Bombardment Creek.

This little eight-mile creek had cut a fabulous gorge between Hanging Glacier rising 4,000 feet above it to the west and Doonerak rising 6,000 feet directly to the east. Higher and higher, as we ascended the valley, the great rock crags of these two towering mountain masses rose. Loftier and loftier grew the sheer rock faces. At places waterfalls dropped over them, a hundred, two hundred, even three hundred feet high.

With mosquitoes swarming about us all the time, we picked a route just below the base of the precipices, on unstable slide-rock slopes, lying at too steep an angle for repose. Every now and then we would start small avalanches. After three and a half miles we came to a sharp turn in the valley beyond which, we decided, it was not safe to go, with the rain making the rock so slippery and with frequent slides starting from the mountainside above. Even while we were discussing the return, a small rock from far up the mountainside went bounding over Harvey's head.

The downhill route over the slide rock was much easier than the ascent. We reached Bombardment Creek just below its plunge over a 125-foot fall. We followed up the narrow gorge, crawled under a massive icebank which overhung for ten feet, and stood in the spray at the base of the fall, which dropped through a narrow chute, rock on one side and ice pillar on the other. At one place the chute was not more than eighteen inches wide. The fall set up a strong breeze, which, together with the cold of the surrounding ice chased away the mosquitoes which had followed us all evening.

The two following nights were also stormy. Jesse and I spent the first in camp, while Harvey and Nutirwik went hunting—and came back empty-handed, because they would not shoot a ewe with a lamb. The second evening it rained only intermittently, so I decided to climb a gray foothill of Mount Doonerak about three miles west of camp, from which I would get a better view of the north side of the mountain and look directly down on what the autumn before had appeared to be a glacier. Harvey and Nutirwik went out after sheep again.

The sky cleared to the north and west, and I climbed 3,000 feet through a garden of bright flowers, keeping pace with the setting sun as shadows rose ever higher on the mountain. Growing luxuriantly were the many-blossomed white heads of bear cabbage (*Veratrum*), the gold of the arctic poppy and the buttercup, the sparkling white of *Dryas octopetala* nodding above its fernlike leaves, the deep purple clumps of phlox.

Now I could look directly over to the black pinnacle of Mount Doonerak, jutting almost straight up for 4,000 feet. It seemed utterly unscalable from this side. At the lower edge of this wall was the glacier indeed, darkened by centuries of tumbling rocks which had mingled with the ice. It was half a mile away and five hundred feet below me. There appeared to be no possible way of climbing to the glacier for measurements. I estimated it was 2,000 feet long and 800 feet wide, and the surface sloped at thirty degrees. The face must have been about 50 feet thick, and a large chunk had apparently broken off just a few days before, because it lay yet unmelted where it had tumbled into a hollow a thousand feet below.

At eleven-fifteen the sun finally dipped behind the mountains across the North Fork and I returned to Bombardment Creek camp. An hour later, Harvey, Nutirwik, and Moose trudged in under the load of a large sheep. Since we were all back in camp by one-thirty in the morning, we decided this would be a good time to change from night to day schedule, which would be better for climbing mountains.

In the later morning, after breakfast, our first job was to cut up the meat, set it on poles under willow shade, and protect it from flies by a mosquito net. The sky was overcast, but the clouds were high and the top of Mount Doonerak clear, so we decided to make an attempt. Unfortunately we started up a ridge which ended in sheer limestone precipices only 3,000 feet above the valley. We were completely stopped for this day, but we could see that the next ridge to the south would permit us to rise higher, even though the summit now appeared impossible.

Next morning the sky was cloudlessly blue. Harvey, Nutirwik, and I set out at six-fifteen, Jesse remaining in camp as his one arm made steep rock work not feasible. We followed up the bench above Bombardment Creek for a mile and then started up a steep, green shoulder leading to the ridge we had, on the previous day, decided to follow. When we reached it we got a fine view into the upper gorge of Bombardment Creek where, to our amazement, we saw a half-mile-long lake which was still frozen on this July 5. Below it, Bombardment Creek spilled over a waterfall, a hundred feet high.

As we followed the ridge on good footing we were suddenly face to face with Mount Doonerak. About half a mile away its north-westerly abutment rose straight up for 2,000 feet. Nowhere did we see a chance to scale it, and yet from a distance this had seemed the most feasible side. The only other remote possibility was some shoulder leading up from the northeast.

We continued climbing easily until we were nearly 6,000 feet high. Then we had precarious footing for a quarter of a mile over tumbling slide rocks toward the base of a rocky dome, a thousand feet high, to the north of Mount Doonerak itself, but sitting on the same massif. We called this dome North Doonerak and started to work our way up it in the hope that from there we would be able to see what the chances for a northeastern ascent of Doonerak might be. We proceeded with great caution, the rock being loose and crumbly.

We labored up almost vertical chimneys, crawled around the edges of great cliffs, took toe and finger holds and pulled ourselves over ledges. By slow degrees we worked higher until finally, five hours after leaving camp, we reached a knife-edge ridge which dropped precipitously on one side toward the North Fork and on the other toward Bombardment Creek. It was a short and easy climb on the crest of this ridge to the summit of North Doonerak. Here was a most comfortable little flat, about ten by six feet, covered with reindeer moss, *Dryas*, and heather. We sprawled out in comfort and leisure to enjoy mountains everywhere under the blue sky.

Dominating the scene, of course, was the great black face of old Doonerak, less than half a mile away and jutting straight up for nearly 2,000 feet. I did not believe that any climber, however expert, could make that face. The northeast shoulder which had been our one remaining hope, we could now see plainly. Some day, probably, people with years of rope-climbing experience will succeed in reaching the top by this route. We all knew that we never could. . . .* Next morning it was raining intermittently. Having given up Mount Doonerak, this was all right with us, because we had only a short day in mind, to pack six miles to the junction of Amawk Creek and the upper North Fork. The footing was relatively good, there was little climbing, and the journey consequently was easy, although our packs, owing to the large amount of fresh meat, were the heaviest of the trip, weighing about 70 pounds. We camped in a clump of cotton-woods with a fine view up the upper North Fork toward the last spruce trees, less than a mile to the north.

Next morning heavy cumulus clouds hung in the sky. The high mountains were covered with fog. It did not seem a very auspicious day to try one of the higher peaks, but Jesse felt convinced it would clear and that today was a better gamble with weather than tomorrow. We had set as our objective a flat-topped, nonprecipitous mountain, about nine miles away, airline, at the head of Amawk Creek. The summit was about 4,600 feet above camp.

We followed the tumbling, plunging waters of Amawk Creek over boulders ground smooth by constant action until, after three miles, we reached a major fork. The left branch flowed for several miles through a deep lime canyon and headed in high mosslands to the east. The right branch came through a schist canyon after rising in

* [George W. Beadle, Gunnar Bergman, and Alfred Tissieres—a team of scientists from the California Institute of Technology—reached the top of Mount Doonerak by way of the south face on June 30, 1952.]

a series of lakes and springs in a large flat between the upper North Fork and Clear River drainages. A ridge covered with sphagnum, *Dryas*, and Angowuk separated the two and led toward our summit.

We climbed along it for miles. The vegetation became scarcer as the sandy soil diminished, and we found ourselves walking over disintegrated schist, slate, quartzite, and volcanic tuff. The whole mountain seemed to be crumbling away at a rapid rate, entirely unlike any other peak we had seen in this arctic territory. To pick one's way through this loose, sliding, rock rubble was like climbing in loose snow. When we occasionally reached a ledge which had not disintegrated, it was a relief to take a few steps in substantial footing before bucking the rubble again.

Of great assistance through this loose footing were the trails which sheep had walked over so much that at places they appeared almost graded. Near the top we followed them altogether. The sheep had plowed out a path even over several large snowbanks which we had to cross.

The summit of the mountain was a flat, thirty or forty acres in extent, covered entirely with fine, disintegrated rock, except for one point, a few feet higher than the rest, which was solid slate. To this very summit not only the sheep had climbed, but also their chief predatory enemy, judging by the wolf sign which was lying there. We named the peak Amawk Mountain—Amawk meaning wolf in Eskimo.

But if the crumbling rock and the fresh wolf sign gave one a feeling of wildness, this was mild compared with the feeling aroused by the panorama of jagged mountains and uncharted valleys. Dominating everything was Mount Doonerak, about twelve miles away to the west. It jutted up into the sky more forbidding than ever. It had the shape of an isosceles triangle from here, with the apex angle only a few degrees and the black sides so steep that ascent seemed as impossible as scaling the craters of the moon.

Four miles southeast of us the twin summit of Apoon rose across Kinnorutin Pass from which I had first seen Apoon in midwinter, eight years before. Then the mountain had made an overwhelming impression on me with the highest unbroken snow slope I had ever seen, rising 4,500 feet out of Kinnorutin Creek. Even now in July it had, in the gully leading downward between its two peaks, the deepest midsummer snow of our experience. We estimated its depth at one hundred feet. We were particularly impressed by a great domeshaped mountain northeast of where we stood.

Toward the Arctic, the limestone summits formed an unknown gray ocean. They were the beginning of unmapped country stretching northward to salt water. Eastward, beyond the Middle Fork, were those yellow limestone precipices which had been so impressive when we were climbing beneath them in the short November days of 1930.

We made interesting geographical discoveries. Alinement Creek cut clear around the head of Hammond River, which did not rise in the Arctic Divide as people had been supposing for thirty-five years. The low pass which Ernie had reported leading from Amawk Creek into the Arctic was in reality a very high pass into Hammond River. Three hours passed rapidly here while we sketched watersheds, took compass shots and vertical angles on mountains, took movies and still pictures, and in general enjoyed the vast, extending landscape.

When we finally left the summit at five in the afternoon it had become so chilly that we ran down the slide-rock slope to get warm. On one snowbank we coasted a couple of hundred feet. We dropped 1,600 feet in short order and soon found ourselves at the edge of a deep-blue lake just under the summit. Its elevation of 5,400 feet here probably made it the highest lake in the Brooks Range, so we called it Inyirik Lake, inyirik meaning mountain.

We then skirted the shoulder of a hill and reached a lake-filled benchland extending for miles in every direction. It seemed a trifle crazy to have this smooth, rolling flat right in the midst of these wild mountains. The sun, which had been obscured by clouds much of the afternoon, at last came out to stay and turned the mosses and leafy plants into a carpet of vivid green. Set in this carpet, everywhere as far as the eye could see, was the golden gleam of the arctic poppy and the snow-white petals of the *Dryas*. The green, the gold, the white—all were so unblemished under the bright sunlight, the rich vegetation so entirely untouched by man, and everything around so peaceful and pure that it seemed a pattern for the Eden of man's dreams.

Unfortunately we were only four lucky people among millions in the world to whom this paradise was as unattainable as Mount Doonerak was to us. Besides, if the millions wanted this sort of perfection and could attain it, the values of freshness and remoteness and adventure beyond the paths of men would automatically disappear. The "paradise" would become a green lawn in Prospect Park, covered with picnicking throngs. Actually, only a small minority of the human race will ever consider primeval nature a basic source of happiness. For this minority, tracts of wilderness paradise urgently need preservation. But mankind as a whole is too numerous for its problem of happiness to be solved by the simple expedient of paradise, whether it lies in Eden or the flower-filled Amawk divide.

Jesse's weather sense proved excellent, for the next day it was raining. We spent it chiefly between the tent and the fireplace, except that Nutirwik went out with his .22 on an unsuccessful hunt for a siksikbok. Harvey and I checked our notes and made corrections on the map. Jesse took care of the cooking, and we helped ourselves generously to the last of the sheep meat. We wanted to finish it before packing across the high divide to the Hammond River.

This they did.

Next day was our last one for side trips. Harvey and I decided to spend it climbing Apoon Mountain which was probably higher than any peak ever climbed in arctic Alaska. Jesse and Nutirwik were going to spend the day taking life easy and doing a little fishing.

The summit of Apoon was only about five miles airline to the northwest of camp. We forded Hammond River and followed up Shinningnellichshunga ("I Am Sleepy") Creek which I had named eight years before on my hike to the head of Hammond. Harvey was still jocularly rolling the name on his tongue. Jesse boycotted it and refused to say anything lengthier than Sleepy Creek. This morning, however, we were wide awake and covered four uphill miles in little more than an hour. Then we left the creek and started the real climb. It was steeply but not precipitously up, first over flowers and green vegetation, then over loose slide rock, finally on sharply rising bedrock which varied from slate to quartz to andesite. At one place a 20-foot sheer drop on a knife-edge ridge made us backtrack and detour, using fingerholds to get around a minor bump on the skyline which we had not noticed from Amawk and Alhamblar. Here it took us fifty minutes to gain 150 feet in elevation.

Mostly, however, the going was good, and less than five hours after leaving camp we stood on a wild summit in the midst of the Koyukuk's most spectacular topography. Across the Clear River country we could see an arctic thunderstorm was just breaking over Boreal, giving an exceptional impression of nature unconquerable and infinitely more powerful than man.

To the right of the storm was Doonerak, just as unconquered as the thunder. There it rose, crowned by 2,000 feet of bleak rock precipice—as unconquerable to us in 1939 as the Atlantic Ocean must have seemed five hundred years ago.

The ascent of Doonerak had been the first objective of our journey. We had intensely wanted to climb the mountain. Now, obviously, our goal was unattainable for us. We had made and would make first ascents of many lesser peaks, but someone else would accomplish the superlative, not we.

Our view, to be sure, was gorgeous perfection. Not even Mount Doonerak could have surpassed it. Indeed, we tried to persuade ourselves that the greater height of Mount Doonerak would tend to flatten the appearance of lesser summits and of the jaggedness of the topography. Also, the storm had spread northward from Boreal, and Mount Doonerak's tip was just being enveloped in clouds. We speculated that if we were now on that peak, there would be no more enjoyment of scenery, but a hasty retreat from the storm. Nevertheless, Mount Doonerak alone could have brought highest fulfillment, the highest honor.

Was our happiness on Apoon diminished because we could not climb 2,000 feet of sheer rock? Is it possible to reconcile oneself to the second best and feel satisfied with the best one can attain? That was the question in everything. One in a million, perhaps, could be a Nobel Prize winner or a President of the United States. The other 999,999 might burden their lives in gnashing their teeth over unrealized ambitions for greatness, or they might adjust to limitations and get the greatest possible happiness out of the North Dooneraks, the Amawks, and the Apoons which they could attain. Perhaps this philosophizing on a windswept pinnacle of rock might seem a little forced, but I could not help it, because I had talked only recently with an assistant manager, an associate professor, and a division chief whose lives for several years had been unhappy because they had not been promoted to head manager, full professor, and bureau chief.

The storm was swinging eastward. Boreal and Doonerak, emerging from the clouds, were saturated in a weird light, as if they had suddenly dissolved in air but not yet blown away. In the opposite direction, far to the east across the deep valley of Hammond River, beyond the widely branching drainage of the Middle Fork, far out among the unknown, unexplored source streams of the Chandalar, against the most distant horizon where fact and infinity merged, the sun was shining brilliantly on countless lofty peaks without name and beyond the scope of human knowledge. All around us were gorges, thousands of feet deep, great snowbanks, bright green valleys, gaily colored rocks. All was peace and strength and immensity and coordination and freedom.

Next morning we broke camp in the rain and started our fifty-three miles of back packing necessary to get back to Wiseman. We all hated the thought of the approaching end. The longer you are out on a wilderness trip, the smoother things work. Making and breaking camp, and all the little chores go more and more automatically. You become so used to your equipment and its inevitable limitations that soon the fact that you have just twenty inches between your head and the back wall of the fly for storing equipment which you want to keep dry has become entirely accepted. All the time you are getting physically hardened so that 55 pounds, which seemed like quite a load whether you had come fresh from a winter of shoveling gravel or of sitting at a Washington desk, is now an easy pack. Saddest of all was the thought of leaving these fine partners—these energetic, stimulating, considerate, kindly, intelligent men, with whom not a single harsh word had been exchanged during the entire journey.

The first day we reeled off fourteen miles along the gravel bars of the Hammond River. We traveled again in fifty-minute shifts with ten-minute rests between. It rained all day steadily but not hard. By ten in the evening we had reached the yellow reindeer moss flats at the mouth of Kalhabuk Creek.

While the fellows were setting up camp and preparing supper, I walked three and a half miles up the right branch of Kalhabuk Creek to Kaaruk Lake on the low divide between Hammond and Dietrich rivers, sparkling with the freshness of arctic moss and arctic flowers at arctic midnight. At the lake a bull moose was feeding with no concern for the first man to visit his domain in many years.

Not the first visitor, however, for old ax marks along the creek indicated both Eskimo and white-man invasions in the past. Later, when we compared notes with Verne Watts after our return, we found that he and three partners had camped at the mouth of Kalhabuk Creek for one mid-winter night when they saw in the new year of 1902.

Next day we covered eighteen easy miles to Canyon Creek, a tributary of the Hammond River, where we spent our last night together, just beyond the zone of men. It was one of our most comfortable camps, although I chided Nutirwik jokingly for the large-size sticks he started to incorporate in the bed.

"Nutirwik, those spruce boughs you've got there, are more like spruce logs."

"Big sticks good for you," he replied. "Get up early, no loaf in bed."

Next day at noon at a mining camp on Swift Creek we saw the first people outside of our party that we had seen in twenty-two days. We learned from them that it was Sunday, that the whole world was not yet at war as it had appeared to be when we emerged from the wilderness the year before, and that Joe Louis had knocked out Tony Galento in four rounds.

We had only half a mile of trail and seven miles of "auto road" from Swift Creek to Wiseman. The auto road was actually being used for the first time since the previous summer by the Koyukuk's one and only car, with whose owner, Joe Ulen, we chatted briefly. Half an hour later we walked up to the Wiseman roadhouse.

Now we were back among people in Wiseman. In a day I should be in Fairbanks, in two more in Juneau, in a week in Seattle and the great, thumping, modern world. I should be living once more among the accumulated accomplishments of man. The world with its present population needs these accomplishments. It cannot live on wilderness, except incidentally and sporadically. Nevertheless, to four human beings, just back from the source streams of the Koyukuk, no comfort, no security, no invention, no brilliant thought which the modern world had to offer could provide half the elation of the days spent in the little-explored, uninhabited world of the arctic wilderness.

NATHANIEL HAWTHORNE

Hobnobbing

"According to my invariable custom, I mistook my way . . ."

Nathaniel Hawthorne did not walk so much as he floundered; so he confessed. But whatever else he was—and he shows here a certain priggishness—Hawthorne was an honest man. Less private than Thoreau and less popular than Emerson, he wore his heart on his sleeve and bore its wounds with a stubborn resignation. In the following selections from his American Notebooks, *Hawthorne struggles desperately with the descriptive art; he engages Margaret Fuller, the most formidable woman of his time, in the discussion of Deep Questions; he snubs the illustrious Emerson; and he strolls the woods of Walden Pond long before his Concord neighbor went there to "live alone, in the woods, a mile from any neighbor, in a house which I had built myself."*

I took a walk through the woods, yesterday afternoon, to Mr. Emerson's, with a book which Margaret Fuller had left behind her, after a call on Saturday eve. I missed the nearest way, and wandered into a very secluded portion of the forest—for forest it might justly be called, so dense and sombre was the shade of oaks and pines. Once I wandered into a tract so overgrown with bushes and underbrush that I could scarcely force a passage through. Nothing is more annoying than a walk of this kind—to be tormented to death by an innumerable host of petty impediments; it incenses and depresses me at the same time. Always when I flounder into the midst of a tract of bushes, which cross and intertwine themselves about my legs, and brush my face, and seize hold of my clothes with a multitudinous gripe—always, in such a difficulty, I feel as it were almost as well to lie down and die in rage and despair, as to go one step further. It is laughable, after I have got out of the scrape, to think how miserably it affected me for the moment; but I had better learn patience betimes; for there are many such bushy tracts in this vicinity, on the margins of meadows; and my walks will often lead me into them. Escaping from the bushes, I soon came to an open space among the woods—a very lonely spot, with the tall old trees standing around, as quietly as if nobody had intruded there throughout the whole summer. A company of crows were holding their sabbath in the tops of some of the trees; apparently they felt themselves injured or insulted by my presence; for, with one consent, they began to caw–caw–caw—and launching themselves sullenly on the air, took flight to some securer solitude. Mine, probably, was the first human shape that they had seen, all day long—at least, if they had been stationary in that spot; but perhaps they had winged their way over miles and miles of country—had breakfasted on the summit of Graylock and dined at the base of Wachusett, and were merely come to sup and sleep among the quiet woods of Concord. But it was my impression, at the time, that they had sat still and silent in the tops of the trees, all through the Sabbath-day; and I felt like one who should unawares disturb an assembly of worshippers. A crow, however, has no real pretensions to religion, in spite of their gravity of mien and black attire—they are certainly thieves, and probably infidels. Nevertheless, their voices, yesterday, were in admirable accordance with the influences of the quiet, sunny, warm, yet autumnal afternoon; they were so far above my head, that their loud clamor added to the quiet of the scene, instead of disturbing it. There was no other sound, except the song of the crickets. . . .

After leaving the book at Mr. Emerson's, I returned through the woods, and entering Sleepy Hollow, I perceived a lady reclining near the path which bends along its verge. It was Margaret herself. She had been there the whole afternoon, meditating or reading; for she had a book in her hand, with some strange title, which I did not understand and have forgotten. She said that nobody had broken her solitude, and was just giving utterance to a theory that no inhabitant of Concord ever visited Sleepy Hollow, when we saw a whole group of people entering the sacred precincts. Most of them followed a path that led them remote from us; but an old man passed near us, and smiled to see Margaret lying on the ground, and me sitting by her side. He made some remark about the beauty of the afternoon, and withdrew himself into the shadow of the wood. Then we talked about Autumn—and about the pleasures of getting lost in the woods—and about the crows, whose voices Margaret had heard—and about the experiences of early childhood, whose influence remains upon the character after the collection of them has passed away—and about the sight of mountains from a distance, and the view from their summits—and about other matters of high and low philosophy. In the midst of our talk, we heard footsteps above us, on the high bank; and while the intruder was still hidden among the trees, he called to Margaret, of whom he had gotten a glimpse. Then he emerged from the green shade; and, behold, it was Mr. Emerson, who, in spite of his clerical consecration, had found no better way of spending the Sabbath than to ramble among the woods. He appeared to have had a pleasant time; for he said that there were Muses in the woods to-day, and whispers to be heard in the breezes. It being now nearly six o'clock, we separated, Mr. Emerson and Margaret towards his house, and I towards mine, where my little wife was very busy getting tea. By the bye, Mr. Emerson gave me an invitation to dinner to-day, to be complied with or not, as might suit my convenience at the time; and it happens not to suit. . . .

Yesterday afternoon . . . I took a solitary walk to Walden Pond. It was a cool, north-west windy day, with heavy clouds rolling and tumbling about the sky, but still a prevalence of genial autumn sunshine. The fields are still green, and the great masses of the woods have not yet assumed their many-colored garments; but here and there, are solitary oaks of a deep, substantial red, or maples of a more brilliant hue, or chestnuts, either yellow or of a tenderer green than in summer. Some trees seem to return to their hue of May or early July, before they put on the brighter autumnal tints. In some places, along the borders of low and moist land, a whole range of trees were clothed in the perfect gorgeousness of autumn, of all shades of brilliant color, looking like the palette on which Nature was arranging the tints wherewith to paint a picture. These hues appeared to be thrown together without design; and yet there was perfect harmony among them, and a softness and delicacy made up of a thousand different brightnesses. . . . But it is vain for me to attempt to describe these autumnal brilliancies, or to convey the impression which they make on me. I have tried a thousand times, and always without the slightest self-satisfaction. . . .

Walden Pond was clear and beautiful, as usual. It tempted me to bathe; and though the water was thrillingly cold, it was like the thrill of a happy death. Never was there such transparent water as this. I threw sticks into it, and saw them float suspended on an almost invisible medium; it seemed as if the pure air was beneath them, as well as above. If I were to be baptized, it should be in this pond; but then one would not wish to pollute it by washing off his sins into it. . . .

In a small and secluded dell, that opens upon the most beautiful cove of the whole lake, there is a little hamlet of huts or shanties, inhabited by the Irish people who are at work upon the rail-road. There are three or four of these habitations, the very rudest, I should imagine, that civilized men ever made for themselves, constructed of rough boards, with protruding ends. Against some of them the earth is heaped up to the roof, or nearly so; and when the grass has had time to sprout upon them, they will look like small natural hillocks, or a species of ant-hill, or something in which Nature has a larger share than man. These huts are placed beneath the trees (oaks, walnuts, and white pines), wherever the trunks give them space to stand; and by thus adapting themselves to natural interstices instead of making new ones, they do not break or disturb the solitude and seclusion of the place. Voices are heard, and the shouts and laughter of children, who play about like sunbeams that come down through the branches. Women are washing beneath the trees, and long lines of whitened clothes are extended from tree to tree, fluttering and gambolling in the breeze. A pig, in a stye even more extemporary than the shanties, is grunting, and poking his snout through the clefts of his habitation. The household pots and kettles are seen at the doors, and a glance within shows the rough benches that serve for chairs, and the bed upon the floor. The visiter's nose takes notice of the fragrance of a pipe. And yet, with all these homely items, the repose and sanctity of the old wood do not seem to be destroyed or prophaned; she over-shadows these poor people, and assimilates them, somehow or other, to the character of her natural inhabitants. Their presence did not shock me, any more than if I had merely discovered a squirrel's nest in a tree. To be sure, it is a torment to see the great, high, ugly embankment of the rail-road, which is here protruding itself into the lake, or along its margin, in close vicinity to this picturesque little hamlet. I have seldom seen anything more beautiful than the cove, on the border of which the huts are situated; and the more I looked, the lovelier it grew. The trees overshadowed it deeply; but on one side there was some brilliant shrubbery which seemed to light up the whole picture with the effect of a sweet and melancholy smile. I felt as if the spirits were there—or as if these shrubs had a spiritual life—in short, the impression was undefinable; and after gazing and musing a good while, I retraced my steps through the Irish hamlet, and plodded on along a wood-path.

According to my invariable custom, I mistook my way, and emerging upon a road, I turned my back, instead of my face, towards Concord, and walked on very diligently, till a guide-board informed me of my mistake. I then turned about, and was shortly overtaken by an old yeoman in a chaise, who kindly offered me a ride, and shortly set me down in the village.

LOREN EISELEY

The Hounds of Darkness

"You can sense their eyes upon you . . ."

Someone—undoubtedly a walker—once wrote that the democracy of the road by day gives way to the aristocracy of the road by night. Loren Eiseley found it so, and discovered something else as well: aristocracy without its retainers can be a chilling affair. An outstanding anthropologist, teacher, writer and contemplative naturalist, Eiseley was born in Nebraska in 1907. He has always searched for "the point at which the mundane world gives way to quite another dimension." He found it here, alone and on foot near the Rocky Mountains. He declines even today to say precisely where.

I have been over into that nocturnal country, as I will presently recount, and though I stand in awe of it, it has also stimulated my curiosity. In fact, though I hesitate to speak openly of the matter, I have a faint, though not too secure, feeling of kinship with certain creatures I have encountered there.

Sometimes in a country lane at midnight you can sense their eyes upon you—the eyes that by daylight may be the vacuous protuberant orbs of grazing cattle or the good brown eyes of farm dogs. But there, in the midnight lane, they draw off from you or silently watch you pass from their hidden coverts in the hedgerows. They are back in a secret world from which man has been shut out, and they want no truck with him after nightfall. Perhaps it is because of this that more and more we employ machines with lights and great noise to rush by these watchful shadows. My experience, therefore, may be among the last to be reported from that night world, which, with our machines to face, is slowly ebbing back into little patches of wilderness behind lighted signboards. It concerns a journey. I will not say where the journey began, but it took place in the years that have come to be called the Great Depression and was made alone and on foot. Finally I had come to a place where, far off over an endless blue plain, I could see the snow on the crests of the mountains. The city to which I was journeying lay, I knew, at the foot of the highest peak. I would keep the mountains in sight, I thought to myself, and find my own path to the city.

I climbed over a barbed-wire fence and marched directly toward the city through the blue air under the great white peak. I think sometimes now, long afterward, that it was the happiest, most independent day of my entire life. No one waited for me anywhere. I was complete in myself like a young migrating animal whose world exists totally in the present moment. The range with its drifting cattle and an occasional passing bird began to unroll beneath my stride. I meant to be across that range and over an escarpment of stone to the city at the mountain's foot before the dawn of another morning. During the entire walk I was never to meet another human being. The lights and showers of that high landscape, the moving shadows of the clouds, shone upon or darkened my face alternately, but I was destined to share the experience with no one.

In the later afternoon, after descending into innumerable arroyos and scrambling with difficulty up the vertical bank of the opposite side, I began to grow tired. Coming out finally into a country that was less trenched and eroded, I was trudging steadily onward when I came upon a pond. At least for all purposes it could answer to the name, though it was only a few inches deep—mere standing rainwater caught in a depression of impermeable soil and interspersed with tufts of brown buffalo grass. I hesitated by it for a moment, somewhat disturbed by a few leeches which I could see moving among the grass stems. Then, losing my scruples, I crouched and drank the bitter water. The hollow was sheltered from the wind that had been sweeping endlessly against me as I traveled. I found a dry spot by the water's edge and stretched out to rest a moment. In my exhaustion the minute must have stretched into an hour. Something, some inner alarm, brought me to my senses.

Long shadows were stealing across the pond water and the light was turning red. One of those shadows, I thought dimly as I tried to move a sleep-stiffened elbow from under my head, seemed to be standing right over me. Drowsily I focused my sight and squinted against the declining sun. In the midst of the shadow I made out a very cold yellow eye and then saw that the thing looming over me was a great blue heron.

He was standing quietly on one foot and looking, like an expert rifleman, down the end of a bill as deadly as an assassin's dagger. I had seen, not long before, a man with his brow split open by a half-grown heron which he had been rash enough to try and capture. The man had been fortunate, for the inexperienced young bird had driven for his eye and missed, gashing his forehead instead.

The bird I faced was perfectly mature and had come softly down on a frog hunt while I slept. Why was he now standing over me? It was certain that momentarily he did not recognize me for a man. Perhaps he was merely curious. Perhaps it was only my little brown eye in the mud that he wanted. As this thought penetrated my sleeping brain I rolled, quick as a frog shrieking underfoot, into the water. The great bird, probably as startled as I, rose and beat steadily off into the wind, his long legs folded gracefully behind him.

A little shaken, I stood up and looked after him. There was nothing anywhere for miles and he had come to me like a ghost. How long he had been standing there I did not know. The light was dim now and the cold of the high plains was rising. I shivered and mopped my wet face. The snow on the peak was still visible. I got my bearings and hurried on, determined to make up for lost time. Again the long plain seemed to pass endlessly under my hastening footsteps. For hours I moved under the moon, not too disastrously, though once I fell. The sharp-edged arroyos had appeared again and were a menace in the dark. They were very hard to see, and some were deep.

It was some time after the moon rose that I began to realize that I was being followed. I stopped abruptly and listened. Something, several things, stopped with me. I heard their feet put down an instant after mine. Dead silence. "Who's there?" I said, trying to make the words adjustable and appeasing to any kind of unwanted companion. There was no answer, though I had the feel of several shapes just beyond my range of vision. There was nothing to do. I started on again and the footsteps began once more, but always they stopped and started with mine. Finally I began to suspect that the number of my stealthy followers was growing and that they were closing up the distance between us by degrees.

I had a choice then: I had been realizing it for some time. I could lose my nerve, run, and invite pursuit, possibly breaking my leg in a ditch, or, like a sensible human being a little out of his element perhaps, I could go back and see what threatened me. On the instant, I stopped and turned.

There was a little clipclop of sound and dead silence once more, but this time I heard a low uneasy snuffling that could only come from many noses. I groped in the dark for a stick or a stone but could find none. I ran three steps back in a threatening manner and raised a dreadful screech that caused some shifting of feet and a little rumble of menacing sound. The screech had nearly shattered my own nerves. My heart thumped as I tried to recover my poise.

Cattle.

What was it that gave them this eerie behavior in the dark?

I affected to ignore them. I started on again, whistling, but my mouth was dry. Range cattle, something spelled out in my mind—wild, used to horsemen—what are they like to a man on foot in the dark? They were getting ominously close—that was certain; even if they were just curious, that steady trampling bearing down on my heels was nerve-wracking. Ahead of me at that instant I saw a section of barbed wire against the moon, and behind it a wide boulder-strewn stream bed.

The stream was dry and the starlight shone on the white stones. I swung about and yelled, making a little rush back. Then, without waiting to observe the effects, I turned and openly ran for it. There was a growing thunder behind me. I heard it as I vaulted the fence and landed eight feet down in the sand of the stream bed. Above me I heard a sound like a cavalry troop wheeling off into the night. A braver man might have stood by the fence and waited to see what would happen, but in the night there is this difference that comes over things. I sat on a stone in the stream bed and breathed hard for a long time. Then the chill forced me up again. The arroyo twisted in the direction I was headed. I wandered down it, feeling safer among the stones that reflected light and half-illuminated my path.

Somewhere along a section of damp sand I encountered several large toads who were also making a night journey and who hopped clumsily for a little way with me. There was something so attractive about their little bursts of energy that, tired as I was, I began to skip with them. I was delighted now to have even lowly company. First one would hop and then another, and I began to take my turn automatically with the rest. I do not know where they might have eventually led me, though I had a feeling that if I stayed and hopped with them long enough I might acquire this knowledge in some primordial manner.

With this thought I parted from them at a turn in the stream bed and made my way again over open rolling foothills in the dark. The land was rising. I was approaching the escarpment which I knew overhung the deeper valley in which lay the city at the mountain's foot.

I met nothing living now except small twisted pines. Boulders swelled up from the turf like huge white puff balls, and there was a flash of lightning off to the south that lit for one blue, glistening instant a hundred miles of churning, shifting landscape. I have

thought since that each stone, each tree, each ravine and crevice echoing and re-echoing with thunder tells us more at such an instant than any daytime vision of the road we travel. The flash hangs like an immortal magnification in the brain, and suddenly you know the kind of country you pass over, and the powers abroad in it. It was at that moment that I reached the edge of the escarpment and looked down.

The night lights of the city glistened in hundreds far out on the plain, but I had chosen a bad pathway. I was high up on a clifflike eminence, and a straight descent in the dark was dangerous. As far as I could see there was no break to right or left. I was tired and hungry—too weary to go on circling in the dark and too cold to sit and wait for dawn. I decided to climb down, though with the utmost caution. Those faraway street lights beneath me were an irresistible attraction. They were the world I knew. The mind inside us is vaster than the world outside and I had been wrestling with its terrors for a long time now.

I began with discretion, working my way by inches down a precipitous gully. After a while the gully ended and I seemed to be looking out through a tree root at a solitary light on a mine tipple still far beneath me. I must have stayed there an hour groping about in the dark. Then I found a ledge along which I edged farther until I knocked over a stone that went rolling and grinding downward. Gaining momentum, it began to leap and volley against unseen stumps and boulders, making a hideous din.

As soon as the echoes died I knew I was in for trouble. I was well down from the summit now and there was no way back up that mountain wall in the dark. I heard them coming before I saw them— two huge watch dogs from the mine property. They barked with great night-foggy voices and leaped and slavered at me up the cliff. The sound was enough to wake the dead, and I expected at first that someone, a watchman, might appear. I hoped to be able to explain myself and have the man get the dogs under control. The dogs, however, happened to be alone. Nobody came and there I hung, a few feet up the cliff, while that formidable chorus played up and down my spine. The grip of my hands was growing tired and I thought with sudden careful prevision: If you wait till you're tired and fall, you won't be able to fight them off.

I climbed on then, slowly working downward along the ledge. I didn't want to have to drop suddenly in their midst. It would startle them, and if I were unlucky enough to fall they might spring on me.

In fact, it looked as though they were going to spring in any case. But there it was. I tried to choose a moment when they seemed tired from their own great bellowing exertions. In a pause I vaulted down onto their own level from the wall.

I said something in a voice I tried to keep confident and friendly. I held one arm over my throat and stood stock-still. They came up to me warily, but one made a small woofing sound in his throat and I could see the motion of his tail in the dark. Seeing this, I dropped one hand on his head and the other on the other beast whose jaws had closed with surprising gentleness about my ankle. I stood there for long minutes talking and side-thumping and trying all the dog language I knew.

At the end of that time my foot was reluctantly released and the great hounds, with the total irrationality that prevails over the sheer cliff of Chaos, leaped and bounded about me, as though I were their returning master. Did they take me finally, because of my successful descent, as a demon like themselves—for, if I had fallen, they had given every indication of devouring me—or are the dogs of Cerberus, the hoarse-voiced, much feared guardian of Darkness, actually abysmally lonely and friendly creatures?

Since that long agonizing descent before I reached the city on the plain, I have never been quite sure. When I come to the Final Pit in which they howl, I shall, without too great a show of confidence, put out my hand and speak once more. Perhaps the great hounds of fear may wait with wagging tails for a voice which knows them. And what dog is there that knows how to tell one demon from another in the dark?

By the eyes, some will say, but I think not, really, for to the spectral tarsier in the bush, or to the owl in the churchyard tower, man and his lights must truly hold a demonic menace. Having journeyed once along the dark side of the planet, I am willing to testify that it is a shifting and unmapped domain of terrors. But as one demon to another, in memory of that hour on a cliff wall, I have helped a bat to escape from a university classroom, and I have never told on a frightened owl I once saw perched on the curtain rod above a Pullman berth. Somewhere in the blasts over the roaring cliff of Chaos I may meet their like again. It will be all one in that place, light and dark, big and small eyes, and the true demon will not fear his brother from another element. No. I think now the great dogs will know me. At least I shall put out my hand and speak.

JOHN DAVIS

A Wag's Progress

"To travel on foot, is to travel like Plato and Pythagoras . . ."

John Davis was born in a momentous year—1776—in Salisbury, England. He went to sea at the tender age of 11, and was only 22 when his wanderings brought him to the shores of America. In New York he lodged with a certain Doctor De Bow, a man with little practice in his profession and less inclination to increase it; while the doctor read Cervantes, Davis translated Buonaparte's Campaign in Italy *from the French, and set out with a full purse for the backwoods. He supported himself, when necessary, as a tutor. While he could not escape the stilted syntax of his time, his account of four years on foot in the new nation cannot be matched for wit and winsomeness. Portions of three of his journeys are included here—the beginning of his long pilgrimage, from New York to Philadelphia; a stroll through South Carolina (present U.S. 17 follows his route through Jacksonboro, Coosawatchie and Ashepoo); and a tour up the wooded Potomac, where women posed greater dangers than any wild beast.*

These accounts are from John Davis' Travels of Four Years and a Half in the United States of America During 1798, 1799, 1800, 1801, and 1802, *published in London in 1803. His more elaborate asides and perorations have been omitted but his spelling and punctuation retained.*

My occupations at New-York, however agreeable, did not repress my desire to explore the continent before me; and I thought it best to travel while I had some crowns left in my purse. I felt regret at the thought of separating from the Doctor, whom I was attached to from habit; but the Doctor soon relieved me by saying, he would accompany me whithersoever I went; that no man loved travelling better than he, and that he would convert his medicines into money to defray his expences on the road.

But tell me, said the Doctor, are you fond of walking? I assured him no person could be more so. Then, resumed he, let us each provide ourselves with a good cudgel, and begin our journey on foot. I will put a case of instruments into my pocket, and you can slip into yours the campaign of *Buonaparte* in *Italy*.

But whither, replied I, do you propose to go; and what, I beseech you, is the object of your travelling? To see the world, assuredly, said he; to eat, drink, and laugh away care on the road. How Doctor, said I, would you approve of a walk to Philadelphia? I should like it of all things, said the Doctor. In our way to it we should go through the place of my birth; you have heard, I guess, of Hackinsac; and at Philadelphia I could get somebody to introduce me to the great Doctor Rush. All we have to do is send on our trunks in the coach, and trudge after them on foot.

Our resolution was no sooner taken than executed. The Doctor got an apothecary, who lived opposite, to purchase what few drugs were contained in his painted drawers; and having dispatched our trunks forward by coach, we began our journey to Philadelphia.

Having crossed the Hudson, which separates York-Island from the shore of the Jerseys, we were landed at a Tavern delightfully situated on the bank of the river. The Doctor having once reduced a fractured leg for the landlord, proposed dining at the Tavern; he will certainly charge us nothing, said he, for I once reduced his leg, when the Tibia and Fibula were both badly fractured. It was a nice case, and I will put him in mind of it.

But *you charged him!* Doctor! did you not, said I. No matter for that, replied he. I should have been expelled from the College of Whigs, had I not put in my claim.

The landlord of the tavern was a portly man, who in the middle of the day was dressed in a loose night-gown and mocossins; he recognized the Doctor, whom he shook heartily by the hand, and turning to a man in company said, "they may talk of Doctor Rush, Doctor Mitchell, or Doctor Devil, but I maintain Doctor De Bow is the greatest Doctor of them all."

It was difficult to refrain from laughing aloud; but the speech of the landlord inspired the Doctor with very different emotions; he made an inclination of his head, adjusted his spectacles, and assumed a profound look, that assented to the justness of the remark.

What, gentlemen, said the landlord, would you chuse for dinner? It is now the hottest part of the day, and if you are walking to Newark, you will find the evening more pleasant. How comes on trade, Doctor, at New-York? I warrant you have got your share.

Why, Mr. Clinch, replied the Doctor, I cannot complain. There have been several cases of fever to which I was called. And the patients were right, said Mr. Clinch, for they could not have called a better Doctor had they sent over the four quarters of the globe for him. Well, it is true, God sends the country fevers, but he also sends us Doctors who are able to cure them. It is like the State I was born in: Virginia is infested with snakes, but it abounds with roots to cure their bite. Come walk in, gentlemen, walk in. I will get dinner ready directly.

Our dinner was a miserable one; but the landlord seasoned his dishes with flattery, and the Doctor found it very palatable. We went forward in the cool; nor did my friend hesitate to pay his club towards two dollars for our repast: it was high, the Doctor whispered, but continued he, when a man's consequence is known at a tavern it always inflames the bill.

It was our original design to have gone through Hackinsack, a little village that claimed the honor of my companion's nativity; but it was getting late; the road to it was circuitous, and we wished much that night to travel to Elizabeth Town. The Doctor consoled himself for not visiting his family by observing that no man was a prophet at home.

We did not stop long at Newark, but prosecuted our walk, after taking shelter from a shower of rain in one of its sylvan habitations. The sun, which had been obscured, again gladdened the plains; and the birds which had ceased awhile singing, again renewed their harmony.

We reached Elizabeth Town a little while after the stage-coach. My companion being somewhat fatigued, retired early to bed, but I devoted great part of the night to the refined pleasures of reading and reflecting. There is no life so unsettled but a lover of reading will find leisure for the acquisition of knowledge, an acquisition that depends not on either seasons or place. To know the value of time, we must learn to appreciate every particle of it; and remember that moments, however trifling in appearance, form the year by accumulation.

When I went to bed there was little sleep to be obtained; for a huge mastiff in the yard, notwithstanding the Doctor put his head out of the window and vociferated to him repeatedly, did not remit barking the whole of the night. We therefore rose without being called, and pursued our journey to Prince-town, a place more famous for its College than its learning.

The road from Prince-town to Trenton offers little matter for speculation. I know that in some places there were battles fought between the British and their revolted Colonists; but the recollection of it tends to no use, and, I am sure, it cannot be pleasing.

At Trenton, the Doctor, who was afflicted with sore eyes, declined proceeding any further. It was to no purpose that I expostulated with him on the folly of his conduct, and urged that we had not many more miles to travel. The son of *Paracelsus* was inexorable, and it only remained for me to perform the last office of friendship, which was to tie a bandage over his eyes, and lead him blindfolded to his room.

From Trenton I was conveyed over the Delaware in the ferry-boat, with an elderly man, clad in the garb of a Quaker. His looks beamed benignity, and his accents breathed kindness: but, as the great Master of Life observes, there is no art can find the mind's construction in the face.

We had scarce landed on the opposite bank of the river, when a poor cripple in a soldier's jacket, advanced towards the Quaker, holding both his crutches in one hand, and taking half a hat from his head with the other:—Bestow your charity, cried the beggar, on a poor worn-out soldier, who fought for your liberty during a long war, and got wounded by a Hessian at the very place you have just left. Refuse not your charity to an old soldier in distress.

Alas! exclaimed the Quaker, this comes of war. Shame on our nature. Beasts live in concord, men only disagree. Had thou taken the advice of scripture, thou wouldest have escaped thy wounds!

What, Master, is that?

Why, Friend, if a man smite thee on one cheek, turn to him the other.

And were you to take the advice of scripture, you would not refuse me your alms.

What, Friend, is that?

Why when a man wants to borrow of thee, turn not thou away.

I remember no such passage, replied the Quaker.

It is in the New Testament, said the beggar.

The text has been corrupted, cried the Quaker, hastening away through a field.

Won't you give me a copper? bawled the beggar, limping after the Quaker.

Charity begins at home, said the Quaker, accelerating his pace.

The Lord help thee, exclaimed the beggar, halting almost breathless on his crutch. But here perhaps is a gentleman who has more of the milk of human kindness.

To become acquainted with human life, the traveller must not mingle only with the sons of opulence and ease; these know no greater fatigue than the hurry of preparation for a ball, and experience no higher mortification than the disappointment of pride. Such beings who pass their days in solemn pomp and plenty, can display no examples of fortitude, of serenity, or patience; their wishes are anticipated, and their mandates obeyed. It is among the children of adversity that we must look for resignation under misfortune; it is from the indigent only we can be instructed to bear calamities without repining.

Impressed with this conviction, I entered into discourse with the cripple, whom I found to be a man not without reflection. He had seen better days, and hoped for their return. Though my present appearance, said he, shews I am in the most wretched state of poverty, there was a time when I knew the comforts of a home and fireside. These are past, but there is a pleasure in the recollection of them; for no man who has enjoyed the comforts of life, is ever without hope that he shall enjoy them again.

I had walked about a mile along the bank of the Delaware, when the coach to Philadelphia overtook me, and finding the road dusty I complied with the invitation of the driver to get into the vehicle. At Bristol we took up two young women, clad in the habit of Quakers, whom I soon, however, discovered to be girls of the town; and who, under pretence of shewing me a letter, discovered their address.

The winters of Carolina, however piercing to a native, who during the summer months may be said to bask rather than breathe, are mild to an Englishman accustomed to the frosts of his island. In the month of November my engagement led me to Coosobatchie, an insignificant village about seventy-eight miles from Charleston; for the plantation of Mr. Drayton was in the neighbouring woods. The serenity of the weather invited the traveller to walk, and, at an early hour of the morning, I departed on foot from Charleston.

The foot-traveller need not be ashamed of his mode of journeying. To travel on foot, is to travel like Plato and Pythagoras; and to these examples may be added the not less illustrious ones of Goldsmith and Rousseau. The rambles of the ancient sages are at this distance of time uncertain; but it is well known, that Goldsmith made his tour of Europe on foot, and that Rousseau walked, from choice, through a great part of Italy.

An agreeable walk of ten miles, brought me to the bank of

Ashley River, where I breakfasted in a decent public-house, with the landlord and his family. Having crossed the ferry, I resumed my journey through a country which might be assimilated to one continued forest. Tall trees of pine, planted by the hand of nature in regular rows, bordered the road I travelled; and I saw no other animals, but now and then a flock of deer, while ceasing to browse, looked up at me with symptoms of wonder rather than fear.

At three in the afternoon I reached Jacksonborough, the only town on the road from Charleston to Coosobatchie. Though a foot-traveller, I was received at the tavern with every demonstration of respect; the landlord ushered me into a room which afforded the largest fire I had ever seen in my travels: yet the landlord, rubbing his hands, complained it was cold, and exclaimed against his negroes for keeping so bad a fire. Here, Syphax, said he, be quick and bring more wood: you have made, you rascal, a *Charleston* fire: fetch a stout back-log, or I'll make a back-log of you.

The exclamations of the landlord brought his wife into the room. She curtsied, and made many eloquent apologies for the badness of the fire; but added, that her waiting man Will had run away, and having whipped Syphax till his back was raw, she was willing to try what gentle means would do.

A dinner of venison, and a pint of Madeira, made me forget I had walked thirty miles; and it being little more than four o'clock, I proceeded forward on my journey. The vapours of a Spanish segar promoted cogitation, and I was lamenting the inequality of conditions in the world, when night overtook me.

I now redoubled my pace, not without apprehension that I should have to seek my lodgings in some tree, to avoid the beasts that prowled nightly in the woods; but the moon, which rose to direct me in my path, alleviated my perturbation, and in another hour I descried the blaze of a friendly fire through the casements of a log house. Imaginary are worse than real calamities; and the apprehension of sleeping in the woods was by far more painful than the actual experience of it would have been. The same Being who sends trials, can also inspire fortitude.

The place I had reached was Asheepo, a hamlet consisting of three or more log-houses; and the inhabitants of every sex and age had collected round a huge elephant, which was journeying with his master to Savannah.

Fortune had therefore brought me into unexpected company,

and I could not but admire the docility of the elephant, who in solemn majesty received the gifts of the children with his trunk. But not so the monkey. This man of Lord *Monboddo* was inflamed with rage at the boys and girls; nor could the rebukes of his master calm the transports of his fury.

I entered the log house which accommodated travellers. An old negro-man had squated himself before the fire. Well, old man, said I, why don't you go out to look at the elephant? Hie! Massa, he calf! In fact the elephant had come from Asia, and the negro from Africa, but he had seen the same species of animal, but of much greater magnitude.

Travelling, says Shakespeare, acquaints a man with strange bed-fellows; and there being only one bed in the log-house, I slept that night with the elephant-driver. Mr. Owen was a native of Wales, but he had been a great traveller, and carried a map of his travels in his pocket.—Nothing shortens a journey more than good company on the road; so I departed after breakfast from Asheepo, with Mr. Owen, his elephant, and his monkey.

Mr. Owen related to me the wonders of his elephant, which at some future day, I may perhaps publish in a separate treatise; but they would be irrelevant to my present journey, which towards noon I was left to prosecute alone. The elephant, however docile, would not travel without his dinner; and Mr. Owen halted under a pine-tree to feed the mute companion of his toils.

For my own part, I dined at a solitary log-house in the woods, upon exquisite venison. My host was a small Planter, who cultivated a little rice, and maintained a wife and four children with his rifled-barrel-gun. He had been Overseer to a Colonel Fishborne, and owned half a dozen negroes; but he observed to me his property was running about at large, for four of them had absconded.

As I purposed to make Pocotaligo the end of my day's journey, I walked forward at a moderate pace; but towards evening I was roused from the reveries into which my walking had plunged me, by a conflagration in the woods. On either side of the road the trees were in flames, which extending to their branches, assumed an appearance both terrific and grotesque. Through these woods, belching flames and rolling smoke, I had to travel nearly a mile, when the sound of the negro's ax chopping of wood, announced that I was near Pocotaligo.

At Pocotaligo I learned that the conflagration in the woods arose from the carelessness of some back-wood-men, who having neglected to extinguish their fires, the flames had extended in succession to the herbage and the trees.

I was somewhat surprised on entering the tavern at Pocotaligo, to behold sixteen or more chairs placed round a table which was covered with the choicest dishes; but my surprise ceased when the Savannah and Charleston stage-coaches stopped at the door, and the passengers flocked to the fire before which I was sitting. In the Charleston coach came a party of comedians. Of these itinerant heroes the greater part were my countrymen; and, as I was not travelling to see Englishmen, but Americans, I was not sorry when they retired to bed.

I was in a worse condition at Pocotaligo than Asheepo; for at Pocotaligo the beds were so small that they would hold only respectively one person. Finding there was no bed to be procured, I seated myself in a nook of the chimney, called for wine and segars, and either attended to the conversation of the negro-girls who had spread their blankets on the floor, or entertained myself with the half-formed notions of the landlord and coachman, who had brought their chairs to the fire, and were disputing on politics. Both Americans and English are subject to loquacious imbecility. Their subjects only differ. The American talks of his government, the Englishman of himself.

Early in the morning, I resumed my journey in the coach that was proceeding to Savannah; I had but a short distance more to go; for Coosobatchie is only ten miles from Pocotaligo.

It was the latter part of March when I left the once-flourishing town of Baltimore, and again directed my steps towards the imperial city. But my mind was somewhat altered. Experience had cured me of illusions. I was no longer elated with the hope of being lifted above the crowd; but my ambition was contented with the harmless drudgery of teaching children their rudiments.

After walking a few miles, I turned into a wood to call at the house of a brother-pedagogue, who had invited me the preceding evening at a public-house, to visit him in his literary retirement. Boys and girls rent the air with their acclamations as I approached the dwelling; but the School-master's daughter, a lusty lass of nineteen, escaped into the woods, and I could only catch a glimpse of her flying across the green. I was not *Apollo*, or I should have followed this *Daphne*.

The board placed over Mr. Macdonald's sylvan Academy, diverted me not a little. "Anthony Macdonald teaches boys and girls their grammar tongue; also Geography terrestrial and celestial.—Old hats made as good as new."

But Mr. Macdonald was not at home; his daughter had fled; and I trod back the path to the main-road, where I sought an asylum under the roof of Widow Smith, who regales the woe-begone Traveller with whiskey. Old age is garrulous, and the Widow did not want for talk. She admired that Miss Macdonald instead of staying in the house to receive a stranger, should run into the woods. For her part she was never scared of folks, however well-dressed; and yet all her life she had lived in the country.

Pursuing my journey, I arrived at Elk-Ridge Landing, where I supped at a genteel tavern with the hostess and her sister, who are remarkable for the elegance of their conversation, and the amenity of their manners. I found the old Manor-house of Charlotte Smith lying on the table, of which the concluding part seemed to have been moistened with tears of sensibility.

The next day I resumed my walk; refreshing myself at Spurrier's, carousing at Dent's, and sleeping at Drummond's; three public-houses on the road, which the Traveller passes in succession. The weather was somewhat warm in the middle of the day; but this only made the springs more grateful, at whose waters I stopped to allay the thirst produced by walking.

Rousseau in enumerating the pleasures of pedestrian travelling, makes no mention of the joy with which the solitary walker beholds a spring on the road; from which omission I am inclined to believe that the foot-travels of the eloquent Swiss were performed round his chamber.

The next morning proceeding forward, I reached Bladensburgh before the going down of the sun; and at night-fall to my great satisfaction I entered the imperial city. The moon was rising from the woods, and I surveyed the Capitol by its light, meditating on the future state of the Western Empire; the clash of interests, the commotions of Demagogues, and the disunion of the States! But dumb be the Oracle of Prediction!

Having amused myself a few days at the imperial city, I rose with the sun, and pursued my journey along the banks of the Potomac. About nine in the morning I reached the bridge at the Little Falls; a bridge that raises the admiration of an American, but provokes only the contempt of an European. In fact, art in America would not detain an intelligent Traveller one hour; but nature would perhaps enchain his attention for years.

Near the bridge at the Little Falls my journey was suspended by the rain, and I found a reception in the tavern of Mr. Slimmer, a German, who at the age of threescore was smitten by a young English woman, whom he had taken for his wife, and who had brought him a child; a child the darling of his dotage, which he ludicrously termed "his little young woman cut shorter."

The rain not remitting its violence, I was obliged to pass the night under the roof of this fond couple, whom, I, however, left at an early hour the next morning to prosecute my journey; purposing to take the more circuitous road of the Great Falls of the Potomac.

I pass over in silence the common occurances of the road; the waggoners who returned no answer to my interrogations, and the plantation-curs that disturbed my reveries with their barking. About noon I reached the cross roads, and taking to the right, I could every minute hear more distinctly the roar of the Great Falls. At length I came to a spacious stream called "Difficult Run;" an appellation derived from the difficulty in crossing it. But no place could be more romantic. On one bank towered a majestic mountain, from the side of which rocks hanging in fragments menaced the Traveller with destruction; while others that had tumbled into the stream inter-rupted its course, producing a tumultuous roar that absorbed the cry of the water fowl hovering over the waves.

I was in suspense whether to ford this Run, or wait for a guide on its bank, when I descried two boys on the opposite shore who obeyed my call with alacrity; leaping from rock to rock till they reached the spot where I stood. With the assistance of a pole they conducted me to the opposite bank, where I learned that one of my young guides was called Basil Hurdle, and the other Jack Miller.

I now ascended a hill that led to the Great Falls, and on a sudden my steps were suspended by the conflict of elements, the strife of nature. I beheld the course of a large river abruptly ob-structed by rocks, over which it was breaking with a tremendous roar; while the foam of the water seemed ascending to the clouds, and the shores that confined it to tremble at the convolution. I gazed for some time in silent awe at this war of elements, when having recovered from my admiration, I could not help exclaiming to the Great Maker of Heaven and of Earth, "Lord! What is man that thou art mindful of him, or the son of man, that thou regardest him!"

For several hours I continued gazing at these Falls, lost in musing over the grandest object the Universe can supply; and when I beheld the wilderness around me, I could not but be impressed with the idea that nature delighted to perform her wonders in the secrecy of solitude.

A little below the Falls, on the bank of the Potomac, stand a few scattered buildings, which form a kind of hamlet called Charlotte-ville. The first settler in this savage wilderness was the Lady of General Lee, from whose christian name the place takes its appel-lation.

At a house of entertainment kept by Widow Myers, I was accommodated with a supper and a bed. This buxom Widow was by persuasion a Methodist, and possessed of considerable property.

On leaving the Great Falls of the Potomac I was followed by a dog, whose attendance I rather encouraged than repulsed. I was tired of travelling alone, and I wanted a companion.

An European who has confined his travels to his own country, can have but a very imperfect idea of the forest scenery of America. His imagination, familiar only with open and clear grounds, will scarce form an adequate conception of the endless and almost im-penetrable woods in the Western Continent: It was through such woods that I now journeyed with an accession of cheerfulness from the company of my dog; and smoking tobacco in my march, with which I never went unprovided.

I never remember to have felt a more perfect exemption from care than in my journey from the Potomac Falls. I rioted in health, and I walked forward *oblitus meorum et obliviscendus ab illis.* I embraced the Universe as my country, and it was wholly indifferent to me where I terminated my pilgrimage; for whether I ended my days in the wilds of the Potomac, or the close of Salisbury, the earth and its bands would have been about me for ever.

I eat my dinner in a log-house on the road. It was kept by a small planter of the name of Homer. Such a tavern would have raised the thunder and lightning of anger in the page of my brother-travellers in America. But the lamented scarcity of American inns is easily ac-counted for. In a country where every private house is a temple dedicated to hospitality, and open alike to Travellers of every descrip-tion, ought it to excite surprize that so few good taverns are to be found? When, therefore, the Travellers through the United States, curse, in their pages of calamity the musquitoes, and fleas, and bugs, and ticks that interrupt their slumbers, they make the eulogium of American hospitality.

The inhabitants of these woods are remarkably prolific; they obey at least one of the divine injunctions,—they increase and multiply their species. Mr. Homer was out felling the lofty trees of the forest, but Mrs. Homer was sitting by the fire, surrounded by half a dozen girls and boys, and giving a bosom of maternal exuberance to a child she held in her arms. A curly-pated boy and girl were eating their dinner on the hearth: it seemed to be short commons; for after thrusting their fingers into the platter, they licked them with great gusto. Come, you eat the sop, cried the boy, the egg belongs to me. No it don't, said the girl, for mammy's hen laid it.

Leaving the hut of Mr. Homer, I walked vigorously forward, indulging the hope I should get to Frying-Pan before night. But before dusk I found myself bewildered in the woods, whose solitude was rendered more melancholy from the cry of the owl. I had given myself up for lost, and was taking the flint from my pocket to kindle a fire, and pass the night under a tree, when the sound of the axe chopping wood rejoiced my hearing. Not more delightful was sleep ever to the weary, or water to the thirsty, than the sound to my ear.

Guided by the noise of the axe, I got to a tobacco plantation; but I had scarce leaped the fence when a couple of huge dogs assailed me, barking, advancing and retreating, all in a breath. Now, thought I, if these curs were to devour me, what an ignominious death would terminate my pilgrimage on earth. Fear is not only an ignoble, but dangerous passion; and, had I turned and endeavoured to escape from these bloodhounds, it is a hundred to one but I had been seized in that part where honour is said to be lodged.

I, therefore, stood my ground, and called lustily to the house. My cry was not unheard; the door was opened, and a lad advanced with a light, which he had fixed in a calabash.

The way, my friend, if you please, to Frying-Pan.

"Frying-Pan! 'Tis a right difficult road to find in the dark. You must keep along the worm fence——*Jowler!* begone——hush your mouth, there, you *Rover!*——begone, I say, you bloody——You must keep strait along the worm [i.e. crooked] fence, till you come to a barn——but I would advise you to avoid the brushwood about the barn, because of a nest of rattlesnakes——and the old one is mighty savage.——Well——when you have left the barn on your right, take the path that leads into the woods, and keep the main road the whole way, without turning either to the right or left, till you come to the track of the wheel——then cross right over into the next wood, and that will bring you to Frying-Pan Run——and, then, you could not go wrong if you was to try at it."

My friend, will you favour me with a draught of water?

Yes, sure. Come walk with me into the house. You *Rover!*—— hush your noise, you *negur.*——*Jowler!* if you don't hush, I'll make you rally for something.

On entering the log-house, I found a man sitting with his wife and five children, before a blazing fire of wood. My reader, do you not envy me the sensations with which the strings of my heart vibrated on beholding this domestic group? The weary Traveller, after losing his way in the awful woods of America, stoops to enter at the door of a little log-house, and happy to be once more in the society of his fellow-creatures, finds the roof under which he has got shelter large enough for his heart's desire.

Hospitality is the prominent feature in the character of a Virginian; and I had a presentiment that I was housed for the night. When I had drunk my water, which tasted the more delicious, from being administered to me by a fine girl of seventeen, (she had two pitch-balls stuck in her head for eyes,) I rose to depart; but the man of the house accosted me, saying, "Be content, I pray you, and tarry here all night; the day is grown to an end: to-morrow I will send my son to put you in the way."

The children now considered me as one of the family, and, moving their chairs, made room for me within their circle.

My dogs, said the man, gave you a rally. But I reckon it was the little dog you brought with you, that made them so savage.

Oh! My! what a pretty little lap Foist, cried the eldest girl. Indeed, indeed, he's right beautiful.

Mary, said a boy about nine years old, he's for all the world like the little dog that Jack Hatchet bought of 'Squire Carter's driver. He's spotted just like him. I'll lay you that he came out of the same bitch.

Do hush, Bill, said Mary. The gentleman brought the dog with him from England.

Supper (that is tea) was now got ready; nor was it without a grateful emotion that I beheld the mother of this worthy family unlock her Sunday cupboard, and hand her eldest daughter part of a loaf of sugar to break for the repast.

Wilmot, the eldest son, now departed. I discovered afterwards that he was courting the daughter of Mr. Strangeways' neighbour, whom he never failed to visit after the labour of the day. It was plain he was a lover by the care he took in adorning his person; changing his leggings for a pair of Philadelphia-made boots, and his frock for a fashionable coatee. The first character of love is a diffidence of pleasing.

As the night advanced, I could not but meditate upon the place my worthy host designed for my repose. I formed a hundred conjectures. He surely would not cherish me in the bosom of his numerous family? And yet I could perceive only one room in the house.

There were three beds in the room. Of these I discovered that the back one belonged to the two eldest girls; for while Mr. Strangeways, his wife, and I were yawning in concert over the fire, I perceived Mary, from the corner of my eye, steal softly to her nest, and slip in under the clothes; an example that was quickly followed by Eliza, who, with equal archness, crept in by her side.

Pure and simple innocence! To dread no eye, and to suspect no tongue, is the prerogative of the family to whom these manners belong.

At length Mr. Strangeways asked me if I was willing to go to bed, and, upon my replying in the affirmative, he fetched a ladder from an out-house into the room, and having placed it against the wall, he ascended a few steps, and opened a trap-door in the rafters, which I had not perceived led to a cock-loft.

Did you ever mount a ship's ladder, said Mr. Strangeways?

I replied, that I had a thousand.

Then, said he, be kind enough to follow me.

I followed, without betraying the least emotion of surprise; none but a rustic would have uttered an exclamation at the novelty of the staircase. I found a decent bed in the room appropriated to my reception; and, when Mr. Strangeways had opened and closed the shutter of the window in a manner which, after travelling so long in America, I could not but understand; the worthy man bade me a good night, and left me to my repose. I soon fell asleep; nor were my slumbers disturbed by the vision of an exorbitant landlord, appearing, to levy contributions on my purse, with a long bill in his hand.

I rose the next morning with the sun, and descended my ladder. The family were all stirring. The father and sons were at the plough, the mother was getting ready breakfast, and the two girls were at their spinning-wheels. The sound of these instruments was not quite so harmonious as that of a piano; but I know not whether a woodland nymph giving rapid motion to her spinning-wheel, be not a more captivating object than a haughty town-dame running her fingers disdainfully over the keys of a harpsichord.

And now it was necessary to separate from the family of the log-house in the woods. Yet, I could not leave Mary without emotion. Oh! my reader, if you are a lover of a happy face, it would have done your heart good to have beheld the countenance of this Virginian damsel. Mary was sitting cross-legged (I hope I need not gut this naughty word of its vowels) in her chair; and had placed on her lap a little looking-glass, in which she was beholding herself. She uttered not a word. Real happiness is not loquacious; the mind under its influence is content with its own sensations.

I now rose to go. The mother and Mary were the only tenants of the log-house. I bade the Dame good bye.

I wish, said the worthy woman, that Wilmot was here. The gentleman will never find his way out of the woods. My daughter, do put on your bonnet, and shew the gentleman the way to the main-road.

Mary rose with alacrity; she slipped on her bonnet; and having taken a parting look at the glass, conducted me through the plan-tation.

I gave the little wood-nymph my arm, and we walked forward together. The mocking-bird was singing; his song never appeared to me so sweet before.

At length, after walking half a mile, we emerged from the wood, and reached the track of the wheel.

And now, Mary, said I, once more farewell. Her cheek was crimsoned, and the redness of her lips heightened, from the exercise of walking. I would fain have tasted them; coral was not to be compared to their hue; and the nether one, a little more prominent than the other, looked as if some bee had newly stung it.

We both stood some minutes in silence. If peradventure, now, thought I, I should give a pressure to that lip, what effects might ensue. There may be a subtile poison lurking in its moisture. It might doom me to pass the remainder of my days in a house roofed with shingles.

Mary, said I, farewell. And let my advice go with you. Confide not for ornament in the rings that hang to thy ears, but in the virtue that dwells in thy bosom.

After walking a mile and a half, I met a boy sauntering along, and whistling, for want of thought. How far, my boy, said I, is it to Frying-Pan? You be in the pan now, replied the oaf. I be, be I, said I. Very well.

Fying-Pan is composed of four log-huts and a Meetinghouse. It took its name from a curious circumstance. Some Indians having encamped on the Run, missed their frying-pan in the morning, and hence the name was conferred on the place.

I did not deign to stop at Frying-Pan, but prosecuted my walk to Newgate; where in the piazza of Mr. Thornton's tavern I found a party of gentlemen from the neighbouring plantations carousing over a bowl of toddy, and smoking segars. In a moment there was room made for me to sit down; a new bowl was called for, and every one who addressed me did it with a smile of conciliation.

At Newgate my pilgrimage was nearly at an end; for Mr. Ball's plantation was only distant eight miles,—and it was he whom I was going to visit. But it was now necessary to bestride a horse; for in Virginia no man is respected who travels on foot; and as a man of sense will conform with the customs of every country, and at Rome, as my Lord Chesterfield elegantly observes, kiss either the Pope's great toe, or his b——k——e, I put myself to the expence of a horse, and with the argument of a stick I prevailed on him to advance.

ENOS A. MILLS

Walking Blind

"*Darkness did not matter, my light had failed at noon . . .*"

When Enos Abijah Mills died in 1922—exhausted and broken-hearted, some said, in the struggle to preserve the Rocky Mountain wilderness he loved—his eulogists compared him with John Muir and John Burroughs. Less felicitous than these patriarchs, he was nevertheless an energetic popularizer of the mountains, and was recognized as the moving force behind the creation of Rocky Mountain National Park in Colorado. Enos Mills had come from Kansas around the turn of the century to homestead at the base of Long's Peak; from his isolated outpost, he made many solitary journeys into the mountains. His most memorable adventure follows—snowblind on the summit.

This account is from The Adventures of a Nature Guide, *by Enos A. Mills.*

As I climbed out of the dwarfed woods at timberline in the Rocky Mountains, and started across the treeless white summit, the terrific sun glare on the snow warned me of the danger of snow-blindness. I had lost my snow glasses. But the wild attractions of the heights caused me to forget the care of my eyes and I lingered to look down into cañons and to examine magnificent snow cornices. A number of mountain sheep also interested me. Then for half an hour I circled a confiding flock of ptarmigan and took picture after picture.

Through the clear air the sunlight poured with burning intensity. I was 12,000 feet above the sea. Around me there was not a dark crag nor even a tree to absorb the excess of light. A wilderness of high, rugged peaks stood about—splendid sunlit mountains of snow. To east and west they faced winter's noonday sun with great shadow mantles flowing from their shoulders.

As I started to hurry on across the pass I began to experience the scorching pains that go with seared, sunburnt eyes—snow-blindness. Unfortunately, I had failed to take even the precaution of blackening my face, which would have dulled the glare. At the summit my eyes became so painful that I could endure the light only a few seconds at a time. Occasionally I sat down and closed them for a minute or two. Finally, while doing this, the lids adhered to the balls and the eyes swelled so that I could not open them.

Blind on the summit of the Continental Divide! I made a grab
for my useful staff which I had left standing beside me in the snow.
In the fraction of a second that elapsed between thinking of the staff
and finding it my brain woke up to the seriousness of the situation.
To the nearest trees it was more than a mile, and the nearest house
was many miles away across ridges of rough mountains. I had matches
and a hatchet, but no provisions. Still, while well aware of my peril, I
was only moderately excited, feeling no terror. Less startling incidents
have shocked me more, narrow escapes from street automobiles have
terrified me.

It had been a wondrous morning. The day cleared after a heavy
fall of fluffy snow. I had snowshoed up the slope through a ragged,
snow-carpeted spruce forest, whose shadows wrought splendid black-
and-white effects upon the shining floor. There were thousands of
towering, slender spruces, each brilliantly laden with snow flowers,
standing soft, white, and motionless in the sunlight. While I was
looking at one of these artistically decorated trees, a mass of snow
dropped upon me from its top, throwing me headlong and causing me
to lose my precious eye-protecting snow glasses. But now I was blind.

With staff in hand, I stood for a minute or two planning the best
manner to get along without eyes. My faculties were intensely awake.
Serious situations in the wilds had more than once before this stimulated them to do their best. Temporary blindness is a good stimulus
for the imagination and memory—in fact, is good educational train-
ing for all the senses. However perilous my predicament during a
mountain trip, the possibility of a fatal ending never even occurred to
me. Looking back now, I cannot but wonder at my matter-of-fact
attitude concerning the perils in which that snow blindness placed
me.

I had planned to cross the pass and descend into a trail at timberline. The appearance of the slope down which I was to travel was
distinctly in my mind from my impressions just before darkness
settled over me.

Off I slowly started. I guided myself with information from feet
and staff, feeling my way with the staff so as not to step off a cliff or
walk overboard into a cañon. In imagination I pictured myself following the shadow of a staff-bearing and slouch-hatted form. Did mountain sheep, curious and slightly suspicious, linger on crags to watch
my slow and hesitating advance? Across the snow did the shadow of a
soaring eagle coast and circle?

I must have wandered far from the direct course to timberline. Again and again I swung my staff to right and left hoping to strike a tree. I had travelled more than twice as long as it should have taken to reach timberline before I stood face to face with a low-growing tree that bristled up through the deep snow. But had I come out at the point for which I aimed—at the trail? This was the vital question.

The deep snow buried all trail blazes. Making my way from tree to tree I thrust an arm deep into the snow and felt of the bark, searching for a trail blaze. At last I found a blaze and going on a few steps I dug down again in the snow and examined a tree which I felt should mark the trail. This, too, was blazed.

Feeling certain that I was on the trail I went down the mountain through the forest for some minutes without searching for another blaze. When I did examine a number of trees not another blaze could I find. The topography since entering the forest and the size and character of the trees were such that I felt I was on familiar ground. But going on a few steps I came out on the edge of an unknown rocky cliff. I was now lost as well as blind.

During the hours I had wandered in reaching timberline I had had a vague feeling that I might be travelling in a circle, and might return to trees on the western slope of the Divide up which I had climbed. When I walked out on the edge of the cliff the feeling that I had doubled to the western slope became insistent. If true, this was most serious. To reach the nearest house on the west side of the range would be extremely difficult, even though I should discover just where I was. But I believed I was somewhere on the eastern slope.

I tried to figure out the course I had taken. Had I, in descending from the heights, gone too far to the right or to the left? Though fairly well acquainted with the country along this timberline, I was unable to recall a rocky cliff at this point. My staff found no bottom and warned me that I was at a jumping-off place.

Increasing coolness indicated that night was upon me. But darkness did not matter, my light had failed at noon. Going back along my trail a short distance I avoided the cliff and started on through the night down a rocky, forested, and snow-covered slope. I planned to get into the bottom of a cañon and follow downstream. Every few steps I shouted, hoping to attract the attention of a possible prospector, miner, or woodchopper. No voice answered. The many echoes, however, gave me an idea of the topography—of the mountain ridges and cañons before me. I listened intently after each shout and noticed the direction from which the reply came, its intensity, and the cross echoes, and concluded that I was going down into the head of a deep, forest-walled cañon, and, I hoped, travelling eastward.

For points of the compass I appealed to the trees, hoping through my knowledge of woodcraft to orient myself. In the study of tree distribution I had learned that the altitude might often be approximated and the points of the compass determined by noting the characteristic kinds of trees.

Cañons of east and west trend in this locality carried mostly limber pines on the wall that faces south and mostly Engelmann spruces on the wall that faces the north. Believing that I was travelling eastward I turned to my right, climbing out of the cañon, and examined a number of trees along the slope. Most of these were Engelmann spruces. The slope probably faced north. Turning about I descended this slope and ascended the opposite one. The trees on this were mostly limber pines. Hurrah! Limber pines are abundant only on southern slopes. With limber pines on my left and Engelmann spruces on my right, I was now satisfied that I was travelling eastward and must be on the eastern side of the range.

To put a final check on this—for a blind or lost man sometimes manages to do exactly the opposite of what he thinks he is doing—I examined lichen growths on the rocks and moss growths on the trees. In the deep cañon I dug down into the snow and examined the faces of low-lying boulders. With the greatest care I felt the lichen growth on the rocks. These verified the information that I had from the trees—but none too well. Then I felt over the moss growth, both long and short, on the trunks and lower limbs of trees, but this testimony was not absolutely convincing. The moss growth was so nearly even all the way around the trunk that I concluded that the surrounding topography must be such as to admit the light freely from all quarters, and also that the wall or slope on my right must be either a gentle one or else a low one and somewhat broken. I climbed to make sure. In a few minutes I was on a terrace—as I expected. Possibly back on the right lay a basin that might be tributary to this cañon. The reports made by the echoes of my shoutings said that this was true. A few minutes of travel down the cañon and I came to the expected incoming stream, which made its swift presence heard beneath its cover of ice and snow.

A short distance farther down the cañon I examined a number of trees that stood in thick growth on the lower part of what I thought was the southern slope. Here the character of the moss and lichens and their abundant growth on the northerly sides of the trees verified the testimony of the tree distribution and of previous moss and lichen growths. I was satisfied as to the points of the compass. I was on the eastern side of the Continental Divide travelling eastward.

After three or four hours of slow descending I reached the bottom. Steep walls rose on both right and left. The enormous rock masses and the entanglements of fallen and leaning trees made progress difficult. Feeling that if I continued in the bottom of the cañon I might come to a precipitous place down which I would be unable to descend, I tried to walk along one of the side walls, and thus keep above the bottom. But the walls were too steep and I got into trouble.

Out on a narrow, snow-corniced ledge I walked. The snow gave way beneath me and down I went over the ledge. As I struck, feet foremost, one snowshoe sank deeply. I wondered, as I wiggled out, if I had landed on another ledge. I had. Not desiring to have more tumbles, I tried to climb back up on the ledge from which I had fallen, but I could not do it. The ledge was broad and short and there appeared to be no safe way off. As I explored again my staff encountered the top of a dead tree that leaned against the ledge. Breaking a number of dead limbs off I threw them overboard. Listening as they struck the snow below I concluded that it could not be more than thirty feet to the bottom.

I let go my staff and dropped it after the limbs. Then, without taking off snowshoes, I let myself down the limbless trunk. I could hear water running beneath the ice and snow. I recovered my staff and resumed the journey.

In time the cañon widened a little and travelling became easier. I had just paused to give a shout when a rumbling and crashing high up the righthand slope told me that a snowslide was plunging down. Whether it would land in the cañon before me or behind me or on top of me could not be guessed. The awful smashing and crashing and roar proclaimed it of enormous size and indicated that trees and rocky debris were being swept onward with it. During the few seconds that I stood awaiting my fate, thought after thought raced through my brain as I recorded the ever-varying crashes and thunders of the wild, irresistible slide.

With terrific crash and roar the snowslide swept into the cañon a short distance in front of me. I was knocked down by the outrush or concussion of air and for several minutes was nearly smothered with the whirling, settling snow-dust and rock powder which fell thickly all around. The air cleared and I went on.

I had gone only a dozen steps when I came upon the enormous wreckage brought down by the slide. Snow, earthy matter, rocks, and splintered trees were flung in fierce confusion together. For three or four hundred feet this accumulation filled the cañon from wall to wall and was fifty or sixty feet high. The slide wreckage smashed the ice and dammed the stream. As I started to climb across this snowy debris a shattered place in the ice beneath gave way and dropped me into the water, but my long staff caught and by clinging to it I saved myself from going in above my hips. My snowshoes caught in the shattered ice and while I tried to get my feet free a mass of snow fell upon me and nearly broke my hold. Shaking off the snow I put forth all my strength and finally pulled my feet free of the ice and crawled out upon the debris. This was a close call and at last I was thoroughly, briefly, frightened.

As the wreckage was a mixture of broken trees, stones, and compacted snow I could not use my snowshoes, so I took them off to carry them till over the debris. Once across I planned to pause and build a fire to dry my icy clothes.

With difficulty I worked my way up and across. Much of the snow was compressed almost to ice by the force of contact, and in this icy cement many kinds of wreckage were set in wild disorder. While descending a steep place in this mass, carrying snowshoes under one arm, the footing gave way and I fell. I suffered no injury but lost one of the snowshoes. For an hour or longer I searched, without finding it.

The night was intensely cold and in the search my feet became almost frozen. In order to rub them I was about to take off my shoes when I came upon something warm. It proved to be a dead mountain sheep with one horn smashed off. As I sat with my feet beneath its warm carcass and my hands upon it, I thought how but a few minutes before the animal had been alive on the heights with all its ever wide-awake senses vigilant for its preservation; yet I, wandering blindly, had escaped with my life when the snowslide swept into the cañon. The night was calm, but of zero temperature or lower. It probably was crystal clear. As I sat warming my hands and feet on the proud master of the crags I imagined the bright, clear sky crowded thick with stars. I pictured to myself the dark slope down which the slide had come. It appeared to reach up close to the frosty stars.

But the lost snowshoe must be found, wallowing through the

deep mountain snow with only one snowshoe would be almost hope-less. I had vainly searched the surface and lower wreckage projections but made one more search. This proved successful. The shoe had slid for a short distance, struck an obstacle, bounced upward over smashed logs, and lay about four feet above the general surface. A few moments more and I was beyond the snowslide wreckage. Again on snowshoes, staff in hand, I countinued feeling my way down the mountain.

My ice-stiffened trousers and chilled limbs were not good travel-ling companions, and at the first cliff that I encountered I stopped to make a fire. I gathered two or three armfuls of dead limbs, with the aid of my hatchet, and soon had a lively blaze going. But the heat increased the pain in my eyes, so with clothes only partly dried, I went on. Repeatedly through the night I applied snow to my eyes trying to subdue the fiery torment.

From timberline I had travelled downward through a green forest mostly of Engelmann spruce with a scattering of fir and limber pine. I frequently felt of the tree trunks. But a short time after leaving my camp-fire I came to the edge of an extensive region that had been burned over. For more than an hour I travelled through dead standing trees, on many of which only the bark had been burned away; on others the fire had burned more deeply.

Pausing on the way down, I thrust my staff into the snow and leaned against a tree to hold snow against my burning eyes. While I was doing this two owls hooted happily to each other and I listened to their contented calls with satisfaction.

Hearing the pleasant, low call of a chickadee I listened. Appar-ently he was dreaming and talking in his sleep. The dream must have been a happy one, for every note was cheerful. Realizing that he probably was in an abandoned woodpecker nesting hole, I tapped on the dead tree against which I was leaning. This was followed by a chorus of lively, surprised chirpings, and one, two, three!—then several —chickadees flew out of a hole a few inches above my head. Sorry to have disturbed them I went on down the slope.

At last I felt the morning sun in my face. With increased light my eyes became extremely painful. For a time I relaxed upon the snow, finding it difficult to believe that I had been travelling all night in complete darkness. While lying here I caught the scent of smoke. There was no mistaking it. It was the smoke of burning aspen, a wood much burned in the cook-stoves of mountain people. Eagerly I rose to find it. I shouted again and again but there was no response. Under favourable conditions, keen nostrils may detect aspen-wood smoke for a distance of two or three miles.

The compensation of this accident was an intense stimulus to my imagination—perhaps our most useful intellectual faculty. My eyes, always keen and swift, had ever supplied me with almost an excess of information. But with them suddenly closed my imagination became the guiding faculty. I did creative thinking. With pleasure I restored the views and scenes of the morning before. Any one seeking to develop the imagination would find a little excursion afield, with eyes voluntarily blind-folded, a most telling experience.

Down the mountainside I went, hour after hour. My ears caught the chirp of birds and the fall of icicles which ordinarily I would hardly have heard. My nose was constantly and keenly analyzing the air. With touch and clasp I kept in contact with the trees. Again my nostrils picked up aspen smoke. This time it was much stronger. Perhaps I was near a house! But the whirling air currents gave me no clue as to the direction from which the smoke came, and only echoes responded to my call.

All my senses worked willingly in seeking wireless news to substitute for the eyes. My nose readily detected odours and smoke. My ears were more vigilant and more sensitive than usual. My fingers, too, were responsive from the instant that my eyes failed. Delightfully eager they were, as I felt the snow-buried trees, hoping with touch to discover possible trail blazes. My feet also were quickly, steadily alert to translate the topography.

Occasionally a cloud shadow passed over. In imagination I often pictured the appearance of these clouds against the blue sky and tried to estimate the size of each by the number of seconds its shadow took to drift across me.

Mid-afternoon, or later, my nose suddenly detected the odour of an ancient corral. This was a sign of civilization. A few minutes later my staff came in contact with the corner of a cabin. I shouted "Hello!" but heard no answer. I continued feeling until I came to the door and found that a board was nailed across it. The cabin was locked and deserted! I broke in the door.

In the cabin I found a stove and wood. As soon as I had a fire going I dropped snow upon the stove and steamed my painful eyes. After two hours or more of this steaming they became more comfortable. Two strenuous days and one toilsome night had made me extremely drowsy. Sitting down upon the floor near the stove I leaned against the wall and fell asleep. But the fire burned itself out. In the night I awoke nearly frozen and unable to rise. Fortunately, I had on my mittens, otherwise my fingers probably would have frozen. By rubbing my hands together, then rubbing my arms and legs, I finally managed to limber myself, and though unable to rise, I succeeded in starting a new fire. It was more than an hour before I ceased shivering; then, as the room began to warm, my legs came back to life and again I could walk.

I was hungry. This was my first thought of food since becoming blind. If there was anything to eat in the cabin, I failed to find it. Searching my pockets I found a dozen or more raisins and with these I broke my sixty-hour fast. Then I had another sleep, and it must have been near noon when I awakened. Again I steamed the eye pain into partial submission.

Going to the door I stood and listened. A camp-bird only a few feet away spoke gently and confidingly. Then a crested jay called impatiently. The camp-bird alighted on my shoulder. I tried to explain to the birds that there was nothing to eat. The prospector who had lived in this cabin evidently had been friendly with the bird neighbours. I wished that I might know him.

Again I could smell the smoke of aspen wood. Several shouts evoked echoes—nothing more. I stood listening and wondering whether to stay in the cabin or to venture forth and try to follow the snow-filled roadway that must lead down through the woods from the cabin. Wherever this open way led I could follow. But of course I must take care not to lose it.

In the nature of things I felt that I must be three or four miles to the south of the trail which I had planned to follow down the mountain. I wished I might see my long and crooked line of footmarks in the snow from the summit to timberline.

Hearing the open water in rapids close to the cabin, I went out to try for a drink. I advanced slowly, blind-man fashion, feeling the way with my long staff. As I neared the rapids, a water ouzel, which probably had lunched in the open water, sang with all his might. I stood still as he repeated his liquid, hopeful song. On the spot I shook off procrastination and decided to try to find a place where someone lived.

After writing a note explaining why I had smashed in the door and used so much wood, I readjusted my snowshoes and started down through the woods. I suppose it must have been late afternoon.

I found an open way that had been made into a road. The woods were thick and the open roadway really guided me. Feeling and thrusting with my staff, I walked for some time at normal pace. Then I missed the way. I searched carefully, right, left, and before me for the utterly lost road. It had forked, and I had continued on the short stretch that came to an end in the woods by an abandoned prospect hole. As I approached close to this the snow caved in, nearly carrying me along with it. Confused by blinded eyes and the thought of oncoming night, perhaps, I had not used my wits. When at last I stopped to think I figured out the situation. Then I followed my snowshoe tracks back to the main road and turned into it.

For a short distance the road ran through dense woods. Several times I paused to touch the trees each side with my hands. When I emerged from the woods, the pungent aspen smoke said that I must at last be near a human habitation. In fear of passing it I stopped to use my ears. As I stood listening, a little girl gently, curiously, asked:

"Are you going to stay here to-night?"

FRANCIS PARKMAN

Brahmin in the Wilderness

"The way was long and the burden heavy . . ."

Born on Boston's Beacon Hill, Francis Parkman was one of America's greatest historians. Within the gathering folds of blindness, and despite recurring headaches which left him without sleep, he vividly recreated the struggle of the French and English for control of the North American continent. But long before illness tested his spirit, he had tested both body and spirit on long walking trips—certain that it was the rigorous prerequisite to his mission as a historian. The following selections from his journal recount parts of two such journeys, undertaken during summer recesses after his freshman and sophomore years at Harvard. The first of these trips, with classmate Dan Slade in 1841 (Parkman was then 18 years old), took him into the White Mountains of New Hampshire and "the most serious adventure it was ever my lot to encounter." The following year found him in the true wilds of northern Maine—as usual, with an aristocratic eye and haughty disdain for the weaknesses of his companions.

July 19th, Monday. I was disappointed of one of my companions, Tower, who fell sick this morning, having imprudently gorged himself with pie yesterday. Dan Slade's horror at so inauspicious an occurrence damped his own ardor and somewhat retarded his preparations, insomuch that I watched from the window, quarter of an hour after the specified time, without beholding the approach of either of my fellow travelers. At length Dan appeared alone, striding along like the colossus; and truly there was need, for we had just five minutes to reach the depot of the railroad, three-quarters of a mile off. By a special providence, a hack was passing; we jumped in, exhorted the driver to use his best speed, and reached the railroad boat at the instant she was leaving the wharf. This was at seven o'clock—at ten we were at Portsmouth—at half-past eleven we were at Dover, and at twelve, *cibo et poto graves*, we were on the way to Alton. Our conveyance was none of the most agreeable. A little carryall whose legitimate freight was four persons, was doomed to transport seven, with baggage more than proportional. Four ladies, or women, were deposited behind, politeness, of course, forbidding Dan and myself to lay claim to back seats. The front seat was all that remained and the driver was a portly man—imagine, then, our condition—uncomfortable, at any rate, but almost insufferable when it be considered that beside being jammed by our disagreeable propinquity, we were obliged to sit bolt upright, for two of the "ladies" occupied the seat just behind, so that we sat back to back with these fair ones, with no guard between; consequently an attempt on our part to lean would have pitched the nymphs, head first, into the laps of their neighbors opposite. This state of thing endured for twenty miles, but the driver being pleasant, civil, and accommodating, the matter was not so bad as it might have been. This "extra accommodation"—for such it was—carried us within twelve miles of Alton. Here we got out, glad of any change, strapped on knapsacks, and entered upon our pedestrian experiences. The way was long and the burden heavy; I particularly had, beside my knapsack, a heavy gun, a ponderous double shot-pouch, well filled, and a powder flask. We travelled on at a tolerably easy rate, until Dan, seating himself on a stone, complained that his darned knapsack hurt his shoulders. He accordingly carried it in his hand a space, but finding this method still more annoying, he again restored it to its rightful position.

"How far to Alton Bay?" we inquired of a rustic who was raking hay in a field. "Two mile strong." "Two miles what?" said we in astonishment. "Two mile strong—rather more nor two mile"; and, accordingly, we found ourselves entering a valley between two ranges of high hills which had appeared to us first, a few hours before, like blue clouds in the distance. The road, flanked by thick woods, wound downwards through the valley; at length we turned an angle of it and saw the waters of the lake glistening through the trees. "There!" cried Dan in exstacy, "there's the lake at last—hope we shall get some good supper—Frank, is my face clean?" Having satisfied Dan on the important subject of this question, I proceeded down with him to a most unpromising-looking tavern on the lake shore. Nevertheless, our lodgings are good and our supper was excellent. We have travelled upwards of a hundred miles today, twelve of them on foot.

July 20th . . . There runs a road along the western banks of the lake, but little travelled, for the first eight or ten miles at least, and commanding fine views of the water and mountains. We left Alton by this path in the morning, doubting nothing to reach Senter Harbor by night, albeit it was a distance of nearly thirty miles. At first we were cool enough, for the road was flanked by deep and dark forests and shaded by wild hills, winding at one time along the edge of the lake and then passing through shaded vallies. But this happy condition of things was not destined to last. The sun grew hotter and hotter and the road more and more open. For the first hour or two, we passed no dwellings but a few log-cabins, with a little clearing in the forest around them. But, alas, the little pathway was widened by the junction of others, and farm houses began to appear, first singly, then in clusters, with clearings extending for miles. The road, too, began to turn from the edge of the lake and to run inland, so that the scenery was no ways so interesting as before. It was almost noon and we toiled up the scorching road, sweating and grumbling at the folly which had deprived us of shelter and comfort by ridiculously burning the forests, in the zeal for making clearings, though the burnt land lays utterly waste and the sole effect of the operation is to ruin the scene and lay the road open to the baking sun. The thermometer was at about 90° and the road had become most disgustingly hilly and dreary. We reached the lake again and bathed—no small relief, for our clothes clung to us with sweat. Next we stopped at a farm house and got some bread and milk, and next made a temporary encampment in a cool piece of wood and rested some time. Then we journeyed on again, and that part of us left undissolved by the heat arrived early in the afternoon at Meredith Bridge, where we lost no time in establishing ourselves at the tavern, wisely relinquishing our purpose of proceeding further. "Last time you catch me walking this time of day," said Dan from his easy chair in the tavern parlor. "Amen," said I, "we will set out before sunrise tomorrow." Meredith Bridge, by the way, is a disgusting little manufacturing village, with no single point of attraction, either as concerns scenery or anything else, if we set aside the six-pound trout sometimes taken there. Indeed, we heard an apocryphal story of a trout ten pounds caught a day or two ago.

July 21st, Wednesday. Agreeably to our resolutions of last night we were up early; nevertheless, the sun from its very rising was insufferably hot, and every well we passed was called upon for our relief. The inhabitants were a kind and hospitable race, to talk like the geography. When we stopped at the cistern, a white-headed brat would generally be despatched out to us with a mug, that we might quench our thirst with the greater convenience, or the master of the house would come himself and hold a talk with us.

We toiled on to Meredith Village—nine miles—where we breakfasted, and finding that we were losing flesh with astounding rapidity and gaining nothing to counterbalance it, we hired a waggon and rode the remaining four miles to Senter Harbor. Here we got rooms, and finding it impossible to stir on account of the heat, we amused ourselves indoors as best we might, Dan with snoring on his bed and I with reading the *Alhambra* on the balcony. There I sat watching the heated air rising from the road and fences and the lake as it lay enduring the heat with Christian resignation, with its surface like glass and all its trees wilting over it. There has been no rain here for weeks; the crops are dried up and all the grass of a straw color. The evening brought some relief, for a party of us, having obtained a leaky boat with infinite difficulty, went out on the pond and landed on some of the islands. Returning, we bathed, to the indescribable horror and inexpressible consternation of a party of ladies who had been out in a leakier boat, and who were advancing in the darkness directly into the midst of us until we signified the peculiar delicacy of our situation by splashings in the water and unequivocal callings to one another. Then, indeed, arose a suppressed murmuring of "Oh's!" and "Ah's!" and "Did you ever's!" as the boat sheered off.

July 24. This morning I went fishing, following downwards the stream of the waterfall which comes down through the Flume. I basketed about thirty trout. The weather was dull and cloudy; the clouds hid the peaks of the mountains and rolled in huge masses along their sides. Early in the morning the mist was rolling, in a constant stream, from the narrow opening at the Notch, like a furnace disgorging its smoke.

This afternoon I achieved the most serious adventure it was ever my lot to encounter. I walked down the Notch to the Willey House and, out of curiosity, began to ascend in the pathway of the avalanche on the mountain directly behind. This pathway is a deep ravine, channelled in the side of the mountain which in this place is ex- tremely steep. In the bottom of this gulf a little stream comes down from a spring above and renders the precipitous rock as slippery as clay. The sides of the ravine, which runs directly up and down the mountain, are of decaying granite, while the bottom is formed by a trap-dike. I ascended at first easily, but the way began to be steeper and the walls on each side more precipitous. Still I kept on until I came to a precipice about forty feet high and not far from perpen- dicular. I could see that this was followed by a similar one above. Professor Silliman, a year or two ago, ascended in this place, until, as he says, "further progress was prevented by inaccessible precipices of the trap rock." The exploit of the professor occurred to me as I stood below and I determined that "inaccessible precipices" which had cooled his scientific ardor should prove no barrier to me. I began to climb; and with considerable difficulty and danger, and with the loss of my stick, which went rattling and bounding down the ravine many rods before it found a resting place, I surmounted both precipices. I climbed on; but finding that I was becoming drenched by the scanty stream, and seeing, moreover, a huge cloud, not far up, settling slowly towards me, I bethought me of retracing my steps. I knew that it would be impossible to descend by the way I had come, and, accordingly, I tried to get out of the ravine to the side of the mountain which was covered with wood, which I could grasp hold of to assist me. But I was enclosed between two walls, (of) fifty feet high and so steep and composed of such material that an attempt to climb would only bring down the rotting granite upon my head. So I began to descend the ravine, nothing doubting that I should find some means of getting out before reaching the critical point. But it was impossible, and I found myself at the top of the precipice with no alternative but to slide down, or clamber the perpendicular and decaying walls to the surface of the mountain. The former was certain destruction, as I proved by suffering a rotten log to slide down. It glanced by the first descent like an arrow, struck at the bottom, bounded six feet into the air, and leaped down the mountain, splintering into twenty pieces as it went. The other method was scarcely less dangerous, but it was my only chance, and I braced my nerves and began to climb. Down went stones and pebbles, clattering hundreds of feet below and giving me a grateful indication of my inevitable fate in case my head should swim or my courage fail. I had got half way up and was clinging to the face of the precipice, when the two stones which supported my feet loosened and leaped down the ravine. My finger-ends, among the rotten gravel, were all which sustained me, and they, of course, would have failed, had I not thought, on the instant, of lowering my body gradually, and so diminishing its weight, until my feet found new supporters. I sank the length of my arms and then hung, for the time, in tolerable safety, with one foot resting on a projecting stone. Loosening the hold of one hand, I took my large jack-knife from my pocket, opened it with the assistance of my teeth, and dug with it a hollow among the decayed stones large enough to receive and support one foot. Then, thrusting the knife as far as possible into the wall to assist my hold, I grasped it and the stones with the unoccupied hand

and raised my foot to the hollow prepared for it. Thus, foot by foot, I made my way, and in ten minutes, as time seemed to me, I seized a projecting root at the top and drew myself up. During the whole time of climbing, I felt perfectly cool, but when fairly up, I confess I shuddered as I looked down at the gulf I had escaped. A large stone, weighing, perhaps, a hundred pounds, lay on the edge. I thrust it off with my foot and down it went, struck the bottom of the ravine with a tremendous crash, and thundered down, leaping from side to side, until it lodged at last, far below, against a projecting rock. I descended the mountain by means of the trees and bushes; cut a fishing pole at the bottom; and, having amused myself with an hour's fishing, went to the tavern, and astonished the company with a recital of my adventure. . . .

July 29th. We set out this morning, before breakfast, to see the Flume. Half-way through the woods, we missed the path, but, guided by the roaring of the water, we found the banks of the Pemigewasset and determined to follow them up until we reach the Flume. Now we were making a grievous mistake, for the Flume is not on the main stream, but on a branch of it in an opposite direction from the one we were pursuing. The forest was dense and dark, and the ground strewed with fallen trunks in various states of decay. The ground was rocky, moreover, and full of ravines and deep holes; and the thick matted undergrowth in nowise facilitated our progress. On we went, stumbling against piles of rotten logs, and switched in all directions by the recoiling twigs. The forest was almost impassable, so we essayed the bank of the river. But the river was full of huge rocks and stones, amongst which the water came racing and foaming down, so that even wading up its bed was impossible. Cliffs (of) sixty feet high, damp and green with moss, and with pine and birch trees growing from their fissures in many places, overhung the water; and along their edges and up and down their sides we must make our way. I was encumbered with gun and shot-pouch, which was a still farther aggravation of my difficulties. Dan stopped short: "Hang your dirty Flume! I move we go back to the house and get the old man to show us the way as he said he would." "We could not find the house, Dan; our only way is to keep on till we come to the Flume. It can't be more than a few rods further."

There was a kind of natural pathway at the foot of the cliffs and we followed it, making our way with difficulty between the rocks on one side and the roaring water on the other. A projecting rock and a slight bend in the stream prevented our seeing further before us, but we heard a loud heavy plunging of water. By swinging from a projecting branch and making a long leap, we gained a flat rock in the middle of the river, and beheld a scene which repaid us for our trouble. A broad circular basin of water was before us, so deep that its waves were of dark green, with huge perpendicular cliffs rising on each hand above it. From the top of the cliffs, trees started out obliquely against the sky and dripping festoons of moss were hanging from every cleft. In front, these same cliffs swept round until they almost met, leaving a narrow passage for the river, through which it plunged, over a wall of rocks, into the basin below. Above, it might be seen again, foaming over a bed of steep rocks, and closing the perspective with a smooth unbroken fall contrasted well with its lashing and white rapids. We looked at it for some time and then began to devise some method of proceeding. It was no easy matter, for the cliffs rose directly from the water and their sides were so steep and smooth that they offered no hold to one passing them. Our only alternative was to scale them where they were less steep, a little way below. We got to the top and began to force our way through the forest again. "Damn the Flume," said Dan, when we had proceeded about quarter of a mile. "We must have missed it," said I, "it can't be farther on than this. This river strikes the road about a mile from here—we had better keep on till we reach it." "Devil take the Flume—I wish we had never come, or else had brought a guide." Thus profanely spoke Dan, but we kept on for half an hour, with toil and suffering, and emerged at length on the road, two miles from the tavern, having forced our way through a mile and a half of forest in the whole, and having two miles more, on the road, to walk before we reached the tavern again. We got there at last, took breakfast, procured a guide, and set out for the Flume a second time. We found to our great satisfaction, that visitors seldom attempted, unattended, to find the place we were searching for, and that when they did they usually returned discouraged and frightened, or else became lost and had to be searched for with shoutings and firings of guns. This Flume is a huge natural trough of rock through which runs, in a succession of falls and rapids, a branch of the river Pemigewasset. On each side of the stream high cliffs rise perpendicularly and run for many rods facing each other. Their black sides are smooth, and continually dropping moisture, for the forest above extends its branches from their edges so that the light of the sun can scarcely penetrate the ravine. Standing on the rocks at the bottom and looking up, you see huge decayed trunks and branches extending across the narrow strip of sky visible between the edges of the cliffs, and the edges themselves overgrown with masses of wet and green moss which hang dripping from them. Knotted and distorted pines, rooted in the crevices, fling their boughs across; and even these, though living, are covered with damp mosses. Midway between the top of the cliffs and the water, and closing the spectator's onward view, hangs a rock, hurled by some convulsion down the ravine and intercepted between its approaching sides. Just beneath this, the stream foams down over a bed of rocks into a deep basin at their foot, then leaps from the basin and rushes forward among the stones and accumulated trunks of trees which intercept its course.

We returned from the Flume and walked back to Franconia Notch, where the tavern is kept by a man named Fifield. He went fishing with us in the afternoon to a little brook at some distance in the woods. I followed the stream upward, while Fifield and Slade went in an opposite direction. Just before sunset, I was half a mile up the brook, with a long string of trout and with the full belief that I knew the direction in which the road lay. I accordingly made all speed through the forest, lest I should be overtaken by the dark. I travelled about a mile, guiding my course by the sun, but the forest seemed deeper and wilder the further I went. At length I caught sight of a mountain peak which I knew, and shaping my course by that, in a few minutes reached the road.

The following summer, Parkman set out with a different companion—Henry Orne White—exploring Lake George, Lake Champlain, northern Vermont and a portion of Quebec Province. In the selections which follow, we pick them up at Stanstead, Quebec; accompany them on a hike to Canaan; and then join them in an exhausting trek through the wilderness of northern New Hampshire, from the Connecticut Lakes to the Little Margalloway River. The Abbot who accompanied them on this latter journey was James Abbot, of Pittsburg, New Hampshire.

Monday, August 1st. Chase had promised to get us a waggon to advance us on our journey. He had it ready quarter before seven and we set out to seek Indian Stream and the Margalloway, that being now our destination, seeing that we are unable to go to Mt. Ktaadin. Chase drove us as far as the town of Barnston, through Stanstead Plain, a very level and fertile country. He says that he should think Stanstead contained 6,000 inhabitants. Dismissing him and his waggon at Barnston—where four or five more soldiers are stationed—we set out on foot for Canaan, which promised land some told us was twenty miles distant, while others reckoned it thirty. The road for a few miles was good, but we were soon compelled to leave it and take a path through the woods. A beautiful river—smooth and rapid—ran across the road under a bridge of logs, between forest-covered banks. Not far from Stanstead, we had crossed a furious stream, answering to the sentimental designation of the Nigger River. We had walked but a few miles when the clouds settled on the hills and it began to rain. We went to a log cabin for shelter. The "old man" was frank and hospitable like all his genus I ever met, and the "old woman"—a damsel of twenty two, who sat combing her hair in the corner—extremely sprightly and talkative. She seemed somewhat moved at heart by the doctrines of Miller, whose apostles are at work all along the Vermont frontier. We abused that holy man to our content and, the rain ceasing, left the cabin. High rolling hills bounded the horizon, all covered with an ocean of forest. The clouds hung heavy upon them, but would break every instant and admit a stream of sunshine, which would pass across the great carpet of woods, illuminate it in spots for an instant, and then give place to the black shadows of the clouds. Soon after leaving this place, we entered the afore-mentioned path through the woods. Now and then there would be a clearing with its charred stumps, its boundary of frowning woods, and its log cabin; but, for the most part, the forest was in its original state. The average depth of the mud in the path was one foot. Scarce a ray of sunlight ever reached there through the thick boughs overhead. The streams that ran through the wood had no bridges, and most of them seemed to have preferred the artificial channel afforded by our path to the one they had worked for themselves among the mossy stones and decayed trunks of the forest. So we had to wade in deep water about two-thirds of the way. Of course, we were soon covered with mud to the eyes. It was not long, however, before we emerged upon a broader path—one practicable to a stout waggon. This, too, led through a dense forest. We stopped at a log cabin at three o'clock and asked for dinner. A decent one was given us. During the process of eating, the "girls" were working at the spinning wheel and giggling among themselves, the boys sat stiff and upright in their chairs—homemade—and contemplated us with great attention. "How far to the next clearing?" we asked. "Eight mile!" and a long eight miles it was to us—a dismal slough of despond the whole way—mud to the knees. But the path was a singularly wild and impressive one—cut through a wilderness. Huge trees flanked and arched it—maple, pine, cedar, cypress, and a thousand others; bending over it, and intertwined with one another, two high walls of foliage and wooden columns. Below, a fringe of high bushes along the path hid the base of the trunks; but, looking through, the ground was hid with matted masses of green mossy logs, and heaps of rot, with a tangled undergrowth, all wet with the moisture that never leaves a forest like this. The day was showery, with occasional glimpses of the sun; so that we were alternately wet and dry. Late in the afternoon we reached a clearing, with a couple of cabins. Two men were mounting their horses to ride through the woods. We gave them the accustomed shake of the hand, etc., walked through another two miles of forest, and came to another clearing, of an aspect so wild and picturesque that a painter might have won the credit of being an outstanding genius by only copying things as they were. At the farther end of this clearing was a stream, swift and cold, into which we walked in order to wash off the superfluous dirt. Thence, passing various dwellings, and holding various colloquies with the inmates, we reached Canaan, and a good tavern.

Thursday, August 4th. Started this morning to strike the Little Margalloway. We proceeded first toward the north, with a path for the first few miles. It soon failed us, and we had to force our way through tangled woods. At about ten o'clock we reached the west bank of the Second Lake. Connecticut is a string of three lakes, on the first of which Abbot's house and all the other settlements are. At this place we met an unexpected delay. The raft, on which we were to have crossed, had broke loose from the bank and gone over the rapids down to the first lake. There was nothing for it but to build another, an operation which took up two hours. We paddled over at last, the mountains which lay between us and the promised river heaving up, ridge over ridge, before us, covered with an unbroken and pathless forest, never trod except by hunters. We landed on this dreary shore—White tumbling over into the water in the attempt—shouldered our packs, and taking a southeast direction by the compass, plunged into the woods. Ten thousand decayed logs scattered here and there—piled one on another, a thick growth of strong and tangled under wood, rocks, fallen trees, gullies, made the forest almost impassable. It was a constant straining of muscle and sinew. Boughs slapped us in the face, swarms of flies stung us; we trod on spots apparently solid and sank to the thighs in masses of rotten timber. White had hurt his foot the day before and constantly lagged behind, so that we had to wait for him every minute, the prey of torturing flies. At length the ascent of the first mountain made the way still more laborious. When at length we reached the top, we could see nothing on account of the thick growth of trees. We passed through a singular piece of boggy ground, of an oblong shape, enclosed in a fringe of cedars, rising one above the other, all hung with tassels of white moss. There was another place, partially open, near the summit. As we passed it, a large buck sprang from the ground, and leaped with long bounds down the mountain, before my rifle was at my shoulder. We heard him crashing the boughs far below. In this spot were several springs of clear, cold water, in broad cup-shaped hollows in the ground, which had probably attracted the deer. We went down the mountain and found a little stream flowing through the valley at the bottom. Both Abbot and myself were for proceeding, but White said he could not go on on account of his foot; so we found a convenient spot and encamped. It was by the stream, flowing half-concealed beneath brushwood and fallen trees, in a thick growth of firs, spruces, and birches. We made a fire, and proceeded to cook our supper. We had brought with us seven pounds of bread, six and a half of rice, and a quantity of butter. We had beside about an ounce of tea, and salt, of course.

We made our fire in the middle of the grove, cut spruce boughs for a bed, lay down on our blankets, and with our knives speedily made way with a mess of rice placed on a broad piece of birch bark amongst us. Then we heaped new wood on the fire, and lay down again, cooled by a gentle rain which just now began to fall. The fire blazed up a column of bright flame, and flung its light deep into the recesses of the woods. In the morning we breakfasted on rice, bread, and tea without sugar and cream, and then—Friday—prepared to resume our course. Abbot led the way, forcing himself with might and main through the bushes and trees, with us following behind. He carried White's blanket, for White professed himself unable, on account of his lame leg. The direction was southeast by compass, up the declivity of the second mountain. White was eternally grumbling and lagging behind. We had to wait for him every few minutes. The guide cursed him to his face, and said he never knew a fellow of so little pluck. At length, after some hours of tedious labor, we stood on the summit, and saw—nothing. The trees crowded round us so dense and thick that our view was confined to a circle of about a rod around, and a few little patches of cloudy sky above; but by climbing to the top of a tall maple, a noble prospect of mountain and wilderness lay before us. Far off rose the Margalloway Mountain, with a sea of smaller hills about it, all pale and indistinct in mist. Lake Connecticut glistened among them like a surface of polished silver. Right beneath us was the valley of [Dead] Diamond Stream. A line of steep and lofty bluffs marked its course, for the river itself was buried too deep among mountains to be visible. In front, close to us, heaved up a long ridge of mountains sloping away to the left, down to the Margalloway.

We set the compass and found the river lay still to the southeast of us. We came down, and pursued that course again. We soon began to ascend [descend] the mountain on the side opposite that which we had ascended. The way was rough and precipitous. White lagged more and more, and provoked Abbot and myself beyond measure. After journeying many hours in this painful style, we heard the plunging of waters in a valley below us, and joyfully turned towards the sound. It grew louder and louder. In five minutes more we emerged from the gloomy forest and stood in the rocky bed of a wild stream that came down in a succession of rapids and falls over broad shelves of granite. Just then the sun came out from the clouds and lit up the long avenue of trees that followed the course of the stream, and made the water sparkle and glisten in welcome contrast to the sombre shades we had just left. We had struck a branch of the Little Margalloway. White's lameness seemed mysteriously to leave him; he seized his fishing tackle and rushed up and down the rocks, pulling a trout from every deep hole and the foot of every waterfall. I soon followed his example. Abbot built a fire by the bank and cooked our fish. We made a plentiful dinner, and then began to follow downward the course of the stream. At first, it was a matter of no difficulty. We could walk well enough down the channel without wading much above the knees in any place, but soon the brooks that poured in from the mountains on all sides increased the depth of the water, so that we had to betake ourselves to the woods again. Four miles below where we struck it, the river was navigable for a canoe; a mile further, and we heard the loud plunging of a fall. We found a ledge of some four feet high stretched across the river, with the water tumbling over it into a deep basin of dark waters. On the right bank, close to the fall, were traces of an old encampment. Night was coming on, so we determined to establish ourselves here, though we had hoped to have reached the forks of the Margalloway, the place where its two branches meet, and where Slade and I made our last camp a year ago. In the middle of the fall there was a rock, to which we waded and caught in ten minutes a dozen of trout averaging a foot in length. We built our fire, split open the fish, broiled them on forked sticks, boiled some rice, made some tea, and supped a very luxurious style. We lay down on our beds of spruce boughs and the monotonous plunge of the falls quickly lulled us to sleep.

Saturday, August 5[6]th. The morning opened with a grand council. How were we to get down the river? Abbot could make a raft, thought he could make a spruce canoe, and was certain that he could make a log one. I told him to make a log one. We roused White from the spruce boughs where he persisted in snoring, in spite of our momentous discussion, and then prepared and ate our breakfast. White went to fishing. Abbot shouldered his axe, and he and I went off together for a suitable pine tree to make our canoe of. He found one to his satisfaction on the other side of the stream, some distance down. I built him a fire to "smudge" the flies, waded back across the stream, and as I ascended the farther bank heard the thundering crash of the falling pine behind me, bellowing over the wilderness, and rolling in echoes far up the mountains. I went back to camp, where White had again betaken himself to his diversion of snoring, took my broken rifle and set out on an exploring expedition to find the basin where the two branches of the Margalloway unite, which I knew could not be far distant. I waded a considerable distance down stream in the water, which varied in depth from the knees to the waist, but finding this method of progression somewhat unpleasing, I took to the woods, forced my way through them in a southerly direction for half a mile, and found at last the object of my search. The old place, though in the midst of a howling wilderness, looked to me quite like home. It was the spot which had listened to Slade's lugubrious lamentations, the extreme point of my last year's pilgrimage; the place where Jerome had joined our party; and to crown all, it was scarce five miles distant from the scene of that astounding exploit of knocking over the wounded moose. There lay the great black basin of dull waters, girt with its fringe of forests, but the appearance of things was altered since I had seen it before. The basin was fuller, the water blacker and deeper. Some hunter—Jerome, we found afterwards—had visited it since Slade and I had been there and made a good camping place of split boards. Two or three vessels of birch bark, a setting pole, and a fishing pole were scattered around. There was a fragrance of rotten fish in the atmosphere which told that the visit had not been many months back. I sat down, dipped a cup of water from the basin, took a biscuit from my pocket, and made a most comfortable luncheon. I took Jerome's pole, went to fishing, and in an hour caught large trout enough for several meals for our whole party. As I went back to camp, I found that Abbot was not at work on his canoe. While I was marvelling at this, I stumbled upon a half-finished sp[r]uce canoe, which Abbot had set out making, having found the pine tree, which he had cut down for his log boat, rotten. I was not much pleased at this change of plan; nevertheless, as the thing was begun I lent him [such] assistance as I could, so that by nightfall we had finished something which had the semblance of a canoe, but, owing chiefly to haste and want of tools, had such a precarious and doubtful aspect that White christened it the *Forlorn Hope*. We put it into the water. It leaked. We took it out and stuffed the seams with pounded spruce bark, chewed spruce gum, and bits of cloth. It still leaked, but we hoped it would do, with diligent baling; so, fastening it to the bank, we cooked our supper, rolled ourselves in our blankets, and went to sleep before the fire.

ODELL SHEPARD

The Peaceable Kingdom

"... *they never mention the terror of solitude.*"

Odell Shepard was an amalgam: he was a newspaper reporter (a pur-
suit he abandoned early with the resolve not to "put in his life with
such shoddy affairs"); an organist and pianist; an essayist; a poet; a
student of Shakespeare and unicorns; a professor of English literature
in Trinity College; the lieutenant governor of Connecticut; a Pulitzer
Prize-winning biographer; and a walker of wistful and leisurely man-
ner. We see him here as a walker through the untenanted townships of
northern Connecticut. Odell Shepard walked with a spirit of repose,
in a peaceable kingdom, yet was ever alert—even in a tame land—to
the mysteries of solitude and the pleasures of a winding road.

At the top of a gradual slope I came to a road running northward
along a ridge, and the borders of it were woven close to left and right
by a thicket of young birches, maples, and aspens. The leaves, already
yellowing, were all atwinkle in the northwest wind, so that the lane
before me was one vista of dazzle and shine. Tall grass grew between
the wheel-ruts. Chicory blossoms lined the way with their deep sky-
blue that the eye can never quite reach the end of, echoed by the
fainter tones of innumerable asters. Hoof-prints of deer were thick in
the softer places. A partridge, with a startling explosion of wings, shot
away through the thicket. A squirrel scolded the intruder in voluble
falsetto. Cedar waxwings fluttered on before me and gathered again in
sibilant twenties and thirties. Robins and bluebirds, lovers of the
open spaces in earlier summer, were here in this upland covert in
multitudes, doing nothing, for their year's work was over, but restless,
flying with faint calls from bush to bough and back again, fluttering
uncertainly, so that all the undergrowth seemed alive with the whir
and beat of aimless wings.

   After a mile of winding between the leaves, my road turned
downhill, and its lyric beauty was changed at once into grandeur. It
opened first into an avenue of leafless ash trees, rigid and gray in
death, standing in strict formation all down the hill and up the
farther slope like a double line of soldiers suddenly destroyed by some
lethal gas but not yet fallen down. On one side ran a huge stone
wall—five feet high, five feet thick, and a mile long—a work of

gigantic toil. Little by little the road discovered a prospect of many-channeled hills to the west and north, rising tier above tier in graduated tones of blue and dimmer blue to the faint horizon. The sun was going down beyond this mysterious country, and the wind that blew from over the heights of Union was the voice of the wilderness. A fiery cloud blotted the sun for a moment, and all the land went suddenly gray. Then I topped the last domelike hill and saw the spire of Fairford church shining far away below me.

There is for some of us a keener thrill of adventure in entering a little town at twilight for the first time than in a first visit to an old and famous city. We know what to expect of London, Paris, Rome, for we have been living there, in a sense, many years; but a town like Fairford is all mystery. It may be the perfect town we have been looking for all our days. Hope revives at the first glimpse of its lighted windows, the heart quickens a little, and we go forward with our illusions carefully wrapped about us, prepared for the impossible.

The long pale finger of Fairford spire, rising slenderly among the trees, is all of the village that one can see at first as he goes down Ragged Hill into the valley of the Natchaug, and round about it the hills make a rich deep setting of verdure and rounded slopes. Then comes an outlying cottage or two, and at last, while the road still plunges down and down, there comes the glint of a stream running smoothly between little hills and among pastures graced by wine-glass elms.

To most of the towns in this neighborhood all the roads must climb, but Fairford lies snug in a twisting valley with the voice of water all about it. Those who know New England well do not need to be told much more about one of its little towns than that it stands on a hill or in a bottom, for either statement paints a picture. The motives that caused our ancestors to settle so frequently on the hilltops, where the soil was thin and the winds of winter bitterest, are not quite clear even to-day, after a good deal of clever theorizing; but at any rate we may say that whereas the hill towns began unconsciously to prepare, two centuries and more ago, for the summer residents of to-day, Fairford began by thinking of itself. Therefore the town is still practically undiscovered. There is no railroad near it, and although it is unfortunately bisected by an automobile highway, its few white houses make only a momentary blur on the landscape for those who hasten through. . . . I do my best to protect its privacy by giving it a ficticious name.

How long this isolation will continue no man can say, but we can be fairly sure that here, as elsewhere, "commonness will prevail." I always feel that I have reached the best places—of which I take Fairford, with all its faults, to be one—just in the nick of time, before they vanish away. It is a world, as some one has probably observed before, of imperfections and approximations, even in Connecticut. Fairford itself is not an ideal town; it only reminds me, vaguely, of the ideal. Otherwise, of course, I should have got no farther. For what is it that makes the rambler buckle on his pack in the early morning, take his stick from the corner, and strike out again on the road that has no end? Simply his dream, never fading because never entirely realized, of "that flying Perfection round which the hands of man shall never close."

I came into Fairford Center just before sunset, was hospitably received at the inn, and then, after telling my host what I would have for dinner, made my way at once to the central ganglion of all such towns as this, the front porch of the post-office and general store. Half a dozen leading citizens were already assembled there for the regular evening session, and with these I ingratiated myself, as much as it is possible for a man in knickerbockers to do with such a group on such short notice, by making humble inquiries about the weather probable for the morrow. These inquiries were referred to the local expert in meteorology, who opined *ex cathedra* that it would rain. (It did not.) The weather gambit led, as it always will when carefully handled, into a discussion of the season's crops, wherein I did not shine, and that in turn led into politics, in which again, for reasons of party affiliation of which I thought best to say nothing, I gave no very brilliant account of myself. At last, with leisurely sweeps, the talk veered round to local gossip, which had been my goal throughout. What I wanted was to hear Fairford talking about itself. Just when it began to do so, I was summoned to supper.

Returning an hour later, I found the witenagemot still in session. The six men on the porch had not changed their positions, apparently, during my absence, and I was delighted to find that the place I had left was still vacant, as though they had expected me to return. (The probability is, however, that no one had felt any desire to move.) I opened this time by asking a granite and sweet-voiced senior, whose white beard I could just see glimmering beside me in the darkness, about a farm-hand by the name of Sheppey with whom I had descended Ragged Hill that afternoon. "He told me," said I, "that he was eighty-two, and yet he hadn't a white hair on his head. And he said that his wife is older still."

The long white beard shook with tolerant laughter, and then the voice remarked, in the tone of a man who has made his peace with all human frailties: "Sheppey always says he's eighty-two. He's been a-sayin' it for years and years. If he keeps on a-sayin' it long enough it'll come true some o' these times, I shouldn't be surprised. An' the way it seems to me is, he says it jest to make hisself seem more interestin' like, as you might say. But if you was to ask me, I don't guess that Sheppey is more than *sixty*-two years old, if he is a day. Why, I know'd that Sheppey when he first come to town. He come from Rhode Island, some town on the Bay . . . I don't just rec'lect the name of it at this present moment. Well, he was quite a young fellow then. Scarcely more'n a boy, as you might say. And yet it don't seem so very long ago to me, either, that he first come here. Eighty-two! Why, that's 'most as old as *I* be! I tell you he jest says that to make hisself more interestin' to strangers like yourself. . . . But his wife, she *is* old. Older than God, seemingly. Joe, how old'd you say Bill Sheppey's wife is now?"

Joe began at once upon an elaborate computation which involved many minute bits of evidence from local history, all of which I found entertaining. (Oh, the peace there is for a man with weary nerves and brain in sitting in the dark on the Fairford post-office porch discussing the ages of Bill Sheppey and his wife! My thoughts flashed back for an instant to the roar of Amsterdam Avenue, and then returned—how willingly!—to those drawling country voices.) This Joe, it appeared, was a brief abstract and chronicle of Fairford times, early and late. The grand total of years he worked out for Bill Sheppey's wife I do not now recall, but I assure the reader that he can hardly imagine her more venerable than she finally turned out to be. I judged that she might easily have been Bill's grandmother. But then, Fairford people are famous, among other things, for longevity. There was a woman then living in the town who confessed to one hundred and seven years, and who, furthermore, was said to be a real daughter of the American Revolution . . . not a daughter several times grand and great, but actually the daughter of a man who bore arms in the Continental Army. This seemed to me just possible, so that I thought it best not to investigate, but to accept the assertion on trust—observing meanwhile how the social value of this particular ancestry seems to increase directly with the remoteness of the descent.

My porch-mates gave me the main outlines of a quarrel that had
been raging for some time between the Methodists and Congregationalists of the town and that was just then coming to a head. As I
recall it, the members of the two denominations had agreed some
months before to hold union meetings in their respective church
buildings for six months at a time, turn and turn about, dividing the
expenses. It was alleged that the Congregationalists had broken the
agreement after the first few months and had gone back to their own
church, taking their funds with them. The entire Methodist population of the town, twelve in number, was to hold a mass meeting on
the next day but one to consider what they should do. The mass
meeting promised to be a lively affair, and I was advised to arrange my
engagements so that I might attend.

Nearly every man on the porch contributed his quota to the
telling of this story, and each man spoke with a complete freedom
from rancor and *odium theologicum* that left me wondering. For I
knew that nearly every person in Fairford who had any religion worth
mentioning must be either Congregational or Methodist, just as every
adult must be either Democrat or Republican. I knew also that
during the long years when religion was more important to Fairford
than all other things together, such a question as this would have set
the whole town—men, women, children, and dogs—by the ears. But
not one of the men on the porch showed the slightest tinge of hatred
for either of the contending parties; rather, they all seemed mildly
amused at both of them. Perhaps they were on their good behavior,
but if so they performed with remarkable unanimity and gave a very
good imitation of brotherly love. A possible explanation, which I hesitate to mention, flashed through my mind—were they all of them
godless free-thinkers?

In the group that gathers nightly at the Fairford post-office could
be found, I think, the same mingling of ignorance and wisdom,
heroism and futility, tragedy and humor and pathos, that Hawthorne
discovered ninety years ago in the similar group at North Adams.
Nothing essential was changed. And when proper allowances are
made for the cramping effects of a narrow social environment, for life-
long toil, for remoteness from the main currents of modern life, these
philosophers of the porch are far from contemptible. I sat with them
for two hours, all the time in darkness, so that I had to judge them
almost entirely by their voices and by what they said. Now and then
some one would touch a match to his pipe, drawing the flame far

down, and then a ruddy face would leap for five seconds out of the gloom—a face I had never seen before and shall not see again. In every instance it was somehow interesting, had some not quite obliterated mark of breeding, was worn by labor and, so it seemed to me, by thought. One or two of these men certainly did think. They seemed to live, indeed, for thinking, and for talk. It was as though they had generalized the determination of the Yankee not to be "taken in" until it had become a mellow scepticism about all things celestial and mundane—and this, of course, is a mental attitude of dignity and charm. They seemed to me clearly superior in knowledge, skill, wisdom, and above all in personality, to the white-collar brigades of the city street. Each man stood out by himself, alone. In those two hours of talk on the dark porch I saw more human nature than I had found during two months in New York City. . . .

A mile or two beyond North Ashford I came to a tiny schoolhouse embowered by birch trees. Asters and goldenrod were blowing in the playground, and the drone of children's voices reading in unison came slumbrously through the open door. A hum of bees, like an echo of that murmur, filled the air with drowsy monotone. The sunshine lay more still and golden here than in the lanes behind me. Spilling from a profound sky, it fell among the chattering birch leaves and was broken into cascades of metallic glitter that gathered again among the grass-roots and slept in a broad pool, soaking slowly into the sod. Here, it seemed to me, a man might almost drown himself in sunshine. I decided to try it. Finding a strip of grass over the path from the school ground, I leant my back against the stone wall and drew forth my luncheon. When this was eaten I found a plentiful dessert of wild grapes hanging in heavy clusters a few feet away.

As I lay there, in the large content of a man who has gathered some part of his own dinner, a huge old farm horse came stumblig down the lane, scattering pebbles before the ponderous tread of his hooves, browsing here and there among the wayside herbage, and blowing mightily from time to time to clear the dust and pollen from his nostrils. He too was living off the country. Without a strap of harness on him, or any other badge of servitude, he looked a perfect symbol of leisure honestly earned. It did me good to gaze at him. The beauty of a nervous thoroughbred is one thing, but the grandeur of his majestic muscles, enormous fetlocks, and mighty mane seemed to me better still because it answered to something deeper in my own mood. He was an epic horse, fit for Odin's riding. He made me understand better than before what the physician meant in telling the overworked and worried Ernest Pontifex to go out to the Zoo and look at the large, grave animals. Small animals, he said, would not do at all, and he advised particularly against monkeys as being too much like the human race.

Solomon was probably right in urging the sluggard to go to the ant, but a tired man should consider a large and lumbering cart-horse on a holiday. There is nothing more therapeutic. Of course I admit that much may be said for cows, but most of it has already been said by Walt Whitman and others. A cow, moreover, can scarcely be said to have any leisure because she never has anything else. Her tranquillity is superb, it is consummate; but then it is also professional. My farm horse was an amateur, enjoying his holiday all the more because it was not to be everlasting. I was hoping at every minute that he would lie down on his back and kick his heels in the air, but probably the lane was too narrow for this supreme exhibition of equine contentment, or else the ground was too rocky. I knew that he had it in him, for there were burrs on his back. He shambled past me without so much as a glance in my direction, planting his huge hoof within six inches of my outstretched foot. I watched him down the hill until he was hidden by the flicker of sun and shade, and sent my blessing after him. More than any other creature that I met in all my journey he seemed bent upon some goalless errand like my own, as though he too had set aside a space of time out of his respectable, strenuous, and law-abiding year in which to drift across the Connecticut landscape thinking idle and self-pleasing thoughts in whatever order they might come. Of course I said to myself that he had the right idea. I thought that he could give lessons in the almost forgotten art of leisure to ninety-nine vacationists in the hundred—to all the fretful human midges that buzz from one excitement to another, that must be always making a noise, always entertained. . . . But then I remembered that only a creature of his ponderous strength could rest so mightily as he. A muscle, I said, is tested by its power of relaxation as much as by its tension, and a man also. If you want to know how a man can work, I said, see how he rests.

And then, as though to make myself the most brilliant possible example of high-power efficiency—for the benefit, perhaps, of the children when they came out of school—I made a pillow of my knapsack, pulled my cap over my eyes, and lay down among the asters with the sunshine splashing all about me. No thought of the indefinite miles that lay between me and any probable bed for the night disturbed my quiet. The busy hum of scholars across the lane and that of bees in the aster-bloom, so far from being a rebuke, was an incentive to slumber. Thoughts of the old farm horse rambling down the lane so full of sleep were a further soporific. I was surprised, not for the first time, to discover how staunchly the planet bears one up when it is allowed to do all the work. Usually, when we overdriven mortals lie down to sleep, we hold some muscle tense, some nerve drawn taut, as though our beds could not quite sustain us; strenuous even in sleep, we feel that we must struggle still against something, even though it be only the force of gravity. But there were eight thousand miles of earth in my mattress and I had put the strenuous life behind me by the width of several townships. The contrast between this nameless lane and Amsterdam Avenue was complete. I slept.

Straight north from Orcuttsville ran my road, deteriorating with gratifying rapidity as it went, so that I feared it might dodge away into Massachusetts and leave me. All it meant, however, was to get round Crow Hill, and when it had done this, skirting the very boundary line of the northern state as a skater does a hole in the ice, it snuggled down into Connecticut again, making for the gap between Bald and Soapstone mountains. The five-mile tramp toward that gap lay through unbroken woodland. I met on the way several families going to church, one hermit who was knocking apples out of a tree above his shack, a man and woman engaged in admiration of the landscape, and a small boy driving a cow. All of these people—a surprising number to find at such a place and time—were foreigners in one sense or another. At last, however, I encountered a native, a specimen of that noble but rapidly disappearing species which should be known as *Homo Connecticutensis*, standing before the door of his house on the loneliest stretch of that lonely road.

He was a man of middle age, well read and well spoken, a college graduate, who had always lived in this house, which he said was the oldest inhabited house in Tolland County, except for the years of his schooling. With him I had some good talk upon solitude, upon which topic I expected to find him an expert, considering that his little farm was beleaguered by the forest and that his nearest neighbor lived a mile away. Unlike the patriarch of North Ashford, he knew the meaning of solitude and admitted the knowledge; but like most sensible men who have had long experience of loneliness, he did not much enjoy it—or perhaps he thought that half a lifetime of it was an overdose. We quoted some of the *loci classici* on the subject, beginning with Scipio's hackneyed *Numquam minus solusquam solus* and coming down to Thoreau's "I have never yet found the companion who is so companionable as solitude." Most of these remarks, we agreed, were only egoism masquerading as philosophy, and few of them were uttered by men who had earned the right to speak. I gave him the gist of a passage from the letters of Thoreau which he had never met with: "It is not that we love to be alone, but that we love to soar, and when we do soar the company grows thinner and thinner till there is none at all. We are not the less to aim at the summits, though the multitude does not ascend them. Use all the society that will abet you." This he thought was good sense, and we agreed that Thoreau often showed good sense when he was not striking attitudes and trying to make people gasp. One convincing proof, I said, that most amateurs of the solitary life—excepting certain hermits of the Thebaid—have not known what they are talking about is that they never mention the terror of solitude, as I had felt it more than once in broad daylight on the tops of the California mountains. He looked at me strangely when I said this, as though he thought, "So you have known that too!" But he did not say that he had.

The road over Skiff Mountain from Sharon to Kent is some thirteen miles in length. On that road I saw perhaps ten houses, and half of these were deserted; for I was coming once more into a region of ghosts. Here again were the old stone walls running through unbroken woodland, and here were apple orchards recaptured by the forest. No better apples are to be had anywhere than the one I picked up in a dense thicket near the top of the mountain. Ages of culture went to the making of that apple, yet there was no sight or sound of human habitation anywhere about—nothing but a brambly wilderness. But going on two hundred yards I saw in the brush beside the way first a ruined chimney and then a worn door-step, with the inevitable lilac bush. They told the story.

It is strange to think as one walks among these untenanted townships that the men who once lived here were an unusually begettive race. Any adjacent graveyard will show that. For the women of Connecticut a century ago child-bearing was a steady occupation, pursued year in and year out, which might well have been classed among the dangerous trades. Hard as the life of the farmer usually was, the graveyard record shows that he frequently outlived three wives. One sees how the economic conditions of the time and place worked together with the Biblical injunction so as to make a virtue of the philoprogenitive instinct, for children provided the cheapest form of labor. For something like a hundred years this haste of the New England Puritans to replenish the earth began to show signs of abatement, and the few that are left have scarcely any children whatever. Of the three last-surviving descendants of Keep-the-Good-Faith Sawyer, John went west and was never heard from again, Sarah died an old maid, and Jake went on the town. To-day you can find only a gaping cellar-hole, a dying lilac bush, several miles of good stone wall, and perhaps one sound apple to mark the scene of the family's long heroic toil.

This part of New England reminds me of the gigantic chestnut cadavers that still hold up their mighty arms here and there in Connecticut, rigid in death, remnants of the host that once peopled all the land. Scions spring every year from their roots, but die before they mature. Yet there is life in these dead trunks even now; they are excellent cradles for woodpecker eggs. Just so there is life in the dead trunk of Connecticut, though it is of a sort that would astonish the founders. The millionaire, the Pole, and the Jew make no more complaint of Connecticut than the woodpecker does of the chestnut. They do not feel that it is old and moribund, but find it quite to their mind. They see no ghosts.

My road was often no more than a cart-track through the woods, and it was printed thickly with hoof-marks of deer. Partridges caromed away with a startling rattle of wings. Once I caught a glimpse of a fox sitting on his haunches in a little clearing twenty paces from the road and staring straight into my eyes. As the afternoon wore away the wind fell and the sky was filled with clouds. The silence of the woods, after a day of stentorian wind-song, deepened my sense of the mystery through which I was walking—a sense that I can express only by saying that I felt suddenly out of time with the place, as though I were intruding upon a scene not meant for me, or for any human witness. It was as though the trees were making some secret preparations, and waited for me to get by. There swept over me a vague feeling that I was being watched by many things at once, from above and below and from all sides. This feeling grew and grew until all the air seemed alive with hostility and menace. And then I came to Desolate Swamp.

The name is my own, for I could not find the place on my map, but it is the source, I think, of Macedonia Brook. I shall remember it always as a perfect symbol of desolation. There were thirty acres of slate-gray water under a slate-gray sky, and in the water two or three hundred drowned trees, some submerged to the knees and others to the armpits, all livid in death. I thought the place was like something Dante had imagined for his *Inferno* but had left out as too terrible for words. Poe's demon had cursed it with silence, and another demon had cursed it with a blank despair which haunted the mind and would make the stoutest beholder quail.

A wholly sentimental traveler would have tried to think Desolate Swamp meaningless, a mere hiatus in nature; but I had been braced by twenty miles of rather hard going over the hills since morning, and so I dared to stand and face the swamp for a few minutes, wondering what it meant. And this is a part of what it said to me—although there are no words to express a message by its essence devoid of human significance:

"Soft and dreamy seeker of pleasant emotions, know that you see no farther into the realities of what you call your 'Mother Nature' than a painted butterfly does in flapping from flower to flower. You too are convinced that the sun shines to warm your wings, and that the meadows are strewn with flowers to flatter your delight in color. The fear that clutches now at your heart is only the fear lest your self-love, your notion of your own importance, may have less warrant than you and your fellows have dreamed. As you stare into my vacant eyes, older than thought, older than mind-stuff, you are learning faster than ever you have in reading the wisest books. Your braggart poets have not told you such things as I tell. They say that 'Nature is ancillary to Man.' On the man-handled meadows of Concord, perhaps, but not on Skiff Mountain, where I still remember the dinosaur's wallowing and the scream of the sabre-tooth. They have said that 'Nature never did betray the heart that loved her.' Ask the ghost of Hendrik Hudson. Ask the spirits of the young men lost on Mount Everest. Ask the woman dying in childbirth. Peer down into the savageries of the under-sea. Think your way out into the infinite of the sky until the brain staggers, or down into the answering infinite of the atom. Or, merely stand and look at me. As I am now, so was the planet for innumerable ages before man came, and so it will be for endless ages after he is gone. . . . Now you may pass on—for I think you will not forget."

No, I shall not soon forget. I had been forced to con the same lesson more than once before. Walking all day in the rain on Exmoor I had read it, and again on the rocky spine of Catalina Island, and once more on a bare mountain slope in Montana. Whenever a man steps a little aside from the thoroughfares of our steam-heated and parlor-cared modernity he is likely to find some dreary page set down for his perusal, and he must deal with it according to whatever philosophy there is in him. Desolate Swamp set all my philosophy at defiance, for it did not pretend to be wise but only final. It made sport of all the heroism I had, for even a man who can face death cannot face the thought that life and death alike are utterly meaningless. It set me for two or three shuddering minutes outside the little circle of the Things We Take for Granted, and I saw how that circle really looks. Once more, for the third or fourth time in my life, I felt the Terror of Solitude.

But it was amusing to observe how my mind began at once to edge away from its lesson. Apparently I was a good deal like the man in Boswell who tried hard for years to be a philosopher, "but cheerfulness was always breaking in." It is natural enough, I said, that there should be some places not yet made ready for man's coming, and we do wrong to stare obtrusively at the vast digestive processes, like that still going forward in Desolate Swamp, by which the planet was prepared for our culminating advent. And then I thought of what a snug and habitable little globe we have made it, after all. I thought of the fires we have kindled here and there—building them on the edges of the abyss, no doubt, and lighting up only our own faces against the ring of darkness, but still . . . fires. I remembered the songs we have made to sing there about the fire, the brave high-hearted songs, as though the darkness were not. And I recalled the pictures we have painted, the music of Mozart, the spire of Salisbury, and some of our pathetic faiths and hopes and illusions.

"Oh well," I said, "we have not done so badly, all things considered. It may be that Nature did not forsee us; but if so we have made her open her eyes! She has brought forth no other such pathetic and marvelous thing in all her kingdoms as this heart of man, so trivial and heroic, so dauntless though so filled with fears, that smiles into the eyes of Death."

Then I thought of my dinner, six miles away, for the sun was setting behind the Catskills. I made the air whistle with a twirl of my stick, twitched my knapsack into position, and set up the rollicking road-song of Autolycus: "Jog on, jog on, the foot-path way."

After leaving Desolate Swamp I passed not a single house, or none that I could see through the gathering darkness, all the way to Kent. For most of that way I burrowed downward through a tunnel of gloom, like a mole, stumbling from rock to rock and feeling the path with my stick, certain only that the water-shed I was descending would take me sooner or later to the Housatonic and so eventually to one of the river towns. An hour or more of this unsatisfactory travel by touch and hearing brought me to the welcome sound of river water, and then there were two miles of valley road still to go. A breeze awoke in the sky and blew bare the new moon, with a planet or two, over Spooner Hill, and by this pale illumination I saw in due time first the buildings of Kent School, then the bridge, and finally, the village street, with the light of my inn at the far end shining.

CLARENCE KING

Silence and Desolation

"Everything may be seen, nothing recognized . . ."

Few accounts of walking in America—or anywhere—can match the drama, the tension and the sense of Olympian enterprise which Clarence King put into his report of scaling Mount Tyndall in California's High Sierra. John Muir proved himself a Scotsman and found it ignored the strict economy of truth; it is a classic nonetheless. King was 22 years old and an unpaid volunteer in a survey party led by William H. Brewer when he and Richard ("Why not?") Cotter shouldered their packs and walked into a wilderness Brewer himself pronounced impassable. At times a dark spirit hovers over these pages: we find King captivated by darkness, by half-light, by Dante upon the peaks, and we recall that the twilight of his life found him in a madhouse, and that he died alone, a free man, but far away from his friends and secret family. Despite this brooding presentiment, Clarence King's saga burns with the light of adventure and danger shared; it is somehow innocent on the face of a hard and treacherous earth. The actual ascent of Tyndall came on July 6, 1864. The other members of Brewer's party mentioned here were James T. Gardner, a geologist and friend of King's, and Charles F. Hoffman, a topographer.

This account is taken from Clarence King's Mountaineering in the Sierra Nevada, *published in 1872.*

Morning dawned brightly upon our bivouac among a cluster of dark firs in the mountain corridor opened by an ancient glacier of King's River into the heart of the Sierras. It dawned a trifle sooner than we could have wished, but Professor Brewer and Hoffman had breakfasted before sunrise, and were off with barometer and theodolite upon their shoulders, purposing to ascend our amphitheatre to its head and climb a great pyramidal peak which swelled up against the eastern sky, closing the view in that direction.

We who remained in camp spent the day in overhauling campaign materials and preparing for a grand assault upon the summits. For a couple of hours we could descry our friends through the field-glasses, their minute black forms moving slowly among piles of giant *débris*; now and then lost, again coming into view, and at last disappearing altogether.

It was twilight of evening and almost eight o'clock when they came back to camp, Brewer leading the way, Hoffman following; and as they sat down by our fire without uttering a word, we read upon their faces terrible fatigue.

So we hastened to give them supper of coffee and soup, bread and venison, which resulted, after a time, in our getting in return the story of the day.

For eight whole hours they had worked up over granite and snow, mounting ridge after ridge, till the summit was made about two o'clock.

These snowy crests bounding our view at the eastward we had all along taken to be the summits of the Sierra, and Brewer had supposed himself to be climbing a dominant peak, from which he might look eastward over Owen's Valley and out upon leagues of desert. Instead of this a vast wall of mountains, lifted still higher than his peak, rose beyond a tremendous cañon which lay like a trough between the two parallel ranks of peaks. Hoffman showed us on his sketch-book the profile of this new range, and I instantly recognized the peaks which I had seen from Mariposa, whose great white pile had led me to believe them the highest points of California.

For a couple of months my friends had made me the target of plenty of pleasant banter about my "highest land," which they lost faith in as we climbed from Thomas's Mill,—I too becoming a trifle anxious about it; but now that the truth had burst upon Brewer and Hoffman they could not find words to describe the terribleness and grandeur of the deep cañon, nor for picturing those huge crags towering in line at the east. Their peak, as indicated by the barometer, was in the region of thirteen thousand four hundred feet, and a level across to the farther range showed its crests to be at least fifteen hundred feet higher. They had spent hours upon the summit scanning the eastern horizon, and ranging downward into the labyrinth of gulfs below, and had come at last with reluctance to the belief that to cross this gorge and ascend the eastern wall of peaks was utterly impossible.

Brewer and Hoffman were old climbers, and their verdict of impossible oppressed me as I lay awake thinking of it; but early next morning I had made up my mind, and, taking Cotter aside, I asked him in an easy manner whether he would like to penetrate the Terra Incognita with me at the risk of our necks, provided Brewer should consent. In a frank, courageous tone he answered after his usual mode,

"Why not?" Stout of limb, stronger yet in heart, of iron endurance, and a quiet, unexcited temperament, and, better yet, deeply devoted to me, I felt that Cotter was the one comrade I would choose to face death with, for I believed there was in his manhood no room for fear or shirk.

It was a trying moment for Brewer when we found him and volunteered to attempt a campaign for the top of California, because he felt a certain fatherly responsibility over our youth, a natural desire that we should not deposit out triturated remains in some undiscoverable hole among the feldspathic granites; but, like a true disciple of science, this was at last over-balanced by his intense desire to know more of the unexplored region. He freely confessed that he believed the plan madness, and Hoffman, too, told us we might as well attempt to get on a cloud as to try the peak.

As Brewer gradually yielded his consent, I saw by his conversation that there was a possibility of success; so we spent the rest of the day in making preparations.

Our walking-shoes were in excellent condition, the hobnails firm and new. We laid out a barometer, a compass, a pocket-level, a set of wet and dry thermometers, note-books, with bread, cooked beans, and venison enough to last a week, rolled them all in blankets, making two knapsack-shaped packs strapped firmly together with loops for arms, which, by Brewer's estimate, weighed forty pounds apiece.

Gardner declared he would accompany us to the summit of the first range to look over into the gulf we were to cross, and at last Brewer and Hoffman also concluded to go up with us.

Quite too early for our profit we all betook ourselves to bed, vainly hoping to get a long refreshing sleep from which we should arise ready for our tramp.

Never a man welcomed those first gray streaks in the east gladder than I did, unless it may be Cotter, who has in later years confessed that he did not go to sleep that night. Long before sunrise we had done our breakfast and were under way, Hoffman kindly bearing my pack, and Brewer Cotter's.

Our way led due east up the amphitheatre and toward Mount Brewer, as we had named the great pyramidal peak.

Awhile after leaving camp, slant sunlight streamed in among gilded pinnacles along the slope of Mount Brewer, touching here and there, in broad dashes of yellow, the gray walls, which rose sweeping up on either hand like the sides of a ship.

Our way along the valley's middle ascended over a number of huge steps, rounded and abrupt, at whose bases were pools of transparent snow-water edged with rude piles of erratic glacier blocks, scattered companies of alpine firs, of red bark and having cypress-like darkness of foliage, with fields of snow under sheltering cliffs, and bits of softest velvet meadow clouded with minute blue and white flowers.

As we climbed, the gorge grew narrow and sharp, both sides wilder; and the spurs which projected from them, nearly overhanging the middle of the valley, towered above us with more and more severe sculpture. We frequently crossed deep fields of snow, and at last reached the level of the highest pines, where long slopes of *débris* swept down from either cliff, meeting in the middle. Over and among these immense blocks, often twenty and thirty feet high, we were obliged to climb, hearing far below us the subterranean gurgle of streams.

Interlocking spurs nearly closed the gorge behind us; our last view was out a granite gateway formed of two nearly vertical precipices, sharp-edged, jutting buttress-like, and plunging down into a field of angular boulders which fill the valley bottom.

The eye ranged out from this open gateway overlooking the great King's Cañon with its moraine-terraced walls, the domes of granite upon Big Meadows, and the undulating stretch of forest which descends to the plain.

The gorge turning southward, we rounded a sort of mountain promontory, which, closing the view behind us, shut us up in the bottom of a perfect basin. In front lay a placid lake reflecting the intense black-blue of the sky. Granite, stained with purple and red, sank into it upon one side, and a broad spotless field of snow came down to its margin on the other.

From a pile of large granite blocks, forty or fifty feet up above the lake margin, we could look down fully a hundred feet through the transparent water to where boulders and pebbles were strewn upon the stone bottom. We had now reached the base of Mount Brewer and were skirting its southern spurs in a wide open corridor surrounded in all directions by lofty granite crags from two to four thousand feet high; above the limits of vegetation, rocks, lakes of deep heavenly blue, and white trackless snows were grouped closely about us. Two sounds, a sharp little cry of martens, and occasional heavy crashes of falling rock, saluted us.

Climbing became exceedingly difficult, light air—for we had already reached twelve thousand five hundred feet—beginning to tell upon our lungs to such an extent that my friend, who had taken turns with me in carrying my pack, was unable to do so any longer, and I adjusted it to my shoulders for the rest of the day.

After four hours of slow laborious work we made the base of the *débris* slope which rose about a thousand feet to a saddle pass in the western mountain wall, that range upon which Mount Brewer is so prominent a point. We were nearly an hour in toiling up this slope over an uncertain footing which gave way at almost every step. At last, when almost at the top, we paused to take a breath, and then all walked out upon the crest, laid off our packs, and sat down together upon the summit of the ridge, and for a few moments not a word was spoken.

The Sierras are here two parallel summit ranges. We were upon the crest of the western ridge, and looked down into a gulf five thousand feet deep, sinking from our feet in abrupt cliffs nearly or quite two thousand feet, whose base plunged into a broad field of snow lying steep and smooth for a great distance, but broken near its foot by craggy steps often a thousand feet high.

Vague blue haze obscured the lost depths, hiding details, giving a bottomless distance out of which, like the breath of wind, floated up a faint tremble, vibrating upon the senses, yet never clearly heard.

Rising on the other side, cliff above cliff, precipice piled upon precipice, rock over rock, up against sky, towered the most gigantic mountain-wall in America, culminating in a noble pile of Gothic-finished granite and enamel-like snow. How grand and inviting looked its white form, its untrodden, unknown crest, so high and pure in the clear strong blue! I looked at it as one contemplating the purpose of his life; and for just one moment I would have rather liked to dodge that purpose, or to have waited, or have found some excellent reason why I might not go; but all this quickly vanished, leaving a cheerful resolve to go ahead.

From the two opposing mountain-walls singular, thin, knife-blade ridges of stone jutted out, dividing the sides of the gulf into a series of amphitheatres, each one a labyrinth of ice and rock. Piercing thick beds of snow, sprang up knobs and straight isolated spires of rock, mere obelisks curiously carved by frost, their rigid, slender forms casting a blue, sharp shadow upon the snow. Embosomed in depressions of ice, or resting on broken ledges, were azure lakes, deeper in tone than the sky, which at this altitude, even at midday, has a violet duskiness.

To the south, not more than eight miles, a wall of peaks stood across the gulf, dividing the King's, which flowed north at our feet, from the Kern River, that flowed down the trough in the opposite direction.

I did not wonder that Brewer and Hoffman pronounced our undertaking impossible; but when I looked at Cotter there was such complete bravery in his eye that I asked him if he was ready to start. His old answer, "Why not?" left the initiative with me; so I told Professor Brewer that we would bid him good by. Our friends helped us on with our packs in silence, and as we shook hands there was not a dry eye in the party. Before he let go of my hand Professor Brewer asked me for my plan, and I had to own that I had but one, which was to reach the highest peak in the range.

After looking in every direction I was obliged to confess that I saw as yet no practicable way. We bade them a "good by," receiving their "God bless you" in return, and started southward along the range to look for some possible cliff to descend. Brewer, Gardner, and Hoffman turned north to push upward to the summit of Mount Brewer, and complete their observations. We saw them whenever we halted, until at last, on the very summit, their microscopic forms were for the last time discernible. With very great difficulty we climbed a peak which surmounted our wall just to the south of the pass, and, looking over the eastern brink, found that the precipice was still sheer and unbroken. In one place, where the snow lay against it to the very top, we went to its edge and contemplated the slide. About three thousand feet of unbroken white, at a fearfully steep angle, lay below us. We threw a stone over and watched it bound until it was lost in the distance; after fearful leaps we could only detect it by the flashings of snow where it struck, and as these were, in some instances, three hundred feet apart, we decided not to launch our own valuable bodies, and the still more precious barometer, after it.

There seemed but one possible way to reach our goal; that was to make our way along the summit of the cross ridge which projected between the two ranges. This divide sprang out from our Mount Brewer wall, about four miles to the south of us. To reach it we must climb up and down over the indented edge of the Mount Brewer wall. In attempting to do this we had a rather lively time scaling a sharp granite needle, where we found our course completely stopped by precipices four and five hundred feet in height. Ahead of us the summit continued to be broken into fantastic pinnacles, leaving us no hope of making our way along it; so we sought the most broken part of the eastern descent, and began to climb down. The heavy knap-sacks, beside wearing our shoulders gradually into a black-and-blue state, overbalanced us terribly, and kept us in constant danger of pitching headlong. At last, taking them off, Cotter climbed down until he had found a resting-place upon a cleft of rock, then I lowered them to him with our lasso, afterwards descending cautiously to his side, taking my turn in pioneering downward, receiving the freight of knapsacks by lasso as before. In this manner we consumed more than half the afternoon in descending a thousand feet of broken, precipitous slope; and it was almost sunset when we found ourselves upon the fields of level snow which lay white and thick over the whole interior slope of the amphitheatre. At our backs the Mount Brewer wall either rose in sheer cliffs or in broken, rugged stairway, such as had offered us our descent. From this cruel dilemma the cross divide furnished the only hope, and the sole chance of scaling that was at its junction with the Mount Brewer wall. Toward this point we directed our course, marching wearily over stretches of dense frozen snow, and regions of *débris*, reaching about sunset the last alcove of the amphitheatre, just at the foot of the Mount Brewer wall. It was evidently impossible for us to attempt to climb it that evening, and we looked about the desolate recesses for a sheltered camping-spot. A high granite wall surrounded us upon three sides, recurring to the southward in long elliptical curves; no part of the summit being less than two thousand feet above us, the higher crags not unfrequently reaching three thousand feet. A single field of snow swept around the base of the rock, and covered the whole amphitheatre, except where a few spikes and rounded masses of granite rose through it, and where two frozen lakes, with their blue ice-disks, broke the monotonous surface. Through the white snow-gate of our amphitheatre, as through a frame, we looked eastward upon the summit group; not a tree, not a vestige of vegetation in sight,—sky, snow, and granite the only elements in this wild picture.

After searching for a shelter we at last found a granite crevice near the margin of one of the frozen lakes,—a sort of shelf just large enough for Cotter and me,—where we hastened to make our bed, having first filled the canteen from a small stream that trickled over the ice, knowing that in a few moments the rapid chill would freeze it. We ate our supper of cold venison and bread, and whittled from the sides of the wooden barometer-case shavings enough to warm water for a cup of miserably tepid tea, and then, packing our provi-

sions and instruments away at the head of the shelf, rolled ourselves
in our blankets and lay down to enjoy the view.

After such fatiguing exercises the mind has an almost abnormal
clearness: whether this is wholly from within, or due to the intensely
vitalizing mountain air, I am not sure; probably both contribute to
the state of exaltation in which all alpine climbers find themselves.
The solid granite gave me a luxurious repose, and I lay on the edge of
our little rock niche and watched the strange yet brilliant scene.

All the snow of our recess lay in the shadow of the high granite
wall to the west, but the Kern divide which curved around us from
the southeast was in full light; its broken sky-line, battlemented and
adorned with innumerable rough-hewn spires and pinnacles, was a
mass of glowing orange intensely defined against the deep violet sky.
At the open end of our horseshoe amphitheatre, to the east, its floor
of snow rounded over in a smooth brink, overhanging precipices
which sank two thousand feet into the King's Cañon. Across the gulf
rose the whole procession of summit peaks, their lower halves rooted
in a deep sombre shadow cast by the western wall, the heights bathed
in a warm purple haze, in which the irregular marbling of snow
burned with a pure crimson light. A few fleecy clouds, dyed fiery
orange, drifted slowly eastward across the narrow zone of sky which
stretched from summit to summit like a roof. At times the sound of
waterfalls, faint and mingled with echoes, floated up through the still
air. The snow near by lay in cold ghastly shade, warmed here and
there in strange flashes by light reflected downward from drifting
clouds. The sombre waste about us; the deep violet vault overhead;
those far summits, glowing with reflected rose; the deep impenetrable
gloom which filled the gorge, and slowly and with vapor-like stealth
climbed the mountain wall extinguishing the red light, combined to
produce an effect which may not be described; nor can I more than
hint at the contrast between the brilliancy of the scene under full
light, and the cold, deathlike repose which followed when the wan
cliffs and pallid snow were all over-shadowed with ghostly gray.

A sudden chill enveloped us. Stars in a moment crowded through
the dark heaven, flashing with a frosty splendor. The snow congealed,
the brooks ceased to flow, and, under the powerful sudden leverage of
frost, immense blocks were dislodged all along the mountain summits
and came thundering down the slopes, booming upon the ice, dashing
wildly upon rocks. Under the lee of our shelf we felt quite safe, but
neither Cotter nor I could help being startled, and jumping just a
little, as these missiles, weighing often many tons, struck the ledge

over our heads and whizzed down the gorge, their stroke resounding fainter and fainter, until at last only a confused echo reached us.

The thermometer at nine o'clock marked twenty degrees above zero. We set the "minimum" and rolled ourselves together for the night. The longer I lay the less I liked that shelf of granite; it grew hard in time, and cold also, my bones seeming to approach actual contact with the chilled rock; moreover, I found that even so vigorous a circulation as mine was not enough to warm up the ledge to anything like a comfortable temperature. A single thickness of blanket is a better mattress than none, but the larger crystals of orthoclase, protruding plentifully, punched my back and caused me to revolve on a horizontal axis with precision and frequency. How I loved Cotter! how I hugged him and got warm, while our backs gradually petrified, till we whirled over and thawed them out together! The slant of that bed was diagonal and excessive; down it we slid till the ice chilled us awake, and we crawled back and chocked ourselves up with bits of granite inserted under my ribs and shoulders. In this pleasant position we got dozing again, and there stole over me a most comfortable ease. The granite softened perceptibly. I was delightfully warm and sank into an industrious slumber which lasted with great soundness till four, when we rose and ate our breakfast of frozen venison.

The thermometer stood at two above zero; everything was frozen tight except the canteen, which we had prudently kept between us all night. Stars still blazed brightly, and the moon, hidden from us by western cliffs, shone in pale reflection upon the rocky heights to the east, which rose, dimly white, up from the impenetrable shadows of the cañon. Silence,—cold, ghastly dimness, in which loomed huge forms,—the biting frostiness of the air, wrought upon our feelings as we shouldered our packs and started with slow pace to climb toward the "divide."

Soon, to our dismay, we found the straps had so chafed our shoulders that the weight gave us great pain, and obliged us to pad them with our handkerchiefs and extra socks, which remedy did not wholly relieve us from the constant wearing pain of the heavy load.

Directing our steps southward toward a niche in the wall which bounded us only half a mile distant, we travelled over a continuous snow-field frozen so densely as scarcely to yield at all to our tread, at the same time compressing enough to make that crisp frosty sound which we all used to enjoy even before we knew from the books that it had something to do with the severe name of regelation.

As we advanced, the snow sloped more and more steeply up

toward the crags, till by and by it became quite dangerous, causing us
to cut steps with Cotter's large bowie-knife,—a slow, tedious operation, requiring patience of a pretty permanent kind. In this way we
spent a quiet social hour or so. The sun had not yet reached us, being
shut out by the high amphitheatre wall; but its cheerful light reflected
downward from a number of higher crags, filling the recess with the
brightness of day, and putting out of existence those shadows which
so sombrely darkened the earlier hours. To look back when we
stopped to rest was to realize our danger,—that smooth swift slope of
ice carrying the eye down a thousand feet to the margin of a frozen
mirror of ice; ribs and needles of rock piercing up through the snow,
so closely grouped that, had we fallen, a miracle only might save us
from being dashed. This led to rather deeper steps, and greater care
that our burdens should be held more nearly over the centre of
gravity, and a pleasant relief when we got to the top of the snow and
sat down on a block of granite to breathe and look up in search of a
way up the thousand-foot cliff of broken surface, among the lines of
fracture and the galleries winding along the face.

It would have disheartened us to gaze up the hard, sheer front of
precipices, and search among splintered projections, crevices, shelves,
and snow-patches for an inviting route, had we not been animated by
a faith that the mountains could not defy us.

Choosing what looked like the least impossible way, we started;
but, finding it unsafe to work with packs on, resumed the yesterday's
plan,—Cotter taking the lead, climbing about fifty feet ahead, and
hoisting up the knapsacks and barometer as I tied them to the end of
the lasso. Constantly closing up in hopeless difficulty before us, the
way opened again and again to our gymnastics, till we stood together
upon a mere shelf, not more than two feet wide, which led diagonally
up the smooth cliff. Edging along in careful steps, our backs flattened
upon the granite, we moved slowly to a broad platform, where we
stopped for breath.

There was no foothold above us. Looking down over the course
we had come, it seemed, and I really believe it was, an impossible
descent; for one can climb upward with safety where he cannot
downward. To turn back was to give up in defeat; and we sat at least
half an hour, suggesting all possible routes to the summit, accepting
none, and feeling disheartened. About thirty feet directly over our
heads was another shelf, which, if we could reach, seemed to offer at
least a temporary way upward. On its edge were two or three spikes

of granite; whether firmly connected with the cliff, or merely blocks of *débris*, we could not tell from below. I said to Cotter, I thought of but one possible plan: it was to lasso one of these blocks, and to climb, sailor-fashion, hand over hand, up the rope. In the lasso I had perfect confidence, for I had seen more than one Spanish bull throw his whole weight against it without parting a strand. The shelf was so narrow that throwing the coil of rope was a very difficult undertaking. I tried three times, and Cotter spent five minutes vainly whirling the loop up at the granite spikes. At last I made a lucky throw, and it tightened upon one of the smaller protuberances. I drew the noose close, and very gradually threw my hundred and fifty pounds upon the rope; then Cotter joined me, and, for a moment, we both hung our united weight upon it. Whether the rock moved slightly or whether the lasso stretched a little we were unable to decide; but the trial must be made, and I began to climb slowly. The smooth precipice-face against which my body swung offered no foothold, and the whole climb had therefore to be done by the arms, an effort requiring all one's determination. When about halfway up I was obliged to rest, and, curling my feet in the rope, managed to relieve my arms for a moment. In this position I could not resist the fascinating temptation of a survey downward.

Straight down, nearly a thousand feet below, at the foot of the rocks, began the snow, whose steep, roof-like slope, exaggerated into an almost vertical angle, curved down in a long white field, broken far away by rocks and polished, round lakes of ice.

Cotter looked up cheerfully and asked how I was making it; to which I answered that I had plenty of wind left. At that moment, when hanging between heaven and earth, it was a deep satisfaction to look down at the wide gulf of desolation beneath, and up to unknown dangers ahead, and feel my nerves cool and unshaken.

A few pulls hand over hand brought me to the edge of the shelf, when, throwing an arm around the granite spike, I swung my body upon the shelf and lay down to rest, shouting to Cotter that I was all right, and that the prospects upward were capital. After a few moments' breathing I looked over the brink and directed my comrade to tie the barometer to the lower end of the lasso, which he did, and that precious instrument was hoisted to my station, and the lasso sent down twice for knapsacks, after which Cotter came up the rope in his very muscular way without once stopping to rest. We took our loads in our hands, swinging the barometer over my shoulder, and climbed up a shelf which led in a zigzag direction upward and to the south, bringing us out at last upon the thin blade of a ridge which connected a short distance above with the summit. It was formed of huge blocks, shattered, and ready, at a touch, to fall.

So narrow and sharp was the upper slope, that we dared not walk, but got astride, and worked slowly along with our hands, pushing the knapsacks in advance, now and then holding our breath when loose masses rocked under our weight.

Once upon the summit, a grand view burst upon us. Hastening to step upon the crest of the divide, which was never more than ten feet wide, frequently sharpened to a mere blade, we looked down the other side, and were astonished to find we had ascended the gentler slope, and that the rocks fell from our feet in almost vertical preci-pices for a thousand feet or more. A glance along the summit toward the highest group showed us that any advance in that direction was impossible, for the thin ridge was gashed down in notches three or four hundred feet deep, forming a procession of pillars, obelisks, and blocks piled upon each other, and looking terribly insecure.

We then deposited our knapsacks in a safe place, and, finding that it was already noon, determined to rest a little while and take a lunch at over thirteen thousand feet above the sea.

West of us stretched the Mount Brewer wall with its succession of smooth precipices and amphitheatre ridges. To the north the great gorge of the King's River yawned down five thousand feet. To the south the valley of the Kern, opening in the opposite direction, was broader, less deep, but more filled with broken masses of granite. Clustered about the foot of the divide were a dozen alpine lakes; the higher ones blue sheets of ice, the lowest completely melted. Still lower in the depths of the two cañons we could see groups of forest trees; but they were so dim and so distant as never to relieve the prevalent masses of rock and snow. Our divide cast its shadow for a mile down King's Cañon in dark blue profile upon the broad sheets of sunny snow, from whose brightness the hard splintered cliffs caught reflections and wore an aspect of joy. Thousands of rills poured from the melting snow, filling the air with a musical tinkle as of many accordant bells. The Kern Valley opened below us with its smooth oval outline, the work of extinct glaciers, whose form and extent were evident from worn cliff-surface and rounded wall; snow-fields, relics of the former *névé*, hung in white tapestries around its ancient birth-place; and, as far as we could see, the broad, corrugated valley, for a breadth of fully ten miles, shone with burnishings wherever its granite surface was not covered with lakelets or thickets of alpine vegetation.

Through a deep cut in the Mount Brewer wall we gained our first view to the westward, and saw in the distance the wall of the South King's Cañon, and the granite point which Cotter and I had climbed a fortnight before. But for the haze we might have seen the plain; for above its farther limit were several points of the Coast Ranges, isolated like islands in the sea.

The view was so grand, the mountain colors so brilliant, immense snow-fields and blue alpine lakes so charming, that we almost forgot we were ever to move, and it was only after a swift hour of this delight that we began to consider our future course.

The King's Cañon, which headed against our wall, seemed untraversable,—no human being could climb along the divide; we had then but one hope of reaching the peak, and our greatest difficulty lay at the start. If we could climb down to the Kern side of the divide, and succeed in reaching the base of the precipices which fell from our feet, it really looked as if we might travel without difficulty among the *roches moutonnées* to the other side of the Kern Valley, and make our attempt upon the southward flank of the great peak. One look at the sublime white giant decided us. We looked down over the precipice, and at first could see no method of descent. Then we went back and looked at the road we had come up, to see if that were not possibly as bad; but the broken surface of the rocks was evidently much better climbing-ground than anything ahead of us. Cotter, with danger, edged his way along the wall to the east, and I to the west, to see if there might not be some favorable point; but we both returned with the belief that the precipice in front of us was as passable as any of it. Down it we must.

After lying on our faces, looking over the brink, ten or twenty minutes, I suggested that by lowering ourselves on the rope we might climb from crevice to crevice; but we saw no shelf large enough for ourselves and the knapsacks too. However, we were not going to give it up without a trial; and I made the rope fast round my breast, and, looping the noose over a firm point of rock, let myself slide gradually down to a notch forty feet below. There was only room beside me for Cotter, so I made him send down the knapsacks first. I then tied these together by the straps with my silk handkerchiefs, and hung them off as far to the left as I could reach without losing my balance, looping the handkerchiefs over a point of rock. Cotter then slid down the rope, and, with considerable difficulty, we whipped the noose off its resting-place above, and cut off our connection with the upper world.

"We're in for it now, King," remarked my comrade, as he looked aloft, and then down; but our blood was up, and danger added only an exhilarating thrill to the nerves.

The shelf was hardly more than two feet wide, and the granite so smooth that we could find no place to fasten the lasso for the next descent; so I determined to try the climb with only as little aid as possible. Tying it round my breast again, I gave the other end into Cotter's hands, and he, bracing his back against the cliff, found for himself as firm a foothold as he could, and promised to give me all the help in his power. I made up my mind to bear no weight unless it was absolutely necessary; and for the first ten feet I found cracks and protuberances enough to support me, making every square inch of surface do friction duty, and hugging myself against the rocks as tightly as I could. When within about eight feet of the next shelf, I twisted myself round upon the face, hanging by two rough blocks of protruding feldspar, and looking vainly for some further handhold; but the rock, beside being perfectly smooth, overhung slightly, and my legs dangled in the air. I saw that the next cleft was over three feet broad, and I thought, possibly, I might, by a quick slide, reach it in safety without endangering Cotter. I shouted to him to be very careful and let go in case I fell, loosened my hold upon the rope, and slid quickly down. My shoulder struck against the rock and threw me out of balance; for an instant I reeled over upon the verge, in danger of falling, but, in the excitement, I thrust out my hand and seized a small alpine goose-berry bush, the first piece of vegetation we had seen. Its roots were so firmly fixed in the crevice that it held my weight and saved me.

I could no longer see Cotter, but I talked to him, and heard the two knapsacks come bumping along till they slid over the eaves above me, and swung down to my station, when I seized the lasso's end and braced myself as well as possible, intending, if he slipped, to haul in slack and help him as best I could. As he came slowly down from crack to crack, I heard his hobnailed shoes grating on the granite; presently they appeared dangling from the eaves above my head. I had gathered in the rope until it was taut, and then hurriedly told him to drop. He hesitated a moment, and let go. Before he struck the rock I had him by the shoulder, and whirled him down upon his side, thus preventing his rolling overboard, which friendly action he took quite coolly.

The third descent was not a difficult one, nor the fourth; but when we had climbed down about two hundred and fifty feet, the rocks were so glacially polished and water-worn that it seemed impossible to get any farther. To our right was a crack penetrating the rock perhaps a foot deep, widening at the surface to three or four inches, which proved to be the only possible ladder. As the chances seemed rather desperate, we concluded to tie ourselves together, in order to share a common fate; and with a slack of thirty feet between us, and our knapsacks upon our backs, we climbed into the crevice, and began descending with our faces to the cliff. This had to be done with unusual caution, for the foothold was about as good as none, and our fingers slipped annoyingly on the smooth stone; besides, the knapsacks and instruments kept a steady backward pull, tending to overbalance us. But we took pains to descend one at a time, and rest wherever the niches gave our feet a safe support. In this way we got down about eighty feet of smooth, nearly vertical wall, reaching the top of a rude granite stairway, which led to the snow; and here we sat down to rest, and found to our astonishment that we had been three hours from the summit.

After breathing a half-minute we continued down, jumping from rock to rock, and, having, by practice, become very expert in balancing ourselves, sprang on, never resting long enough to lose the *aplomb*, and in this manner made a quick descent over rugged *débris* to the crest of a snow-field, which, for seven or eight hundred feet more, swept down in a smooth, even slope, of very high angle, to the borders of a frozen lake.

Without untying the lasso which bound us together, we sprang upon the snow with a shout, and glissaded down splendidly, turning now and then a somersault, and shooting out like cannon-balls almost to the middle of the frozen lake; I upon my back, and Cotter feet first, in a swimming position. The ice cracked in all directions. It was only a thin, transparent film, through which we could see deep into the lake. Untying ourselves, we hurried ashore in different directions, lest our combined weight should be too great a strain upon any point.

With curiosity and wonder we scanned every shelf and niche of the last descent. It seemed quite impossible we could have come down there, and now it actually was beyond human power to get back again. But what cared we? "Sufficient unto the day—" We were bound for that still distant, though gradually nearing, summit; and we had come from a cold shadowed cliff into deliciously warm sunshine, and were jolly, shouting, singing songs, and calling out the companionship of a hundred echoes. Six miles away, with no grave danger, no great difficulty, between us, lay the base of our grand mountain. Upon its skirts we saw a little grove of pines, an ideal bivouac, and toward this we bent our course.

After the continued climbing of the day, walking was a delicious rest, and forward we pressed with considerable speed, our hobnails giving us firm footing on the glittering glacial surface. Every fluting of the great valley was in itself a considerable cañon, into which we descended, climbing down the scored rocks, and swinging from block to block, until we reached the level of the pines. Here, sheltered among *roches moutonnées*, began to appear little fields of alpine grass, pale yet sunny, soft under our feet, frequently jewelled with flowers of fairy delicacy, holding up amid thickly clustered blades, chalices of turquoise and amethyst, white stars, and fiery little globes of red. Lakelets, small but innumerable, were held in glacial basins, the striae and grooves of that old dragon's track ornamenting their smooth bottoms.

One of these, a sheet of pure beryl hue, gave us much pleasure from its lovely transparency, and because we lay down in the necklace of grass about it and smelled flowers, while tired muscles relaxed upon warm beds of verdure, and the pain in our burdened shoulders went away, leaving us delightfully comfortable.

After the stern grandeur of granite and ice, and with the peaks and walls still in view, it was a relief to find ourselves again in the region of life. I never felt for trees or flowers such a sense of intimate relationship and sympathy. When we had no longer excuse for resting, I invented the palpable subterfuge of measuring the altitude of the spot, since the few clumps of low, wide-boughed pines near by were the highest living trees. So we lay longer with less and less will to rise, and when resolution called us to our feet the getting-up was sorely like Rip Van Winkle's in the third act.

The deep glacial cañon-flutings across which our march then led proved to be great consumers of time; indeed it was sunset when we reached the eastern ascent, and began to toil up through scattered pines, and over trains of moraine rocks, toward the great peak. Stars were already flashing brilliantly in the sky, and the low glowing arch in the west had almost vanished when we reached the upper trees, and threw down our knapsacks to camp. The forest grew on a sort of plateau-shelf with a precipitous front to the west,—a level surface which stretched eastward and back to the foot of our mountain, whose lower spurs reached within a mile of camp. Within the shelter lay a huge fallen log, like all these alpine woods one mass of resin, which flared up when we applied a match, illuminating the whole grove. By contrast with the darkness outside, we seemed to be in a vast, many-pillared hall. The stream close by afforded water for our blessed teapot; venison frizzled with mild, appetizing sound upon the ends of pine sticks; matchless beans allowed themselves to become seductively crisp upon our tin plates. That supper seeemed to me then the quintessence of gastronomy, and I am sure Cotter and I must have said some very good *après-dîner* things, though I long ago forgot them all. Within the ring of warmth, on elastic beds of pine-needles, we curled up, and fell swiftly into a sound sleep.

I woke up once in the night to look at my watch, and observed that the sky was overcast with a thin film of cirrus cloud to which the reflected moonlight lent the appearance of a glimmering tint, stretching from mountain to mountain over cañons filled with impenetrable darkness, only the vaguely lighted peaks and white snow-fields distinctly seen. I closed my eyes and slept soundly until Cotter woke me at half past three, when we arose, breakfasted by the light of our fire, which still blazed brilliantly, and, leaving our knapsacks, started for the mountain with only instruments, canteens, and luncheon.

In the indistinct moonlight climbing was very difficult at first, for we had to thread our way along a plain which was literally covered with glacier boulders, and the innumerable brooks which we crossed were frozen solid. However, our march brought us to the base of the great mountain, which, rising high against the east, shut out the coming daylight, and kept us in profound shadow. From base to summit rose a series of broken crags, lifting themselves from a general slope of *débris*. Toward the left the angle seemed to be rather gentler, and the surface less ragged; and we hoped, by a long *détour* round the base, to make an easy climb up this gentler face. So we toiled on for an hour over the rocks, reaching at last the bottom of the north slope. Here our work began in good earnest. The blocks were of enormous size, and in every stage of unstable equilibrium, frequently rolling over as we jumped upon them, making it necessary for us to take a second leap and land where we best could. To our relief we soon surmounted the largest blocks, reaching a smaller size, which served us as a sort of stairway.

The advancing daylight revealed to us a very long, comparatively even snow-slope, whose surface was pierced by many knobs and granite heads, giving it the aspect of an ice-roofing fastened on with bolts of stone. It stretched in far perspective to the summit, where already the rose of sunrise reflected gloriously, kindling a fresh enthusiasm within us.

Immense boulders were partly embedded in the ice just above us, whose constant melting left them trembling on the edge of a fall. It communicated no very pleasant sensation to see above you these immense missiles hanging by a mere band, and knowing that, as soon as the sun rose, you would be exposed to a constant cannonade.

The east side of the peak, which we could now partially see, was too precipitous to think of climbing. The slope toward our camp was too much broken into pinnacles and crags to offer us any hope, or to divert us from the single way, dead ahead, up slopes of ice and among fragments of granite. The sun rose upon us while we were climbing the lower part of this snow, and in less than half an hour, melting, began to liberate huge blocks, which thundered down past us, gathering and growing into small avalanches below.

We did not dare climb one above another, according to our ordinary mode, but kept about an equal level, a hundred feet apart, lest, dislodging the blocks, one should hurl them down upon the other.

We climbed alternately up smooth faces of granite, clinging simply by the cracks and protruding crystals of feldspar, and then hewed steps up fearfully steep slopes of ice, zigzagging to the right and left to avoid the flying boulders. When midway up this slope we reached a place where the granite rose in perfectly smooth bluffs on either side of a gorge,—a narrow cut, or walled way, leading up to the flat summit of the cliff. This we scaled by cutting ice steps, only to find ourselves fronted again by a still higher wall. Ice sloped from its front at too steep an angle for us to follow, but had melted in contact with it, leaving a space three feet wide between the ice and the rock. We entered this crevice and climbed along its bottom, with a wall of rock rising a hundred feet above us on one side, and a thirty-foot face of ice on the other, through which light of an intense cobalt-blue penetrated.

Reaching the upper end, we had to cut our footsteps upon the ice again, and, having braced our backs against the granite, climb up to the surface. We were now in a dangerous position: to fall into the crevice on one side was to be wedged to death between rock and ice·

to make a slip was to be shot down five hundred feet, and then hurled over the brink of a precipice. In the friendly seat which this wedge gave me, I stopped to take wet and dry observations with the thermometer,—this being an absolute preventive of a scare,—and to enjoy the view.

The wall of our mountain sank abruptly to the left, opening for the first time an outlook to the eastward. Deep—it seemed almost vertically—beneath us we could see the blue water of Owen's Lake, ten thousand feet down. The summit peaks to the north were piled in titanic confusion, their ridges overhanging the eastern slope with terrible abruptness. Clustered upon the shelves and plateaus below were several frozen lakes, and in all directions swept magnificent fields of snow. The summit was now not over five hundred feet distant, and we started on again with the exhilarating hope of success. But if Nature had intended to secure the summit from all assailants, she could not have planned her defences better; for the smooth granite wall which rose above the snow-slope continued, apparently, quite round the peak, and we looked in great anxiety to see if there was not one place where it might be climbed. It was all blank except in one place; quite near us the snow bridged across the crevice, and rose in a long point to the summit of the wall,—a great icicle-column frozen in a niche of the bluff,—its base about ten feet wide, narrowing to two feet at the top. We climbed to the base of this spire of ice, and, with the utmost care, began to cut our stairway. The material was an exceedingly compacted snow, passing into clear ice as it neared the rock. We climbed the first half of it with comparative ease; after that it was almost vertical, and so thin that we did not dare to cut the footsteps deep enough to make them absolutely safe. There was a constant dread lest our ladder should break off, and we be thrown either down the snow-slope or into the bottom of the crevasse. At last, in order to prevent myself from falling over backwards, I was obliged to thrust my hand into the crack between the ice and the wall, and the spire became so narrow that I could do this on both sides; so that the climb was made as upon a tree, cutting mere toe-holes and embracing the whole column of ice in my arms. At last I reached the top, and, with the greatest caution, wormed my body over the brink, and, rolling out upon the smooth surface of granite, looked over and watched Cotter make his climb. He came steadily up, with no sense of nervousness, until he got to the narrow part of the ice, and here he stopped and looked up with a forlorn face at me; but as he climbed up over the edge the broad smile came back to his face, and he asked me if it had occurred to me that we had, by and by, to go down again.

We had now an easy slope to the summit, and hurried up over rocks and ice, reaching the crest at exactly twelve o'clock. I rang my hammer upon the topmost rock; we grasped hands, and I reverently named the great peak MOUNT TYNDALL. . . .

Fronting us stood the west chain, a great mural ridge watched over by two dominant heights, Kaweah Peak and Mount Brewer, its wonderful profile defining against the western sky a multitude of peaks and spires. Bold buttresses jut out through fields of ice, and reach down stone arms among snow and *débris*. North and south of us the higher, or eastern, summit stretched on in miles and miles of snow-peaks, the farthest horizon still crowded with their white points. East the whole range fell in sharp, hurrying abruptness to the desert, where, ten thousand feet below, lay a vast expanse of arid plain intersected by low parallel ranges, traced from north to south.

Upon the one side a thousand sculptures of stone, hard, sharp, shattered by cold into infiniteness of fractures and rift, springing up, mutely severe, into the dark, austere blue of heaven; scarred and marked, except where snow or ice, spiked down by ragged granite bolts, shields with its pale armor these rough mountain shoulders; storm-tinted at summit, and dark where, swooping down from ragged cliff, the rocks plunge over cañon-walls into blue, silent gulfs.

Upon the other hand, reaching out to horizons faint and remote, lay plains clouded with the ashen hues of death; stark, wind-swept floors of white, and hill-ranges, rigidly formal, monotonously low, all lying under an unfeeling brilliance of light, which, for all its strange, unclouded clearness, has yet a vague half-darkness, a suggestion of black and shade more truly pathetic than fading twilight. . . .

The serene sky is grave with nocturnal darkness. The earth blinds you with its light. That fair contrast we love in lower lands between bright heavens and dark cool earth here reverses itself with terrible energy. You look up into an infinite vault, unveiled by clouds, empty and dark, from which no brightness seems to ray, an expanse with no graded perspective, no tremble, no vapory mobility, only the vast yawning of hollow space.

With an aspect of endless remoteness burns the small white sun, yet its light seems to pass invisibly through the sky, blazing out with intensity upon mountain and plain, flooding rock details with painfully bright reflections, and lighting up the burnt sand and stone of the desert with a strange, blinding glare. There is no sentiment of beauty in the whole scene; no suggestion, however far remote, of sheltered landscape; not even the air of virgin hospitality that greets us explorers in so many uninhabited spots which by their fertility and loveliness of grove or meadow seem to offer man a home, or us no-mads a pleasant camp-ground. Silence and desolation are the themes which nature has wrought out under this eternally serious sky. A faint suggestion of life clings about the middle altitudes of the east-ern slope, where black companies of pine, stunted from breathing the hot desert air, group themselves just beneath the bottom of perpetual snow, or grow in patches of cloudy darkness over the moraines, those piles of wreck crowded from their pathway by glaciers long dead. Something there is pathetic in the very emptiness of these old glacier valleys, these imperishable tracks of unseen engines. . . .

I thoroughly enjoyed the silence, which, gratefully contrasting with the surrounding tumult of form, conveyed to me a new senti-ment. I have lain and listened through the heavy calm of a tropical voyage, hour after hour, longing for a sound; and in desert nights the dead stillness has many times awakened me from sleep. For mo-ments, too, in my forest life, the groves made absolutely no breath of movement; but there is around these summits the soundlessness of a vacuum. The sea stillness is that of sleep. The desert of death, this silence is like the waveless calm of space.

All the while I made my instrumental observations the fascina-tion of the view so held me that I felt no surprise at seeing water boiling over our little fagot blaze at a temperature of one hundred and ninety-two degrees F., nor in observing the barometrical column stand at 17.99 inches; and it was not till a week or so after that I realized we had not felt none of the conventional sensations of nausea, headache, and I don't know what all, that people are sup-posed to suffer at extreme altitudes; but these things go with guides and porters, I believe, and with coming down to one's hotel at eve-ning there to scold one's picturesque *aubergiste* in a French which strikes upon his ear as a foreign tongue; possibly all that will come to us with advancing time, and what is known as "doing America." They are already shooting our buffaloes; it cannot be long before they will cause themselves to be honorably dragged up and down our Sierras, with perennial yellow gaiter, and ostentation of bathtub.

Having completed our observations, we packed up the instruments, glanced once again around the whole field of view, and descended to the top of our icicle ladder. Upon looking over, I saw to my consternation that during the day the upper half had broken off. Scars traced down upon the snow-field below it indicated the manner of its fall, and far below, upon the shattered *débris*, were strewn its white relics. I saw that nothing but the sudden gift of wings could possibly take us down to the snow-ridge. We held council and concluded to climb quite round the peak in search of the best mode of descent.

As we crept about the east face, we could look straight down upon Owen's Valley, and into the vast glacier gorges, and over piles of moraines and fluted rocks, and the frozen lakes of the eastern slope. When we reached the southwest front of the mountain we found that its general form was that of an immense horseshoe, the great eastern ridge forming one side, and the spur which descended to our camp the other, we having climbed up the outer part of the toe. Within the curve of the horseshoe was a gorge, cut almost perpendicularly down two thousand feet, its side rough-hewn walls of rocks and snow, its narrow bottom almost a continuous chain of deep blue lakes with loads of ice and *débris* piles. The stream which flowed through them joined the waters from our home grove, a couple of miles below the camp. If we could reach the level of the lakes, I believed we might easily climb round them, and out of the upper end of the horseshoe, and walk upon the Kern plateau round to our bivouac.

It required a couple of hours of very painstaking deliberate climbing to get down the first descent, which we did, however, without hurting our barometer, and fortunately without the fatiguing use of the lasso; reaching finally the uppermost lake, a granite bowlful of cobalt-blue water, transparent and unrippled. So high and enclosing were the tall walls about us, so narrow and shut in the cañon, so flattened seemed the cover of sky, we felt oppressed after the expanse and freedom of our hours on the summit.

The snow-field we followed, descending farther, was irregularly honeycombed in deep pits, circular or irregular in form, and melted to a greater or less depth, holding each a large stone embedded in the bottom. It seems they must have fallen from the overhanging heights with sufficient force to plunge into the snow. . . .

Mile after mile we walked cautiously over the snow, and climbed around the margins of lakes, and over piles of *débris* which marked the ancient terminal moraines. At length we reached the end of the horseshoe, where the walls contracted to a gateway, rising on either side in immense vertical pillars a thousand feet high. Through this gateway we could look down the valley of the Kern, and beyond to the gentler ridges where a smooth growth of forest darkened the rolling plateau. Passing the last snow, we walked through this gateway and turned westward round the spur toward our camp. The three miles which closed our walk were alternately through groves of *Pinus flexilis* and upon plains of granite. . . .

The sun was still an hour high when we reached camp, and with a feeling of relaxation and repose we threw ourselves down to rest by the log, which still continued blazing. We had accomplished our purpose.

During the last hour or two of our tramp Cotter had complained of his shoes, which were rapidly going to pieces. Upon examination we found to our dismay that there was not over half a day's wear left in them, a calamity which gave to our difficult homeward climb a new element of danger. The last nail had been worn from my own shoes, and the soles were scratched to the quick, but I believed them stout enough to hold together till we should reach the main camp.

We planned a pair of moccasins for Cotter, and then spent a pleasant evening by the camp-fire, rehearsing our climb to the detail, sleep finally overtaking us and holding us fast bound until broad daylight next morning, when we woke with a sense of having slept for a week, quite bright and perfectly refreshed for our homeward journey.

After a frugal breakfast, in which we limited ourselves to a few cubic inches of venison, and a couple of stingy slices of bread, with a single meagre cup of diluted tea, we shouldered our knapsacks, which now sat lightly upon toughened shoulders, and marched out upon the granite plateau.

We had concluded that it was impossible to retrace our former way, knowing well that the precipitous divide could not be climbed from this side; then, too, we had gained such confidence in our climbing powers, from constant victory, that we concluded to attempt the passage of the great King's Cañon, mainly because this was the only mode of reaching camp, and since the geological section of the granite it exposed would afford us an exceedingly instructive study. . . .

The morning was wholly consumed in walking up this gently inclined plane of granite, our way leading over the glacier-polished foldings and along graded undulations among labyrinths of alpine garden and wildernesses of erratic boulders, little lake-basins, and scattered clusters of dwarfed and sombre pine.

About noon we came suddenly upon the brink of a precipice which sunk sharply from our feet into the gulf of the King's Cañon. Directly opposite us rose Mount Brewer and up out of the depths of those vast sheets of frozen snow swept spiry buttress-ridges, dividing the upper heights into those amphitheatres over which we had struggled on our outward journey. Straight across from our point of view was the chamber of rock and ice where we had camped on the first night. The wall at our feet fell sharp and rugged, its lower two-thirds hidden from our view by the projections of a thousand feet of crags. Here and there, as we looked down, small patches of ice, held in rough hollows, rested upon the steep surface, but it was too abrupt for any great fields of snow. I dislodged a boulder upon the edge and watched it bound down the rocky precipice, dash over eaves a thousand feet below us, and disappear; the crash of its fall coming up to us from the unseen depths fainter and fainter, until the air only trembled with confused echoes.

A long look at the pass to the south of Mount Brewer, where we had parted from our friends, animated us with courage to begin the descent, which we did with utmost care, for the rocks, becoming more and more glacier-smoothed, afforded us hardly any firm footholds. When down about eight hundred feet we again rolled rocks ahead of us, and saw them disappear over the eaves, and only heard the sound of their stroke after many seconds, which convinced us that directly below lay a great precipice.

At this juncture the soles came entirely off Cotter's shoes, and we stopped upon a little cliff of granite to make him moccasins of our provision bags and slips of blanket, tying them on as firmly as we could with the extra straps and buckskin thongs.

Climbing with these proved so insecure that I made Cotter go behind me, knowing that under ordinary circumstances I could stop him if he fell.

Here and there in the clefts of the rocks grew stunted pine bushes, their roots twisted so firmly into the crevices that we laid hold of them with the utmost confidence whenever they came within our reach. In this way we descended to within fifty feet of the brink, having as yet no knowledge of the cliffs below, except our general memory of their aspect from the Mount Brewer wall.

The rock was so steep that we descended in a sitting posture, clinging with our hands and heels.

I heard Cotter say, "I think I must take off these moccasins and try it barefooted, for I don't believe I can make it." These words were instantly followed by a startled cry, and I looked around to see him slide quickly toward me, struggling and clutching at the smooth granite. As he slid by I made a grab for him with my right hand, catching him by the shirt, and, throwing myself as far in the other direction as I could, seized with my left hand a little pine tuft, which held us. I asked Cotter to edge along a little to the left, where he could get a brace with his feet and relieve me of his weight, which he cautiously did. I then threw a couple of turns with the lasso round the roots of the pine bush, and we were safe, though hardly more than twenty feet from the brink. The pressure of curiosity to get a look over that edge was so strong within me, that I lengthened out sufficient lasso to reach the end, and slid slowly to the edge, where, leaning over, I looked down, getting a full view of the wall for miles. Directly beneath, a sheer cliff of three or four hundred feet stretched down to a pile of *débris* which rose to unequal heights along its face, reaching the very crest not more than a hundred feet south of us. From that point to the bottom of the cañon broken rocks, ridges rising through vast sweeps of *débris*, tufts of pine and frozen bodies of ice, covered the further slope.

I returned to Cotter, and, having loosened ourselves from the pine bush, inch by inch crept along the granite until we supposed ourselves to be just over the top of the *débris* pile, where I found a firm brace for my feet, and lowered Cotter to the edge. He sang out "All right!" and climbed over on the uppermost *débris*, his head only remaining in sight of me; when I lay down upon my back, making knapsack and body do friction duty, and, letting myself move, followed Cotter and reached his side.

From that point the descent required us two hours of severe constant labor, which was monotonous of itself, and would have proved excessively tiresome but for the constant interest of glacial geology beneath us. When at last we reached bottom and found ourselves upon a velvety green meadow, beneath the shadow of wide-armed pines, we realized the amount of muscular force we had used up, and threw ourselves down for a rest of half an hour, when we rose, not quite renewed, but fresh enough to finish the day's climb.

In a few minutes we stood upon the rocks just above King's

River,—a broad white torrent fretting its way along the bottom of an impassable gorge. Looking down the stream, we saw that our right bank was a continued precipice, affording, so far as we could see, no possible descent to the river's margin, and indeed, had we gotten down, the torrent rushed with such fury that we could not possibly have crossed it. To the south of us, a little way up stream, the river flowed out from a broad oval lake, three quarters of a mile in length, which occupied the bottom of the granite basin. Unable to cross the torrent, we must either swim the lake or climb round its head. Upon our side the walls of the basin curved to the head of the lake in sharp smooth precipices, or broken slopes of *débris*; while on the opposite side its margin was a beautiful shore of emerald meadow, edged with a continuous grove of coniferous trees. Once upon this other side, we should have completed the severe part of our journey, crossed the gulf, and have left all danger behind us; for the long slope of granite and ice which rose upon the west side of the cañon and the Mount Brewer wall opposed to us no trials save those of simple fatigue.

Around the head of the lake were crags and precipices in singular forbidding arrangement. As we turned thither we saw no possible way of overcoming them. At its head the lake lay in an angle of the vertical wall, sharp and straight like the corner of a room; about three hundred feet in height, and for two hundred and fifty of this, a pyramidal pile of blue ice rose from the lake, rested against the corner, and reached within forty feet of the top. Looking into the deep blue water of the lake, I concluded that in our exhausted state it was madness to attempt to swim it. The only other alternative was to scale that slender pyramid of ice and find some way to climb the forty feet of smooth wall above it; a plan we chose perforce, and started at once to put it into execution, determined that if we were unsuccessful we would fire a dead log which lay near, warm ourselves thoroughly, and attempt the swim. At its base the ice mass overhung the lake like a roof, under which the water had melted its way for a distance of not less than a hundred feet, a thin eave overhanging the water. To the very edge of this I cautiously went, and, looking down into the lake, saw through its beryl depths the white granite blocks strewn upon the bottom at least one hundred feet below me. It was exceedingly transparent, and, under ordinary circumstances, would have been a most tempting place for a dive; but at the end of our long fatigue, and with the still unknown tasks ahead, I shrunk from a swim in such a chilly temperature.

We found the ice-angle difficultly steep, but made our way successfully along its edge, clambering up the crevices melted between its body and the smooth granite to a point not far from the top, where the ice had considerably narrowed, and rocks overhanging it encroached so closely that we were obliged to leave the edge and make our way with cut steps out upon its front. Streams of water, dropping from the overhanging rock-eaves at many points, had worn circular shafts into the ice, three feet in diameter and twenty feet in depth. Their edges offered us our only foothold, and we climbed from one to another, equally careful of slipping upon the slope itself, or falling into the wells. Upon the top of the ice we found a narrow, level platform, upon which we stood together, resting our backs in the granite corner, and looked down the awful pathway of King's Cañon, until the rest nerved us up enough to turn our eyes upward at the forty feet of smooth granite which lay between us and safety.

Here and there were small projections from its surface, little protruding knobs of feldspar, and crevices riven into its face for a few inches.

As we tied ourselves together, I told Cotter to hold himself in readiness to jump down into one of these in case I fell, and started to climb up the wall, succeeding quite well for about twenty feet. About two feet above my hands was a crack, which, if my arms had been long enough to reach, would probably have led me to the very top; but I judged it beyond my powers, and, with great care, descended to the side of Cotter, who believed that his superior length of arm would enable him to make the reach.

I planted myself against the rock, and he started cautiously up the wall. Looking down the glare front of ice, it was not pleasant to consider at what velocity a slip would send me to the bottom, or at what angle, and to what probable depth, I should be projected into the ice-water. Indeed, the idea of such a sudden bath was so annoying that I lifted my eyes toward my companion. He reached my farthest point without great difficulty, and made a bold spring for the crack, reaching it without an inch to spare, and holding on wholly by his fingers. He thus worked himself slowly along the crack toward the top, at last getting his arms over the brink, and gradually drawing his body up and out of sight. It was the most splendid piece of slow gymnastics I ever witnessed. For a moment he said nothing; but when I asked him if he was all right cheerfully repeated, "All right." It was only a moment's work to send up the two knapsacks and barometer, and receive again my end of the lasso. As I tied it round my breast, Cotter said to me, in an easy, confident tone, "Don't be afraid to bear your weight." I made up my mind, however, to make that climb without his aid, and husbanded my strength as I climbed from crack to crack. I got up without difficulty to my former point, rested there a moment, hanging solely by my hands, gathered every pound of strength and atom of will for the reach, then jerked myself upward with a swing, just getting the tips of my fingers into the crack. In an instant I had grasped it with my right hand also. I felt the sinews of my fingers relax a little, but the picture of the slope of ice and the blue lake affected me so strongly that I redoubled my grip, and climbed slowly along the crack until I reached the angle and got one arm over the edge as Cotter had done. As I rested my body upon the edge and looked up at Cotter, I saw that, instead of a level top, he was sitting upon a smooth roof-like slope, where the least pull would have dragged him over the brink. He had no brace for his feet, nor hold for his hands, but had seated himself calmly, with the rope tied round his breast, knowing that my only safety lay in being able to make the climb entirely unaided; certain that the least waver in his tone would have disheartened me, and perhaps made it impossible. The shock I received on seeing this affected me for a moment, but not enough to throw me off my guard, and I climbed quickly over the edge. When we had walked back out of danger we sat down upon the granite for a rest.

In all my experiences of mountaineering I have never known an act of such real, profound courage as this of Cotter's. It is one thing, in a moment of excitement, to make a gallant leap, or hold one's nerves in the iron grasp of will, but to coolly seat one's self in the door of death, and silently listen for the fatal summons, and this all for a friend,—for he might easily have cast loose the lasso and saved himself,—requires as sublime a type of courage as I know.

But a few steps back we found a thicket of pine overlooking our lake, by which there flowed a clear rill of snow-water. Here, in the bottom of the great gulf, we made our bivouac; for we were already in the deep evening shadows, although the mountain-tops to the east of us still burned in the reflected light. It was the luxury of repose which kept me awake half an hour or so, in spite of my vain attempts at sleep. To listen for the pulsating sound of waterfalls and arrowy rushing of the brook by our beds was too deep a pleasure to quickly yield up.

Under the later moonlight I rose and went out upon the open rocks, allowing myself to be deeply impressed by the weird Dantesque surroundings;—darkness, out of which to the sky towered stern, shaggy bodies of rock; snow, uncertainly moonlit with cold pallor; and at my feet the basin of the lake, still, black, and gemmed with reflected stars, like the void into which Dante looked through the bottomless gulf of Dis. A little way off there appeared upon the brink of a projecting granite cornice two dimly seen forms; pines I knew them to be, yet their motionless figures seemed bent forward, gazing down the cañon; and I allowed myself to name them Mantuan and Florentine, thinking at the same time how grand and spacious the scenery, and how powerful their attitude, how infinitely more profound the mystery of light and shade, than any of those hard, theoretical conceptions with which Doré has sought to shut in our imagination. That artist, as I believe, has reached a conspicuous failure from an overbalancing love of solid, impenetrable darkness. There is in all his Inferno landscape a certain sharp boundary between the real and the unreal, and never the infinite suggestiveness of great regions of half-light, in which everything may be seen, nothing recognized. Without waking Cotter, I crept back to my blankets, and to sleep.

The morning of our fifth and last day's tramp must have dawned cheerfully; at least, so I suppose from its aspect when we first came back to consciousness, surprised to find the sun risen from the eastern mountain-wall and the whole gorge flooded with its direct light. Rising as good as new from our mattresses of pine twigs, we hastened to take breakfast, and started up the long, broken slope of the Mount Brewer wall. To reach the pass where we had parted from our friends required seven hours of slow, laborious climbing, in which we took advantage of every outcropping spine of granite and every level expanse of ice to hasten at the top of our speed. Cotter's feet were severely cut, his tracks upon the snow were marked by stains of blood, yet he kept on with undiminished spirit, never once complaining. The perfect success of our journey so inspired us with happiness that we forgot danger and fatigue, and chatted in liveliest strain.

It was about two o'clock when we reached the summit and rested a moment to look back over our new Alps, which were hard and distinct under direct unpoetic light; yet with all their dense gray and white reality, their long, sculptured ranks, and cold, still summits, we gave them a lingering farewell look, which was not without its deep fullness of emotion, then turned our backs and hurried down the *débris* slope into the rocky amphitheatre at the foot of Mount Brewer, and by five o'clock had reached our old camp-ground. We found here a note pinned to a tree informing us that the party had gone down into the lower cañon, five miles below, that they might camp in better pasturage.

The wind had scattered the ashes of our old camp-fire, and banished from it the last sentiment of home. We hurried on, climbing among the rocks which reached down to the crest of the great lateral moraine, and then on in rapid stride along its smooth crest, riveting our eyes upon the valley below, where we knew the party must be camped.

At last, faintly curling above the sea of green tree-tops, a few faint clouds of smoke wafted upward into the air. We saw them with a burst of strong emotion, and ran down the steep flank of the moraine at the top of our speed. Our shouts were instantly answered by the three voices of our friends, who welcomed us to their camp-fire with tremendous hugs.

After we had outlined for them the experience of our days, and as we lay outstretched at our ease, warm in the blaze of the glorious camp-fire, Brewer said to me, "King, you have relieved me of a dreadful task. For the last three days I have been composing a letter to your family, but somehow I did not get beyond 'It becomes my painful duty to inform you.' "

VACHEL LINDSAY

Preaching the Gospel of Beauty

"I say we do not see enough visions . . ."

In the summer of 1912, Vachel Lindsay set out from Springfield, Illinois—the "city of my discontent"—for a walking tour of the West. He was 33 years old and, as his biographer points out, "still without visible occupation or even prospects." Yet he walked with an evangelical fervor, alone save for a packet of rhymes which he hoped to read and trade for bread. His rules were simple: steer away from cities, travel light. They were good rules. Within two years, Lindsay would burst upon the American literary scene as a poet of the first order; but now, like John Muir before him, he was anonymous. We take him as far as Kansas, frightening mules, promising not to work, preaching the gospel of beauty.

These selections are from Vachel Lindsay's Adventures While Preaching the Gospel of Beauty.

Thursday, May 30, 1912. In the blue grass by the side of the road. Somewhere west of Jacksonville, Illinois. Hot sun. Cool wind. Rabbits in the distance. Bumblebees near.

At five last evening I sighted my lodging for the night. It was the other side of a high worm fence. It was down in the hollow of a grove. It was the box of an old box-car, brought there somehow, without its wheels. It was far from a railroad. I said in my heart "Here is the appointed shelter." I was not mistaken.

As was subsequently revealed, it belonged to the old gentleman I spied through the window stemming gooseberries and singing: "John Brown's body." He puts the car top on wagon wheels and hauls it from grove to grove between Jacksonville and the east bank of the Mississippi. He carries sawmill equipment along. He is clearing this wood for the owner, of all but its walnut trees. He lives in the box with his son and two assistants. He is cook, washerwoman and sawmill boss. His wife died many years ago.

The old gentleman let me in with alacrity. He allowed me to stem gooseberries while he made a great supper for the boys. They soon came in. I was meanwhile assured that my name was going into the pot. My host looked like his old general, McClellan. He was eloquent on the sins of preachers, dry voters and pension reformers.

He was full of reiminiscences of the string band at Sherman's head-quarters, in which he learned to perfect himself on his wonderful fiddle. He said, "I can't play slow music. I've got to play dance tunes or die." He did not die. His son took a banjo from an old trunk and the two of them gave us every worthwhile tune on earth: *Money Musk, Hell's Broke Loose in Georgia, The Year of the Jubilee, Sailor's Hornpipe, Baby on the Block, Lady on the Lake,* and *The Irish Washerwoman*, while I stemmed gooseberries, which they protested I did not need to do. Then I read my own unworthy verses to the romantic and violin-stirred company. And there was room for all of us to sleep in that one repentent and converted box-car.

Friday, May 31, 1912. Half an hour after a dinner of crackers, cheese and raisins, provided at my solicitation by the grocer in the general store and post-office, Valley City, Illinois.

I have thought of a new way of stating my economic position. I belong to one of the leisure classes, that of the rhymers. In order to belong to any leisure class, one must be a thief or a beggar. On the whole I prefer to be a beggar, and, before each meal, receive from toiling men new permission to extend my holiday. The great business of that world that looms above the workshop and the furrow is to take things from people by some sort of taxation or tariff or special privilege. But I want to exercise my covetousness only in a retail way, open and above board, and when I take bread from a man's table I want to ask him for that particular piece of bread, as politely as I can.

But this does not absolutely fit my life. For yesterday I ate several things without permission, for instance, in mid-morning I devoured all the cherries a man can hold. They were hanging from heavy, breaking branches that came way over the stone wall into the road.

Another adventure. Early in the afternoon I found a brick farm-house. It had a noble porch. There were marks of old-fashioned distinction in the trimmed hedges and flower-beds, and in the sum-mer-houses. The side-yard and barn-lot were the cluckingest, buzz-ingest kind of places. There was not a human being in sight. I knocked and knocked on the doors. I wandered through all the sheds. I could look in through the unlocked screens and see every sign of present occupation. If I had chosen to enter I could have stolen the wash bowl or the baby-buggy or the baby's doll. The creamery was more tempting, with milk and butter and eggs, and freshly pulled taffy cut in squares. I took a little taffy. That is all I took, though the chickens were very social and I could have eloped with several of them. The roses and peonies and geraniums were entrancing, and there was not a watch dog anywhere. Everything seemed to say *"Enter in and possess!"*

I saw inside the last door where I knocked a crisp, sweet, simple dress on a chair. Ah, a sleeping beauty somewhere about!

I went away from that place.

Tuesday Morning, June 4, 1912. In a hotel bedroom in Laddonia, Missouri. I occupy this room without charge.

Through the mercy of the gateman I crossed the Hannibal toll-bridge without paying fare, and the more enjoyed the pearly Mississippi in the evening twilight. Walking south of Hannibal next morning, Sunday, I was irresistibly reminded of Kentucky. It was the first real "pike" of my journey,—solid gravel, and everyone was exercising his racing pony in his racing cart, and giving me a ride down lovely avenues of trees. Here, as in dozens of other interesting "lifts" in Illinois, I had the driver's complete attention, recited *The Gospel of Beauty* through a series of my more didactic rhymes till I was tired, and presented the *Village Improvement Parade* and the *Rhymes to Be Traded for Bread* and exhorted the comradely driver to forget me never. One colored horseman hitched forward on the plank of his breaking-cart and gave me his seat. Then came quite a ride into New London. He asked, "So you goin' to walk west to the mountains and all around?" "Yes, if this colt don't break my neck, or I don't lose my nerve or get bitten by a dog or anything." "Will you walk back?" "Maybe so, maybe not." He pondered a while, then said, with the Bert Williams manner, *"You'll ride back. Mark my words, you'll ride back!"*

He asked a little later, "Goin' to harves' in Kansas?" I assured him I was not going to harvest in Kansas. He rolled his big white eyes at me: "What in the name of Uncle Hillbilly *air* you up to then?"

In this case I could not present my tracts, for I was holding onto him for dear life. Just then he turned off my road. Getting out of the cart I nearly hung myself; and the colt was away again before I could say "Thank you."

Yesterday I passed through what was mostly a flat prairie country, abounding in the Missouri mule. I met one man on horseback driving before him an enormous specimen tied head to head with a draught-horse. The mule was continually dragging his good-natured comrade into the ditch and being jerked out again. The mule is a perpetual inquisitor and experimenter. He followed me along the fence with the alertest curiosity, when he was inside the field, yet meeting me in the road, he often showed deadly terror. If he was a mule colt, following his mare mamma along the pike, I had to stand in the side lane or hide behind a tree till he went by, or else he would turn and run as if the very devil were after him. Then the farmer on the mare would have to pursue him a considerable distance, and drive him back with cuss words. 'Tis sweet to stir up so much emotion, even in the breast of an animal.

What do you suppose happened in New London? I approached what I thought a tiny Baptist chapel of whitewashed stone. Noting it was about sermon-time, and feeling like repenting, I walked in. Behold, the most harmoniously-colored Catholic shrine in the world! The sermon was being preached by the most gorgeously robed priest one could well conceive. The father went on to show how a vision of the Christ-child had appeared on the altar of a lax congregation in Spain. From that time those people, stricken with reverence and godly fear, put that church into repair, and the community became a true servant of the Lord. Infidels were converted, heretics were confounded.

After the sermon came the climax of the mass, and from the choir loft above my head came the most passionate religious singing I ever heard in my life. The excellence of the whole worship, even to the preaching of visions, was a beautiful surprise.

People do not open their eyes enough, neither their spiritual nor their physical eyes. They are not sensitive enough to loveliness either visible or by the pathway of visions. I wish every church in the world could see the Christ-child on the altar, every Methodist and Baptist as well as every Catholic congregation.

With these thoughts I sat and listened while that woman soloist sang not only through the Mass, but the Benediction of the Blessed Sacrament as well. The whole surprise stands out like a blacking star in my memory.

I say we do not see enough visions. . . .

Friday, June 7, 1912. In the mid-afternoon in the woods, many miles west of Jefferson City. I am sitting by a wild rose bush. I am looking down a long sunlit vista of trees.

Wednesday evening, three miles from Fulton, Missouri, I encountered a terrific storm. I tried one farm-house just before the rain came down, but they would not let me in, not even into the barn. They said it was "not convenient." They said there was another place a little piece ahead, anyway. Pretty soon I was considerably rained upon. But the "other place" did not appear. Later the thunder and lightning were frightful. It seemed to me everything was being struck all around me: because of the sheer downpour it became pitch dark. It seemed as though the very weight of the rain would beat me into the ground. Yet I felt that I needed the washing. The night before I enjoyed the kind of hospitality that makes one yearn for a bath.

At last I saw a light ahead. I walked through more cataracts and reached it. Then I knocked at the door. I entered what revealed itself to be a negro cabin. Mine host was Uncle Remus himself, only a person of more delicacy and dignity. He appeared to be well preserved, though he was eighteen years old when the war broke out. He owns forty acres and more than one mule. His house was sweet and clean, all metal surfaces polished, all wood-work scrubbed white, all linen fresh laundered. He urged me to dry at his oven. It was a long process, taking much fuel. He allowed me to eat supper and breakfast with him and his family, which honor I scarcely deserved. The old man said grace standing up. Then we sat down and he said another. The first was just family prayers. The second was thanksgiving for the meal. The table was so richly and delicately provided that within my heart I paraphrased the twenty-third Psalm, though I did not quote it out aloud: "Thou preparest a table before me in the presence of mine enemies"—(namely, the thunder and lightning, and the inhospitable white man!).

I hope to be rained on again if it brings me communion bread like that I ate with my black host. The conversation was about many things, but began religiously; how "Ol' Master in the sky gave us everything here to take keer of, and said we mussent waste any of it." The wife was a mixture of charming diffidence and eagerness in offering her opinion on these points of political economy and theology.

After supper the old gentleman told me a sweet-singing field-bird I described was called the "Rachel-Jane." He had five children grown and away from home and one sleek first voter still under his roof. The old gentleman asked the inevitable question: "Goin' west harvestin'?"

I said "No" again. Then I spread out and explained *The Village Improvement Parade*. This did not interest the family much, but they would never have done with asking me questions about Lincoln. And the fact that I came from Lincoln's home town was plainly my chief distinction in their eyes. The best bed was provided for me, and warm water in which to bathe, and I slept the sleep of the clean and re-generated in snowy linen. Next morning the sun shone, and I walked the muddy roads as cheerfully as though they were the paths of Heaven. . . .

[*June 10, 1912*]. I feel that in a certain mystical sense I have made myself part of the hundreds and hundreds of farms that lie between me and machine-made America. I have scarcely seen anything but crops since I left home. The whole human race is grubbing in the soil, and the soil is responding with tremendous vigor. By walking I get as tired as any and imagine I work too. Sometimes the glory goes. Then I feel my own idleness above all other facts on earth. I want to get to work immediately. But I suppose I am a minstrel or nothing. (There goes a squirrel through the treetops.)

June 12, 1912. On the banks of a stream west of the town of War-rensburg, Missouri.

Perhaps the problem of a night's lodging has been solved. I seem to have found a substitute for the spare bedrooms and white sheets of Georgia and Pennsylvania. It appears that no livery-stable will refuse a man a place to sleep. What happened at Otterville and Warrens-burg I can make happen from here on in, or so I am assured by a farmhand. He told me that every tiniest village from here to western Kansas has at least two livery-stables and there a man may sleep for the asking. . . . And so, if I am to believe my friend with the red neck, my good times at Warrensburg and Otterville are likely to continue.

Strange as it may seem, sleeping in a hayloft is Romance itself. The alfalfa is soft and fragrant and clean, the wind blows through the big loft door, the stars shine through the cottonwoods. If I wake in the night I hear the stable-boys bringing in the teams of men who have driven a long way and back again to get something;—to get drunk, or steal the kisses of somebody's wife or put over a political deal or get a chance to preach a sermon;—and I get scraps of detail from the stable-boys after the main actors of the drama have gone. It sounds as though all the remarks were being made in the loft instead of on the ground floor. The horses stamp and stamp and the grinding

of their teeth is so close to me I cannot believe at first that the mangers and feed-boxes are way down below.

It is morning before I know it and the gorged birds are singing "shivaree, shivaree, Rachel Jane, Rachel Jane" in the mulberry trees, just outside the loft window. After a short walk I negotiate for breakfast, then walk on through Paradise again and at six negotiate for the paradisical haymow, without looking for supper, and again more sleepy than hungry. The difference between this system and the old one is that about half past four I used to begin to worry about supper and night accommodations, and generally worried till seven. Now life is one long sweet stroll, and I watch the sunset from my bed in the alfalfa with the delights of the whole day renewed in my heart.

Passing through the village of Sedalia I inquired the way out of town to the main road west. My informant was a man named McSweeny, drunk enough to be awfully friendly. He asked me all sorts of questions. He induced me to step two blocks out of my main course down a side-street to his "Restaurant." He said he was not going to let me leave town without a square meal. It was a strange eating-place, full of ditch-diggers, teamsters, red-necked politicians and slender intellectual politicians. In the background was a scattering of the furtive daughters of pleasure, some white, some black. The whole institution was but an annex to the bar room in front. Mr. McSweeny looked over my book while I ate. After the meal he gathered a group of the politicians and commanded me to recite. I gave them my rhyme in memory of Altgeld and my rhyme in denunciation of Lorimer, and my rhyme denouncing all who cooperated in the white slave trade, including sellers of drink. Mr. Mc-Sweeny said I was the goods, and offered to pass the hat, but I would not permit. A handsome black jezebel sat as near us as she dared and listened quite seriously. I am sure she would have put something in that hat if it had gone around.

"I suppose," said Mr. McSweeny, as he stood at his door to bow adieu, "you will harvest when you get a little further west?"

That afternoon I walked miles and miles through rough country, and put up with a friendly farmer named John Humphrey. He had children like little golden doves, and a most hard-working wife. The man had harvested and travelled eight years in the west before he had settled down. He told me all about it. Until late that night he told me endless fascinating stories upon the theme of that free man's land ahead of me. If he had not had those rosy babies to anchor him, he would have picked up and gone along, and argued down my rule to travel alone.

Because he had been a man of the road there was a peculiar feeling of understanding in the air. They were people of much natural refinement. I was the more grateful for their bread when I considered that when I came upon them at sunset they were working together in the field. There was not a hand to help. How could they be so happy and seem so blest? Their day was nearer sixteen than eight hours long. I felt deathly ashamed to eat their bread. I told them so, with emphasis. But the mother said, "We always takes in them that asks, and nobody never done us no harm yet."

That night was a turning point with me. In reply to a certain question I said: "*Yes, I am going west harvesting.*"

I asked the veteran traveller to tell me the best place to harvest. He was sitting on the floor pulling the children's toes, and having a grand time. He drew himself up into a sort of oracular knot, with his chin on his knees, and gesticulated with his pipe.

"Go straight west," he said, "to Great Bend, Barton County, Kansas, the banner wheat country of the United States. Arrive about July fifth. Walk to the public square. Walk two miles north. Look around. You will see nothing but wheat fields, and farmers standing on the edge of the road crying into big red handkerchiefs. Ask the first man for work. He will stop crying and give it to you. Wages will be two dollars and a half a day, and keep. You will have all you want to eat and a clean blanket in the hay."

I have resolved to harvest at Great Bend.

JOHN JAMES AUDUBON

Rambles on the Prairie

"Nothing in the shape of man had I met with . . ."

His passion for wildlife made John James Audubon a great naturalist; necessity made him a frontier storekeeper, a traveling salesman of his Birds of America, *and an itinerant portrait painter. In each of these roles Audubon tramped a good part of pioneer America. The accounts which follow were part of a series accompanying the plates of* Birds of America *and designed to "relieve the tedium of descriptive ornithology." The authenticity of the first—recounting the sinister end to a solitary day on the prairie in 1812—has been mildly disputed; Audubon's biographer finds no reason to doubt its "substantial truth," even if it does read like a dime novel. The second account, which Audubon called* A Tough Walk for Youth, *occurred in 1823 after an unsuccessful tour as a portraitist; it may mark the first time that a walker limped in print "like a lame duck."*

The selections are from the first and third volumes of Audubon's Ornithological Biography, *published in Edinburgh in 1831 and 1835.*

On my return from the Upper Mississippi, I found myself obliged to cross one of the wide Prairies, which, in that portion of the United States, vary the appearance of the country. The weather was fine, all around me was as fresh and blooming as if it had just issued from the bosom of nature. My napsack, my gun, and my dog, were all I had for baggage and company. But, although well moccasined, I moved slowly along, attracted by the brilliancy of the flowers, and the gambols of the fawns around their dams, to all appearance as thoughtless of danger as I felt myself.

My march was of long duration; I saw the sun sinking beneath the horizon long before I could perceive any appearance of woodland, and nothing in the shape of man had I met with that day. The track which I followed was only an old Indian trace, and as darkness overshadowed the prairie, I felt some desire to reach at least a copse, in which I might lie down to rest. The Night-hawks were skimming over and around me, attracted by the buzzing wings of the beetles which form their food, and the distant howling of wolves, gave me some hope that I should soon arrive at the skirts of some woodland.

I did so, and almost at the same instant a fire-light attracting my eye, I moved towards it, full of confidence that it proceeded from the camp of some wandering Indians. I was mistaken:—I discovered by its glare that it was from the hearth of a small log cabin, and that a tall figure passed and repassed between it and me, as if busily engaged in household arrangements.

I reached the spot, and presenting myself at the door, asked the tall figure, which proved to be a woman, if I might take shelter under her roof for the night. Her voice was gruff, and her attire negligently thrown about her. She answered in the affirmative. I walked in, took a wooden stool, and quietly seated myself by the fire. The next object that attracted my notice was a finely formed young Indian, resting his head between his hands, with his elbows on his knees. A long bow rested against the log wall near him, while a quantity of arrows and two or three raccoon skins lay at his feet. He moved not; he apparently breathed not. Accustomed to the habits of the Indians, and knowing that they pay little attention to the approach of civilized strangers (a circumstance which in some countries is considered as evincing the apathy of their character), I addressed him in French, a language not unfrequently partially known to the people in that neighborhood. He raised his head, pointed to one of his eyes with his finger, and gave me a significant glance with the other. His face was covered with blood. The fact was, that an hour before this, as he was in the act of discharging an arrow at a raccoon in the top of a tree, the arrow had split upon the cord, and sprung back with such violence into his right eye as to destroy it forever.

Feeling hungry, I inquired what sort of fare I might expect. Such a thing as a bed was not to be seen, but many large untanned bear and buffalo hides lay piled in a corner. I drew a fine time-piece from my breast, and told the woman that it was late, and that I was fatigued. She had espyed my watch, the richness of which seemed to operate upon her feelings with electric quickness. She told me that there was plenty of venison and jerked buffalo meat, and that on removing the ashes I should find a cake. But my watch had struck her fancy, and her curiosity had to be gratified by an immediate sight of it. I took off the gold chain that secured it from around my neck, and presented it to her. She was all ecstasy, spoke of its beauty, asked me its value, and put the chain around her brawny neck, saying how happy the possession of such a watch should make her. Thoughtless, and, as I fancied myself, in so retired a spot, secure, I paid little attention to her talk or her movements. I helped my dog to a good supper of venison, and was not long in satisfying the demands of my own appetite.

The Indian rose from his seat, as if in extreme suffering. He passed and repassed me several times, and once pinched me on the side so violently, that the pain nearly brought forth an exclamation of anger. I looked at him. His eye met mine; but his look was so forbidding, that it struck a chill into the more nervous part of my system. He again seated himself, drew his butcher-knife from its greasy scabbard, examined its edge, as I would do that of a razor suspected dull, replaced it, and again taking his tomahawk from his back, filled the pipe of it with tobacco, and sent me expressive glances whenever our hostess chanced to have her back towards us.

Never until that moment had my senses been awakened to the danger which I now suspected to be about me. I returned glance for glance to my companion, and rested well assured that, whatever enemies I might have, he was not of their number.

I asked the woman for my watch, wound it up, and under pretence of wishing to see how the weather might probably on the morrow, took up my gun, and walked out of the cabin. I slipped a ball into each barrel, scraped the edges of my flints, renewed the primings, and returning to the hut, gave a favourable account of my observations. I took a few bear-skins, made a pallet of them, and calling my faithful dog to my side, lay down, with my gun close to my body, and in a few minutes was, to all appearance, fast asleep.

A short time had elapsed, when some voices were heard, and from the corner of my eyes I saw two athletic youths making their entrance, bearing a dead stag on a pole. They disposed of their burden, and asking for whisky, helped themselves freely to it. Observing me and the wounded Indian, they asked who I was, and why the devil that rascal (meaning the Indian, who, they knew, understood not a word of English) was in the house. The mother—for so she proved to be, bade them speak less loudly, made mention of my watch, and took them to a corner, where a conversation took place, the purport of which it required little shrewdness in me to guess. I tapped my dog gently. He moved his tail, and with indescribable pleasure I saw his fine eyes alternately fixed on me and raised towards the trio in the corner. I felt that he perceived danger in my situation. The Indian exchanged a last glance with me.

The lads had eaten and drunk themselves into such condition, that I already looked upon them as *hors de combat*; and the frequent visits of the whisky bottle to the ugly mouth of their dam I hoped would soon reduce her to a like state. Judge of my astonishment, reader, when I saw this incarnate fiend take a large carving-knife, and go to the grindstone to whet its edge. I saw her pour the water on the turning machine, and watched her working away with the dangerous instrument, until the sweat covered every part of my body, in despite of my determination to defend myself to the last. Her task finished, she walked to her reeling sons, and said, "There, that'll soon settle him! Boys, kill yon —, and then for the watch."

I turned, cocked my gun-locks silently, touched my faithful companion, and lay ready to start up and shoot the first who might attempt my life. The moment was fast approaching, and that night might have been my last in this world, had not Providence made preparations for my rescue. All was ready. The infernal hag was advancing slowly, probably contemplating the best way of despatching me, whilst her sons should be engaged with the Indian. I was several times on the eve of rising and shooting her on the spot—but she was not to be punished thus. The door was suddenly opened, and there entered two stout travellers, each with a long rifle on his shoulder. I bounced up on my feet, and making them most heartily welcome, told them how well it was for me that they should have arrived at that moment. The tale was told in a minute. The drunken sons were secured, and the woman, in spite of her defence and vociferations, shared the same fate. The Indian fairly danced with joy, and gave us to understand that, as he could not sleep for pain, he would watch over us. You may suppose we slept much less than we talked. The two strangers gave me an account of their once having been themselves in a somewhat similar situation. Day came, fair and rosy, and with it the punishment of the captives.

They were now quite sobered. Their feet were unbound, but their arms were still securely tied. We marched them into the woods off the road, and having used them as Regulators were wont to use such delinquints, we set fire to the cabin, gave all the skins and implements to the young Indian warrior, and proceeded, well pleased, towards the settlements.

About twelve years ago I was conveyed, along with my son Victor, from Bayou Sarah to the mouth of the Ohio, on board the steamer Magnet, commanded by Mr. M'Knight, to whom I here again offer my best thanks for his attentions. The very sight of the waters of that beautiful river filled me with joy as we approached the little village of Trinity, where we were landed along with several other passengers, the water being too low to enable the vessel to proceed to Louisville. No horses could be procured, and as I was anxious to continue my journey without delay, I consigned my effects to the care of the tavern-keeper, who engaged to have them forwarded by the first opportunity. My son, who was not fourteen, with all the ardour of youth considered himself able to accomplish on foot the long journey which we contemplated. Two of the passengers evinced a desire to accompany us, "provided," said the tallest and stoutest of them, "the lad can keep up. My business," he continued, "is urgent, and I shall push for Frankfort pretty fast." Dinner, to which we had contributed some fish from the river, being over, my boy and I took a ramble along the shores of Cash Creek, on which some years before I had been detained several weeks by ice. We slept at the tavern, and next morning prepared for our journey, and were joined by our companions, although it was past twelve before we crossed the creek.

One of our fellow-travellers, named Rose, who was a delicate and gentlemanly person, acknowledged that he was not a good walker, and said he was glad that my son was with us, as he might be able to keep up with the lively youth. The other, a burly personage, at once pushed forward. We walked in Indian file along the narrow track cut through the canes, passed a wood-yard, and entered the burnt forest, in which we met with so many logs and briars, that we judged it better to make for the river, the course of which followed over a bed of pebbles, my son sometimes a-head, and again falling back, until we reached America, a village having a fine situation, but with a shallow approach to the shore. Here we halted at the best house, as every traveller ought to do, whether pedestrian or equestrian, for he is there sure of being well treated, and will not have more to pay than in an inferior place. Now we constituted Mr. Rose purser. We had walked twelve miles over rugged paths and pebbly shores, and soon proceeded along the edge of the river. Seven tough miles ended, we found a house near the bank, and in it we determined to pass the night. The first person we met with was a woman picking cotton in a small field. On asking her if we might stay in her cabin for the night, she answered we might, and hoped we could make a shift with the fare on which she and her husband lived. While she went to the house to prepare supper, I took my son and Mr. Rose to the water, knowing how much we should be refreshed by a bath. Our fellow-traveller refused, and stretched himself on a bench by the door. The sun was setting; thousands of robins were flying southward in the calm and clear air; the Ohio was spread before us smooth as a mirror, and into its waters we leaped with pleasure. In a short time the good man of the hut called us to supper, and in a trice we were at his heels. He was a tall raw-boned fellow, with an honest bronzed face. After our frugal meal, we all four lay down in a large bed spread on the floor, while the good people went up to a loft.

The woodsman having, agreeably to our instructions, roused us at day-break, told us that about seven miles further we should meet with a breakfast much better than the last supper we had. He refused any pecuniary compensation, but accepted from me a knife. So we again started. My dear boy appeared very weak at first, but soon recovered, and our stout companion, whom I shall call S., evidently shewed symptoms of lassitude. On arriving at the cabin of a lazy man blessed with an industrious wife and six healthy children, all of whom laboured for his support, we were welcomed by the woman, whose motions and language indicated her right to belong to a much higher class. Better breakfast I never ate: the bread was made of new corn ground on a tin-grater by the beautiful hands of our blue-eyed hostess; the chickens had been prepared by one of her lovely daughters; some good coffee was added, and my son had fresh milk. The good woman, who now held a babe to her bosom, seemed pleased to see how heartily we all ate; the children went to work, and the lazy husband went to the door to smoke a corn-cob pipe. A dollar was put into the ruddy hand of the chubby urchin, and we bade its mother farewell. Again we trudged along the beach, but after a while betook ourselves to the woods. My son became faint. Dear boy! never can I forget how he lay exhausted on a log, large tears rolling down his cheeks. I bathed his temples, spoke soothingly to him, and chancing to see a fine turkey cock run close by, directed his attention to it, when, as if suddenly refreshed, he got up and ran a few yards towards the bird. From that moment he seemed to acquire a new vigour, and at length we reached Wilcox's, where we stopped for the night. We were reluctantly received at the house, and had little attention paid to us, but we had a meal and went to bed.

The sun rose in all its splendour, and the Ohio reflected its ruddy beams. A finer view of that river can scarcely be obtained than that from the house which we were leaving. Two miles through the intricate woods brought us to Belgrade, and having passed Fort Massacre, we halted and took breakfast. S. gave us to understand that the want of roads made travelling very unpleasant; he was not, he added, in the habit of "skulking through the bushes or tramping over stony bars in the full sunshine," but how else he had travelled was not explained. Mr. Rose kept up about as well as Victor, and I now led the way. Towards sunset we reached the shores of the river, opposite the mouth of the Cumberland. On a hill, the property of a Major B., we found a house, and a solitary woman, wretchedly poor, but very kind. She assured us, that if we could not cross the river, she would give us food and shelter for the night, but said that as the moon was up, she could get us put over when her skiff came back. Hungry and fatigued we laid us down on the brown grass, waiting either a scanty meal, or the skiff that was to convey us across the river. I had already grated the corn for our supper, run down the chickens, and made a fire, when a cry of "Boat coming" roused us all. We crossed half of the Ohio, walked over Cumberland Isle, and after a short ferry found ourselves in Kentucky, the native land of my beloved sons. I was now within a few miles of the spot where, some years before, I had a horse killed under me by lightning.

It is unnecessary to detain you with a long narrative, and state every occurrence until we reached the banks of Green River. We had left Trinity at 12 o'clock of the 15th October, and on the morning of the 18th four travellers descending a hill were admiring the reflection of the sun's rays on the forest-margined horizon. The frost which lay thick on the ground and the fences, glittered in the sheen, and dissolved away; all nature seemed beautiful in its calm repose; but the pleasure which I felt on gazing on the scene was damped by the fatigue of my son, who now limped like a lamed turkey, although, as the rest of the party were not much better off, he smiled, straightened himself, and strove to keep up with us. Poor S. was panting many yards behind, and was talking of purchasing a horse. We had now, however, a tolerably good road, and in the evening got to a house where I inquired if we could have a supper and beds. When I came out, Victor was asleep on the grass, Mr. Rose looking at his sore toes, and S. just finishing a jug of monongahela. Here we resolved that, instead of going by Henderson, we should take a cut across to the right, and made direct for Smith's Ferry, by way of Highland Lick Creek.

Next day we trudged along, but nothing very remarkable occurred excepting that we saw a fine black wolf quite tame and gentle, the owner of which had refused a hundred dollars for it. Mr. Rose, who was an engineer, and a man of taste, amused us with his flageolet, which increased my good opinion of him. At an orchard we filled our pockets with October peaches, and when we came to Trade Water River we found it quite low. The acorns were already drifted on its shallows, and the Wood Ducks were running about picking them up. Passing a flat bottom, we saw a large Buffalo Lick. Where now are the bulls which erst scraped its earth away, bellowing forth their love or their anger?

Good Mr. Rose's feet became sorer and sorer each succeeding day; Mr. S. at length nearly gave up; my son had grown brisker. The 20th was cloudy, and we dreaded rain, as we knew the country to be flat and clayey. In Union County, we came to a large opening, and found the house of a Justice, who led us kindly to the main road, and accompanied us for a mile, giving us excellent descriptions of brooks, woods and barrens, notwithstanding which we should have been much puzzled, had not a neighbour on horseback engaged to shew us the way. The rain now fell in torrents, and rendered us very uncomfortable, but at length we reached Highland Lick, where we stumbled on a cabin, the door of which we thrust open, overturning a chair that had been placed behind it. On a dirty bed lay a man, a table with a journal or perhaps a ledger before him, a small cask in a corner near him, a brass pistol on a nail over his head, and a long Spanish dagger by his side. He rose and asked what was wanted. "The way to a better place, the road to Sugg's." "Follow the road, and you'll get to his house in about five miles!" My party were waiting for me, warming themselves by the fires of the salt-kettles. The being I had seen was an overseer. By-and-by we crossed a creek; the country was hilly, clayey and slippery; Mr. S. was cursing, Rose limped like a lame duck, but Victor kept up like a veteran.

Another day, kind Reader, and I shall for a while shut my journal. The morning of the 21st was beautiful; we had slept comfortably at Sugg's, and we soon found ourselves on pleasant barrens, with an agreeable road. Rose and S. were so nearly knocked up, that they proposed to us to go on without them. We halted and talked a few minutes on the subject, when our companions stated their resolution to proceed at a slower pace. So we bade them adieu. I asked my son how he felt; he laughed and quickened his steps; and in a short time our former associates were left out of sight. In about two hours we were seated in the Green River ferryboat, with our legs hanging in the water. At Smith's Ferry this stream looks like a deep lake; and the thick cane on its banks, the large overhanging willows, and its dark green waters, never fail to form a fine picture, more especially in the calm of an autumnal evening. Mr. Smith gave us a good supper, sparkling cider, and a comfortable bed. It was arranged that he should drive us to Louisville in his dearborne; and so here ended our walk of two hundred and fifty miles.

CHARLES
DUDLEY WARNER

How I Killed a Bear

"The bear was coming on . . ."

Charles Dudley Warner wrote about the wilderness with dry wit and skeptical detachment. Born in Massachusetts in 1829, he went west as a young man to work in the surveys, returned east to study law, practiced for a time in Chicago and then turned to journalism, becoming co-editor of the Hartford Courant. *The Adirondacks were his stamping ground, and his account of how he killed an Adirondack bear deserves to be more widely known. Warner walked only to the blackberry patch. But the brevity of his walk should not count against him, for he was involved in greater things. His quick thinking—indeed the* quantity *of his quick thinking in the face of danger—should inspire all those walkers of today whose thoughts occasionally turn to the possibility of a bear in the trail ahead.*

This account is taken from In the Wilderness, *by Charles Dudley Warner, published in* 1878.

So many conflicting accounts have appeared about my casual en-counter with an Adirondack bear last summer, that in justice to the public, to myself, and to the bear, it is necessary to make a plain statement of the facts. Besides, it is so seldom I have occasion to kill a bear, that the celebration of the exploit may be excused.

The encounter was unpremeditated on both sides. I was not hunting for a bear, and I have no reason to suppose that a bear was looking for me. The fact is, that we were both out blackberrying, and met by chance,—the usual way. There is among the Adirondack visitors always a great deal of conversation about bears,—a general expression of the wish to see one in the woods, and much speculation as to how a person would act if he or she chanced to meet one. But bears are scarce and timid, and appear only to a favored few.

It was a warm day in August, just the sort of day when an adven-ture of any kind seemed impossible. But it occurred to the house-keepers of our cottage—there were four of them—to send me to the clearing, on the mountain back of the house, to pick blackberries. It was rather a series of small clearings, running up into the forest, much overgrown with bushes and briers, and not unromantic. Cows pas-tured there, penetrating through the leafy passages from one opening to another, and browsing among the bushes. I was kindly furnished with a six-quart pail, and told not to be gone long.

Not from any predatory instinct, but to save appearances, I took a gun. It adds to the manly aspect of a person with a tin pail if he also carries a gun. It was possible I might start up a partridge; though how I was to hit him, if he started up instead of standing still, puzzled me. Many people use a shot-gun for partridges. I prefer the rifle: it makes a clean job of death, and does not prematurely stuff the bird with globules of lead. The rifle was a Sharp's, carrying a ball-cartridge (ten to the pound),—an excellent weapon belonging to a friend of mine, who had intended, for a good many years back, to kill a deer with it. He could hit a tree with it—if the wind did not blow, and the atmosphere was just right, and the tree was not too far off—nearly every time. Of course, the tree must have some size. Needless to say that I was at that time no sportsman. Years ago I killed a robin under the most humiliating circumstances. The bird was in a low cherry-tree. I loaded a big shot-gun pretty full, crept up under the tree, rested the gun on the fence, with the muzzle more than ten feet from the bird, shut both eyes, and pulled the trigger. When I got up to see what had happened, the robin was scattered about under the tree in more than a thousand pieces, no one of which was big enough to enable a naturalist to decide from it to what species it belonged. This disgusted me with the life of a sportsman. I mention the incident to show, that, although I went blackberrying armed, there was not much inequality between me and the bear.

In this blackberry-patch bears had been seen. The summer before, our colored cook, accompanied by a little girl of the vicinage, was picking berries there one day, when a bear came out of the woods, and walked towards them. The girl took to her heels, and escaped. Aunt Chloe was paralyzed with terror. Instead of attempting to run, she sat down on the ground where she was standing, and began to weep and scream, giving herself up for lost. The bear was bewildered by this conduct. He approached and looked at her; he walked around and surveyed her. Probably he had never seen a colored person before, and did not know whether she would agree with him: at any rate, after watching her a few moments, he turned about, and went into the forest. This is an authentic instance of the delicate consideration of a bear, and is much more remarkable than the forbearance towards the African slave of the well-known lion, because the bear had no thorn in his foot.

When I had climbed the hill, I set up my rifle against a tree, and began picking berries, lured on from bush to bush by the black gleam of fruit (that always promises more in the distance than it realizes when you reach it); penetrating farther and farther, through leaf-shaded cow-paths flecked with sunlight, into clearing after clearing. I could hear on all sides the tinkle of bells, the cracking of sticks, and the stamping of cattle that were taking refuge in the thicket from the flies. Occasionally, as I broke through a covert, I encountered a meek cow, who stared at me stupidly for a second, and then shambled off into the brush. I became accustomed to this dumb society, and picked on in silence, attributing all the wood-noises to the cattle, thinking nothing of any real bear. In point of fact, however, I was thinking all the time of a nice romantic bear, and, as I picked, was composing a story about a generous she-bear who had lost her cub, and who seized a small girl in this very wood, carried her tenderly off to a cave, and brought her up on bear's milk and honey. When the girl got big enough to run away, moved by her inherited instincts, she escaped, and came into the valley to her father's house (this part of the story was to be worked out, so that the child would know her father by some family resemblance, and have some language in which to address him), and told him where the bear lived. The father took his gun, and, guided by the unfeeling daughter, went into the woods and shot the bear, who never made any resistance, and only, when dying, turned reproachful eyes upon her murderer. The moral of the tale was to be kindness to animals.

I was in the midst of this tale, when I happened to look some rods away to the other edge of the clearing, and there was a bear! He was standing on his hind-legs, and doing just what I was doing,—picking blackberries. With one paw he bent down the bush, while with the other he clawed the berries into his mouth,—green ones and all. To say that I was astonished is inside the mark. I suddenly discovered that I didn't want to see a bear, after all. At about the same moment the bear saw me, stopped eating berries, and regarded me with glad surprise. It is all very well to imagine what you would do under such circumstances. Probably you wouldn't do it; I didn't. The bear dropped down on his fore-feet, and came slowly towards me. Climbing a tree was of no use, with so good a climber in the rear. If I started to run, I had no doubt the bear would give chase; and although a bear cannot run down hill as fast as he can run up hill, yet I felt that he could get over this rough, brush-tangled ground faster than I could.

The bear was approaching. It suddenly occurred to me how I could divert his mind until I could fall back upon my military base. My pail was nearly full of excellent berries,—much better than the bear could pick himself. I put the pail on the ground, and slowly backed away from it, keeping my eye, as beast-tamers do, on the bear. The ruse succeeded.

The bear came up to the berries, and stopped. Not accustomed to eat out of a pail, he tipped it over, and nosed about in the fruit, "gorming" (if there is such a word) it down, mixed with leaves and dirt, like a pig. The bear is a worse feeder than the pig. Whenever he disturbs a maple-sugar camp in the spring, he always upsets the buckets of sirup, and tramples round in the sticky sweets, wasting more than he eats. The bear's manners are thoroughly disagreeable.

As soon as my enemy's head was down, I started and ran. Somewhat out of breath, and shaky, I reached my faithful rifle. It was not a moment too soon. I heard the bear crashing through the brush after me. Enraged at my duplicity, he was now coming on with blood in his eye. I felt that the time of one of us was probably short. The rapidity of thought at such moments of peril is well known. I thought an octavo volume, had it illustrated and published, sold fifty thousand copies, and went to Europe on the proceeds, while that bear was loping across the clearing. As I was cocking the gun, I made a hasty and unsatisfactory review of my whole life. I noted, that, even in such a compulsory review, it is almost impossible to think of any good thing you have done. The sins come out uncommonly strong. I recollected a newspaper subscription I had delayed paying years and years ago, until both editor and newspaper were dead, and which now never could be paid to all eternity.

The bear was coming on.

I tried to remember what I had read about encounters with bears. I couldn't recall an instance in which a man had run away from a bear in the woods and escaped, although I recalled plenty where the bear had run from the man and got off. I tried to think what is the best way to kill a bear with a gun, when you are not near enough to club him with the stock. My first thought was to fire at his head; to plant the ball between his eyes: but this is a dangerous experiment. The bear's brain is very small: and, unless you hit that, the bear does not mind a bullet in his head; that is, not at the time. I remembered that the instant death of the bear would follow a bullet planted just back of his fore-leg, and sent into his heart. This spot is also difficult

to reach, unless the bear stands off, side towards you, like a target. I finally determined to fire at him generally.

The bear was coming on.

The contest seemed to me very different from any thing at Creedmoor. I had carefully read the reports of the shooting there; but it was not easy to apply the experience I had thus acquired. I hesitated whether I had better fire lying on my stomach; or lying on my back, and resting the gun on my toes. But in neither position, I reflected, could I see the bear until he was upon me. The range was too short; and the bear wouldn't wait for me to examine the thermometer, and note the direction of the wind. Trial of the Creedmoor method, therefore, had to be abandoned; and I bitterly regretted that I had not read more accounts of offhand shooting.

For the bear was coming on.

I tried to fix my last thoughts upon my family. As my family is small, this was not difficult. Dread of displeasing my wife, or hurting her feelings, was uppermost in my mind. What would be her anxiety as hour after hour passed on, and I did not return! What would the rest of the household think as the afternoon passed, and no blackberries came! What would be my wife's mortification when the news was brought that her husband had been eaten by a bear! I cannot imagine any thing more ignominious than to have a husband eaten by a bear. And this was not my only anxiety. The mind at such times is not under control. With the gravest fears the most whimsical ideas will occur. I looked beyond the mourning friends, and thought what kind of epitaph they would be compelled to put upon the stone. Something like this:—

HERE LIE THE REMAINS

OF

— — — — — ——,

EATEN BY A BEAR

AUG. 20, 1877.

It is a very unheroic and even disagreeable epitaph. That "eaten by a bear" is intolerable. It is grotesque. And then I thought what an inadequate language the English is for compact expression. It would not answer to put upon the stone simply "eaten;" for that is indefinite, and requires explanation: it might mean eaten by a cannibal. This difficulty could not occur in the German, where *essen* signifies the act of feeding by a man, and *fressen* by a beast. How simple the thing would be in German!—

HIER LIEGT

HOCHWOHLGEBOREN

HERR — — — — —   — — — — —,

GEFRESSEN

AUG. 20, 1877.

That explains itself. The well-born one was eaten by a beast, and presumably by a bear,—an animal that has had a bad reputation since the days of Elisha.

The bear was coming on; he had, in fact, come on. I judged that he could see the whites of my eyes. All my subsequent reflections were confused. I raised the gun, covered the bear's breast with the sight, and let drive. Then I turned, and ran like a deer. I did not hear the bear pursuing. I looked back. The bear had stopped. He was lying down. I then remembered that the best thing to do after having fired your gun is to reload it. I slipped in a charge, keeping my eyes on the bear. He never stirred. I walked back suspiciously. There was a quiver in the hind-legs, but no other motion. Still he might be shamming: bears often sham. To make sure, I approached, and put a ball into his head. He didn't mind it now: he minded nothing. Death had come to him with a merciful suddenness. He was calm in death. In order that he might remain so, I blew his brains out, and then started for home. I had killed a bear!

Notwithstanding my excitement, I managed to saunter into the house with an unconcerned air. There was a chorus of voices:—

"Where are your blackberries?"

"Why were you gone so long?"

"Where's your pail?"

"I left the pail."

"Left the pail? What for?"

"A bear wanted it."

"Oh, nonsense!"

"Well, the last I saw of it, a bear had it."

"Oh, come! You didn't really see a bear?"

"Yes, but I did really see a bear."

"Did he run?"

"Yes: he ran after me."

"I don't believe a word of it. What did you do?"

"Oh! nothing particular—except kill the bear."

Cries of "Gammon!" "Don't believe it!" "Where's the bear?"

"If you want to see the bear, you must go up into the woods. I couldn't bring him down alone."

Having satisfied the household that something extraordinary had occurred, and excited the posthumous fear of some of them for my own safety, I went down into the valley to get help. The great bear-hunter, who keeps one of the summer boarding-houses, received my story with a smile of incredulity; and the incredulity spread to the other inhabitants and to the boarders as soon as the story was known. However, as I insisted in all soberness, and offered to lead them to the bear, a party of forty or fifty people at last started off with me to bring the bear in. Nobody believed there was any bear in the case; but everybody who could get a gun carried one; and we went into the woods armed with guns, pistols, pitchforks, and sticks, against all contingencies or surprises,—a crowd made up mostly of scoffers and jeerers.

But when I led the way to the fatal spot, and pointed out the bear, lying peacefully wrapped in his own skin, something like terror seized the boarders, and genuine excitement the natives. It was a no-mistake bear, by George! and the hero of the fight—well, I will not insist upon that. But what a procession that was, carrying the bear home! and what a congregation was speedily gathered in the valley to see the bear! Our best preacher up there never drew any thing like it on Sunday.

And I must say that my particular friends, who were sportsmen, behaved very well, on the whole. They didn't deny that it was a bear, although they said it was small for a bear. Mr. Deane, who is equally good with a rifle and a rod, admitted that it was a very fair shot. He is probably the best salmon-fisher in the United States, and he is an equally good hunter. I suppose there is no person in America who is more desirous to kill a moose than he. But he needlessly remarked, after he had examined the wound in the bear, that he had seen that kind of a shot made by a cow's horn.

This sort of talk affected me not. When I went to sleep that night, my last delicious thought was, "I've killed a bear!"

COLIN FLETCHER

Leaving the Surface

"I had faced my trial of the spirit . . ."

Colin Fletcher is the complete walker. Born in Wales in 1922 and a Royal Marine Commando during World War II, his penchant for the tough go has taken him alone and afoot through the Grand Canyon and on a thousand-mile hike the length of California. Severe honesty and a sensitivity to both his surroundings and himself carry his narratives beyond simple adventure. In the account which follows, he tells of his first tentative foray into the mysteries of the Grand Canyon—a reconnaissance, as it turned out, of more than merely rock and water.

For two days I moved, very slowly, deeper and deeper into the Canyon. I moved down from Hualpai Canyon into Havasu Canyon. On the third morning I passed through Supai village. And all this time I lived on the surface of things. I accepted the restriction resignedly, for any journey into wilderness involves a curious and stubborn paradox.

You know, of course, that you are going to renounce the complexities of civilization and embrace the simple life. And you know that the simple life can lead to insight: even our brusque Western tradition sometimes admits that it is so. But what you are likely to overlook is that your mutiny means making two separate escapes. Obviously, you have to shake off the myopic thoughtways of our man-centered world. But you discover that the tools you have chosen for the escape—solitude and simplicity—at first build new walls. For the trivia take over. And they screw you tight to the present. You wrestle with blisters and sweat rash and upset stomach, with socks that ruck and clothing that rubs and pack straps that slip and food that persistently burns. You anoint and experiment and adjust and readjust. You worry, all the time, about where the next water is coming from, or the next warmth, or the next shelter. And before long you come to realize that these mundane matters are devouring the days.

A preemptory physical challenge, though it will help in the end, begins by making matters even worse. You are forever checking the map, assessing today's achievements, setting tomorrow's targets. And the rare moments when you have a deep, round thought to contemplate always seem to come just when it is time to push ahead again.

These earthy barriers foil your hopes of a quick and total escape from civilization. Experience may help you to break free more quickly, but that is all. In the end you come to accept as something that has to be faced at the start of every journey the stubborn and inescapable paradox of simple living.

That first stimulating evening on the floor of Hualpai Canyon, when I at least glimpsed the underpinnings of geology, had been a sharp and welcome exception to the paradox. But I knew the general rule. And it had been very much in my mind when I roughed out in advance the probable "shape" of my journey.

First, I had decided, I would spend a week in safe, tourist-visited Havasu Canyon, near Supai village. That week would be part shake-down cruise, part hardening period, part reconnaissance.

Then, provided the weather had been right for rainpockets, I would climb up out of Supai onto a broad and sparsely watered rock terrace, two thousand feet above the Colorado, known as the Esplanade. For two weeks or more I would strike eastward along the Esplanade and its unnamed extension until I came to Bass Trail. I knew that all through those two weeks I would be grappling, close and sweaty, with the trivia.

But beyond Bass Trail the challenge would ease. Water would become a rather less critical problem. I would even find old man-made trails. But the chance of meeting men on them seemed remote, and I hoped that as I moved eastward along the Tonto Platform, still a thousand feet above the river, the hours and days and weeks of solitude would begin to tell.

Roughly halfway I would reach the only inhabited place in the Canyon outside Supai village: Phantom Ranch, a small, Park-concession tourist hotel that stands on the floor of the Canyon, midway on the mule and hikers' trail running directly across from Rim to Rim. On the second half of my journey the water problem would become even less pressing. By then, too, my body would be honed. And time would have deepened the solitude. I was not sure what I would find beyond Phantom, or even what I hoped to find (though I was already intrigued by reports of ancient cliff dwellings and by an account of a "fifty-room Indian village," once discovered but now "lost" again). Yet somehow I felt confident that beyond Phantom I would find whatever uncertain grail I was going down into the Canyon to look for.

The first week of my journey, then, had been set aside as a

combined shakedown cruise, hardening period, and reconnaissance. It turned out to be a more important week than I had expected.

In those first three days, as I moved down deeper into the Canyon—from Hualpai Canyon into Havasu Canyon, and down through Supai village—I cleared up most of the minor equipment difficulties that plague you at the start of any trip. And I began to work myself into shape.

Of course, you always mean to start a long walking trip in good physical condition. Your plans wisely include a series of lengthening workouts with full pack. But the pressure of last-minute preparation always seems to crowd them out, and you arrive at the starting point not only mentally exhausted but equipped with flaccid muscles and slipper-soft feet. This time I was particularly unready. For two frustrating weeks I had lain fallow in Grand Canyon Village while an infected heel cleared up, and now, with a sixty-pound pack on my back, I had to treat feet and muscles with more than usual care.

But new pressures were already building up. Pressures of time and space and weather. My route along the Esplanade became tolerably safe only when storms had punctuated the rock with rainpockets. But the year's winter storms had been light and scattered, and the spring ones had so far failed to materialize. Until heavy rain fell, the Esplanade would be a hazardous proposition.

My only alternative was the Inner Gorge of the Colorado—that narrow final chasm, two thousand feet deep and almost sheer, through which the river often flows.

No one, it seemed, had ever attempted the Gorge on foot. Boat parties who had run the river all reported that in the twenty vital miles above Havasu Creek, the Canyon was at its most awe-inspiring. On either side, they said, a series of rockwalls plunged two thousand feet down to the river. No man could hope to find a way through on foot. But it occurred to me that an unlandlubberly boatman would have his attention riveted on the perils of the river and not on details along its edge. The one short movie sequence and two old photographs of the Gorge that I had seen supported this gleam of hope: all showed a narrow, steeply sloping ledge at the foot of one or both of the rockwalls. I had a bonus going for me too. The Colorado is the third longest river in the United States, and is muscled accordingly. At least, it used to be. But four weeks before I began my journey it had been emasculated. The gates of the new Glen Canyon Dam, sixty miles upstream of the Park, had been closed. And all the time I was in the Canyon the river would probably flow at about one third or one quarter of its previous normal low-water level. No one seemed to have much idea whether this artificial drought would open up sections of gorge previously thought of as impassable, but I meant to find out. Unless rain or snow fell along the Esplanade I had, in any case, precious little choice.

So, late on the fourth day of my journey I left some heavy gear at my campsite near Supai (because I would be returning to the village within three days to pick up supplies for the following week) and set off down Havasu Canyon for a reconnaissance of the Inner Gorge.

Before the day was over I discovered an obstacle that all my careful planning had overlooked.

For almost three hours below Supai I followed, and often waded, the rushing blue-green waters of Havasu Creek. By the time I heard the roar of Beaver Falls, halfway between Supai and the Colorado, the light was failing. Soon I came to a bluff that stretched across the narrow canyon, creating the falls. And at its edge the trail I had been following stopped. Just cut off, dead. It was rather like starting across a high bridge and finding yourself on the brink of a missing span. The bluff dropped away sheer: fifty feet of rough red travertine rock—a limestone coating deposited on the bedrock by the heavily mineralized waters of the creek. In the gathering gloom I could see no way around this bluff. And on either side, little more than a hundred yards apart, towered the huge Redwall cliffs that form the walls of Havasu Canyon.

Standing there irresolute at the abrupt end of the trail I found myself, for the first time since leaving Supai, really looking at the cliffs. Evening had already stolen their color, and they were two soaring, impenetrable blanks. Their rims, almost a thousand feet above me, ran black and stark. The strip of pale sky between them looked very narrow. Until that moment I had not realized how far I had come down into the earth.

Pushing uneasiness aside, I cast about for a way around the bluff. In the half-light I could find no hint of one. And after a while I accepted that there was nothing to do but camp.

Somehow, it seemed a somber decision. I knew, of course, that this was no real check: in daylight the trail would show. But I stood for a moment in the half-darkness, hesitating. The strip of sky between the Redwall cliffs was very pale now, almost ready for the stars. The rims looked an immense distance away. And when I began to

hunt for a campsite among the jumbled rocks I found myself still
acutely aware of the depth of the black chasm in which I would sleep.
The monotonous, booming roar of Beaver Falls seemed to mock my
frailty.

I camped in the only level place I could find, where the trail
zigzagged between two blocks of travertine. As I unrolled my sleeping
bag it occurred to me that I had chosen a perfect place for a bobcat or
mountain lion to turn one of the trail's blind corners and stumble on
my helpless, cocooned figure. I could picture the animal startled into
panic and changing from the timorous and retiring creature that it
normally was into a snarling, clawing menace. Wondering a little at
my sudden timidity, I laid warning blocks across the trail: on the
downwind side, a few sticks of the firewood I had already collected;
on the upwind side, a coil of nylon rope that would hold my scent.
Afterward, I felt better.

Before cooking dinner I rested for a few minutes, stretched out
on my sleeping bag. And it was then, lying on my back and watching
the first stars glimmer their hesitant way into that pale strip of sky,
lying there with the roar of Beaver Falls filling the night around me,
that I felt the weight and power of the Redwall.

A few weeks earlier I had read John Wesley Powell's account of
how the boat party he led downriver in 1869 forced what was almost
certainly the first passage ever made of Grand Canyon. And I had
wondered at the oppression that reverberated through the journal's
pages: Powell, a tough, one-armed Civil War major, was obviously
not the timorous type. But now, lying on my back at the bottom of
the black Redwall gorge, I understood. I was hopelessly insignificant.
And when we humans feel this way we are, inevitably, afraid.

Out in the world you may, very occasionally, look down at night
from a high and lonely vantage point onto the swarming life of a great
city and catch a frightening glimpse of your own personal insignificance. But that is not quite the same thing. You do not feel, achingly,
the utter insignificance of all mankind, and you therefore escape the
sense of final, absolute, overwhelming helplessness.

Beneath the Redwall at Beaver Falls, the helplessness lasted only
a few minutes. But while it was on me I recognized, deep down and
naked, that before I could master the Canyon's physical challenge I
must face, sooner or later, a trial of the spirit.

I sat up and lit my cooking stove. Its roar drowned the roar of the
falls. Soon I had a fire going too. It injected life and warmth into the

red travertine blocks that were my room. It set shadows dancing
behind the room's ornaments: a slender green bush and a prickly pear
set at just the right angle. And it thrust away the night. But when I
lay back on my sleeping bag, waiting for dinner to cook, there was
still, far above, only a starry sliver of night sky clamped between the
two walls of towering and terrible blackness. And there was still, deep
down, the lingering knowledge of my utter insignificance.

Next morning, in daylight, the Redwall once more looked red and
friendly. I found the trail around Beaver Falls without difficulty, and
hurried on down beside Havasu Creek.

Ever since Hualpai Hilltop I had been acutely aware of how
much hinged on my Inner Gorge reconnaissance; and when, a couple
of hours below Beaver Falls, I saw the far rockwall of the Gorge
looming up ahead, I found myself suddenly nervous.

My first glimpse of the Colorado was a moderate relief. The river
was big, but not hopelessly big. If anything, it looked narrower and
less turbulent than I had dared hope. Less intimidating, certainly,
than the huge waterway, three hundred miles downriver, that I had
come to know on another long foot journey—and had come to respect.

But after the relief came doubt. Not the kind of doubt you can
define and exorcise, but a vague and elusive sense of insecurity.

A raw wind was gusting up the Gorge. It brushed ugly patterns
across the river's surface. The river was a somber, muddy brown, and
the dark rock that imprisoned it, pressing in from either side, was
lined and ancient, portentous with age. High above the first cliffs, set
back only a little, rose the Redwall. It did not look very big now. And
above it towered other cliffs. The rims of the Gorge, more than two
thousand feet above the river, thrust jagged buttresses against gray
and threatening cloud banks. Compared with this gloomy chasm, the
Redwall gorge of the night before seemed an almost friendly place.
Here even the silence was somber. The roar of the rapids only
deepened it.

But as soon as I had grasped the new, huge size of things I was
gratefully surprised to find that everything looked much as it had in
an old photograph of this place that I had seen. It was oddly comforting to pick out a familiar triangle of sand at the foot of a cleft, and a
flat rock platform just above the point at which the muddy Colorado
began to snuff out the blue-green waters of Havasu Creek. Best of all,
when I came down to the river's edge and looked upstream I saw,

exactly as the photograph had shown it, a narrow shelf that ran along beside the river at the foot of the first cliff. A jutting outcrop of solid rock hid the beginnings of the shelf, but it looked from a distance as if a man should be able to make his way along it.

I slipped off my pack, unclipped the thermometer from my shirt pocket, and held it in the river. The water felt quite warm. And that was another relief. The rockshelf almost certainly did not extend unbroken along any one side of the Gorge, so I would probably have to cross the river several times. While this prospect would never exactly enthrall me, I knew that the river's temperature could make a critical difference. You cannot swim far in liquid ice, cannot even live in it for very long; but your body will work efficiently for quite a long time in 50-degree water. Because of the new Glen Canyon Dam, no one seemed to know quite how cold the Colorado would be running now; generally speaking, dams tend to lower a river's temperature. After about a minute I took the thermometer out of the water. It read exactly 60 degrees.

Almost cheerfully, I undressed and put on swimming trunks (tourists visiting Supai occasionally came down to this place). Even out of the wind, the air was two degrees colder than the river. I waded Havasu Creek and with wet, bare feet climbed carefully along the jutting outcrop that hid the shelf. Centuries of racing water had polished the black rock to a slippery glaze. But the water had cut fluted depressions, and the inlaid pattern—like a mosaic of black, empty, upturned mussel shells—gave my toes a tenuous, welcome purchase.

As I traversed along the rockledge, gusts of wind whipped rawly across my skin, sucking away the warmth like a vacuum cleaner. I reached the apex of the jutting outcrop. And at once I forgot the wind. For in front of me the ledge tapered off sharply, then vanished. And beyond it a cliff sliced down and away in a savage, unclimbable overhang.

I found myself looking out beyond the overhang. The way along the shelf, the route that would mean success or failure, looked even easier now. And at its near end a sandy beach sloped gently up from the water's edge. But between this beach and me, like a protecting moat, stretched a broad back eddy of the river.

Barely one hundred and fifty feet separated me from the beach and the vital shelf. But I could tell that close against the rock the water was deep. Very deep. Except when the wind daubed on its ugly brush marks, I could see steady upstream movement. Once or twice, swirls broke the surface.

Standing there on the rockledge, already shivering, I knew, and wished I did not know, that a hundred and fifty feet of slow-moving water is to most people no kind of challenge at all. But the thought of swimming more than a few strokes has always alarmed me. The act has never pushed me over the brink of panic; but the threat is always there. Even in calm water, nervousness contracts my muscles and quickly and quite unnecessarily tires them. A hundred and fifty feet was probably close to my unaided limit—and I had always swum in open, sunny, populated places, and never with a heavy pack. The one man who had known anything about hiking deep in the Canyon had told me how even at high water he dog-paddled across the river on an air mattress with his pack slung over one shoulder, half-floating. But he was, his wife had said, "like a seal in the water." As I stood shivering on the black rockledge I knew, miserably, that I was no seal. And I knew that in the Gorge, on such a somber day, there was a lot more to it than that.

I waded back across Havasu Creek and dressed and heated some soup on my little stove. After lunch I sat in the lee of a rock and watched the sullen gray clouds, far overhead. Then I dozed. But when I woke up the wind was still there, and the silence, and the roar of the rapids.

It was four thirty before I made up my mind. All along, there had been only one thing to do; now, with less than three hours of daylight left, I could not put it off any longer. I collected together the few things I would need: air mattress, patching kit, poncho, binoculars, waterproof matchsafe, washcloth, nylon cord, and a large sheet of stout white plastic brought along for just this moment. I took off my warm clothes and boots and socks so that I was wearing only shorts, underpants, and shirt. Then I picked up the boots and socks and the little pile of things I would need and walked away from the comforting reassurance of my pack. I waded Havasu Creek again, climbed carefully along the black rockledge, and once more came face to face with the back eddy.

It looked faster now: easier to drift with, but harder to come back against. I knew that if the back eddy defeated me on the way back, I would have to float down in the main current; and now the current looked much farther out, twice as turbulent, and more perilously and inevitably directed toward the roaring downstream rapids.

The gray cloud banks, far overhead, had grown even more sullen. The gusts of wind came more often; harder, colder, crueller.

I blew up the air mattress, taking great care not to inflate it too hard because I would need a deep V to lie across. I suspect that I did everything with great care at least in part because I was still stringing out every act as far as it would go. I bundled up all my gear in the poncho—clothes, boots, binoculars, and the rest—and wrapped the white plastic sheet around the poncho and then lashed the plastic sheet tight with the nylon cord. By the time I began to knot the nylon, my hands were shivering so violently that the job took even longer than I wanted it to. I think I told myself that it was only the cold making me shiver.

At last I was ready. There was a moment when, with the white bundle in my hands, I hesitated. Then, reluctantly, as if trying it committed me, I lowered the bundle onto the water. It floated, cocked high. I took it out, balanced it on a little level platform of the black rock, and put the air mattress in the river. It was too limp. The hot breath inside had cooled and contracted. I blew it up harder and put it back in the water. This time it looked about right.

There were no more excuses left now. I took a deep breath, then slid down into the river beside the little green air mattress. It did not really feel warmer underwater than out in the air, but it was a relief to escape the wind.

Keeping close to the rock, very close, I pulled the mattress under me until I was lying with my chest across it. The V was just right, and I felt reassured and surprisingly comfortable. Then I looked up at the white bundle. And at once I saw that there was no room to put it on the mattress, as I had intended.

For what seemed a very long time I just lay in the water, looking up at the white bundle on the black rock and thinking that now I would have to abandon the reconnaissance. As I lay there I noticed that water running down from the bundle had turned the black rock even blacker. It seemed an interesting fact. All this time, inevitably, my determination was seeping slowly away. But then, almost as if I were hovering above the water watching my own antics, I saw that all I was doing was continuing to make ridiculous excuses. And then, leaving no time for second thoughts, I had grabbed the bundle and stuffed it under my chest and pushed off.

Over the brink, everything was easier. Very slowly, the back eddy began to carry me upstream. There were cracks in the rock just above water level, and I slipped the fingers of my right hand into them and pulled. Every time I pulled, the rock moved smoothly past. Nothing else existed now except the black rock and the brown river and my little green air mattress. And the river was only a few inches of water between mattress and rock.

All at once, just when there were no cracks for my fingers, a swirl began to carry me out and away. The few inches of water widened to a foot, to three feet, to four. I found myself kicking with suddenly tensed legs, dog-paddling with desperately cupped hands. For a moment I went on moving out into the river. The rapids were suddenly very loud. Then, slowly, I came back to the rock.

Pulling with fingers and kicking with feet, I began to move along with the back eddy again. Soon there were no more cracks in the rock, only the black mussel-mosaic; but the river was still carrying me forward. And then I was under the overhang and the rock had slanted back and left me out on my own. Immediately, the river was very big. And back in the gloom at the base of the overhang, water lapped quietly against black rock.

I was past the swirls now, in quiet water that no longer helped me forward. I began to dog-paddle. As I paddled I kept looking ahead at the beach that sloped up to the shelf. It did not seem to get any closer. The mattress, reassuring though it was, made the dog-paddling hard work, and my muscles began to contract again. Then, almost unexpectedly, the beach looked closer. And then much closer. By the time I let my legs sink and felt toes touch sand, my muscles felt almost relaxed.

Coming up out of the water—clambering up the steep and yielding sand with the white bundle dripping in my arms—was like coming up out of a pit into sunlight. And when I dropped everything and began to dance around on the sand like a dervish I wondered, even while I was dancing, whether the dance was mostly to get warm or mostly to release the great flood of elation that would not stay down.

In the water I had hardly noticed the cold. But now the wind was cruel again on my wet body. As soon as the elation would let me, I stopped dancing and unwrapped the white bundle. Everything was bone dry. I toweled briefly with the washcloth, pulled on my clothes, and ducked thankfully into the poncho, out of the wind. And then I had grabbed the plastic sheet and the air mattress and, with water still dripping from them, was running full tilt up the sloping beach. The first strides brought a promise of real warmth.

The sand ended and the shelf began. The shelf was a sloping layer of small rockledges, each so narrow that at times it would not accept a boot; but all the ledges angled inward, so that even where they had crumbled your feet could not slip. And each time I came to a doubtful place the ledges were still there.

Right from the start I traveled fast. Even with a heavy pack I could have kept moving. The elation, which had started to go the way of wonderful but fragile things, began to bubble up again.

Half an hour later, I had gone what I judged from the map must be almost a mile. Ahead, the shelf curved on and around and out of sight, unchanged. There was another shelf on the far side of the river. And the river did not look too fast. Not impossible for a timid swimmer with an air mattress who could bring himself to try it.

I would have liked to go farther—at least around the first big bend. But on such a gloomy evening, deep in that somber place, it would be dark in less than two hours. And on the way back it might take longer to cross the back eddy.

I sat down and tightened my bootlaces and marshaled my thoughts. But I knew that I did not really have to think. The decision had made itself. Had made itself while I was moving, unchecked, along the shelf.

There could be no certainty, of course, about the vital thirty miles ahead. But in half an hour I had come almost a mile. Obviously, the remaining twenty-nine were worth a try.

I took a last look upriver, saw nothing to dissuade me, and started back along the shelf.

Now that I knew the way, there was time for me to see more than the next step ahead, and as I hurried along I noticed that the threatening gray clouds had dropped down over the rim of the Gorge. Soon it began to rain. A few big drops at first, unsure of what they wanted to do. Then a couple of flurries, press-ganged by the wind. And then at last, after two false starts, a steady, driving attack. The rain fell noiselessly on the brown river and noiselessly on the black rock. Its drumming on the hood of my tight-wrapped poncho only deepened the silence outside. I hurried on. The gloom thickened. Once I found myself stopping to listen. All I could hear was the quiet, indifferent lapping of the Colorado.

I had time now to see that all the rock—the black rock around me and the brown rock above it—was cracked and fissured and waiting. Every poised boulder and every peeling fragment hung imminent. I felt that they must all, any moment now, come crashing down on me. It took tight, determined thinking to convince myself that this was not really so.

As I hurried on downstream through the rain I remembered John Wesley Powell's account of his pioneer passage; remembered the oppression reverberating through its pages. And I understood at last—and knew that under the Redwall at Beaver Falls I had not really understood at all—what the Gorge had done to him, and why three of his companions had finally left him and taken their chance up a sidecanyon in a bid for the sky and freedom. (All three reached the Rim; but just beyond it they were murdered—by either Indians or whites.) Now, deep in the Gorge, I found their choice easy to understand. And as I hurried on with the rain still falling silently through the gloom, I knew that in attempting a passage of the Gorge I would face more than a physical challenge.

It was almost a relief to tackle the back eddy again. There was a moment when the current threatened to defeat me. But then, so that I could dog-paddle more freely, I had wrapped an end of the nylon cord around my arm and was towing the white bundle along behind. And soon I was pulling myself up, relaxed again, onto the black mussel-mosaic of the rockledge. Then I was unwrapping the white bundle and thinking, because my icy fingers could not feel anything in the shorts pockets, that I had lost my washcloth. I was shivering so viciously now, with the rain suddenly over and the wind in command, that all the time I was dressing I kept worrying that I might shake my feet off the wet, smooth rock.

The cold no longer mattered, though. I knew it would pass. But when I looked back up into the silent and somber Gorge, I saw that although the gloom had by now grown deeper, the evening was no longer gloomy; and I knew that merely because I had crossed the back eddy and then had returned, the Gorge would never again seem quite such a terrible place. And I knew that this new response would last.

I climbed along the rockledge, waded Havasu Creek, and came home to my pack. And then at last I was pulling on long whipcord pants and down-filled jacket and waiting for the wonderful warmth to spread to hands and feet.

Almost at once, something made me look up. The clouds had lifted. I could see the rim of the Gorge again. And then, far overhead, the clouds moved apart. Through the gap slanted a shaft of evening sunlight. Just for a minute, or perhaps two minutes, a shining cliff face floated high above the far rim of the Gorge, so bright and clear that I could pick out every detail. But the detail was not ordinary rock detail. The outlines of the cliff had been softened by a thin, uneven coating of white.

Before the clouds closed in again I had checked my map. And then I knew for sure. The white cliff stood opposite the Esplanade. And if snow had fallen along the Esplanade there was only one thing to do.

For a time I just stood beside my pack, looking up at the gray cloud banks and hoping for another glimpse of that shining and beautiful cliff. I know I smiled to myself at the way the Gorge had made me forget, until I saw the snow, what rain would mean up on the Esplanade. But I do not think my mind had quite grasped the new shape of things.

Suddenly I realized that the daylight had almost gone. I still had to spend a night in the Gorge. Then, in the morning, I could start doing what had to be done.

I found a good campsite under an overhang. Soon it was dark, and raining again. I lit a fire with sticks I had gathered just before the rain began. The fire's flickering light transformed the overhang into a cheerful little room. With beans bubbling on the stove I sat back in my sleeping bag, leaning against the pack, waiting. My body was glowing now, and tingling; my mind, glowing and content. It had grasped the new shape of things at last, and I could let myself admit, slowly, the relief I felt because I would probably not need, after all, to face a passage of the Gorge.

But I knew the day had not been wasted. Anything but wasted. It had been a great and wonderful and victorious day. A day to remember. And after a while, as I sat there with the stove roaring and firelight playing red on rock and rain falling silvery in the darkness outside, I understood what the day had meant. It had been, I saw, the vital day. The Gorge no longer seemed a terrible place. And because of that the Canyon would no longer hold for me the worst fear of all—the fear of the unknown. I had faced my trial of the spirit.

ELEANOR
DE LA VERGNE RISLEY

The Road to Wildcat

"O America! Land of peace and plenty. Alabama!
Here we rest!"

Confronted by "invalidism, hospital observation, and insulin"—none of them very appealing—Eleanor Risley set out in the late 1920s for a walking tour of northern Alabama's hill country vowing to die with her boots on. Her excursion was both haunting and harrowing. Peter was her husband; John a mongrel "who just missed being a setter"; Sisyphus their pushcart, a three-wheeled barrow with green galvanized sides and a push-bar in back. Eleanor Risley was born in 1876; at the time she wrote this, she lived on a chicken farm in the unlikely hamlet of Ink, Arkansas.

This account is from Eleanor Risley's The Road to Wildcat, *published in 1930.*

We were resting by the roadside, for it was July and nearing noon. Even in the cool mountains nature makes obeisance to the sun at noonday. The singing birds are already hiding in lost green glades, and the jeweled lizard, forever darting across the white sand, sleeps now, beneath his broad leaf, as still as the pebble beside him. After the joyous allegro of the morning, the crescendo of winds and woods attains the pause before the languid and prolonged adagio of a summer afternoon.

We had been walking since sunrise, up and up the mountain road. Peter, who pushed the cart, was dejected. He had ivy poison. John, the beloved mongrel, was dejected. We had taken away his kitten. Two nights before he had brought a scrawny, badly blondined kitten to camp. He had divided his corn pone with her, and she slept in the ashes of the camp fire by his side. He insisted that she continue the journey with our party. John, who hates cats! The mystery of the masculine mind! A scrawny little blondined cat! Even we objected to hiking accompanied by a yellow cat; so this morning we presented the kitten to a friendly mountain woman. I am persuaded that John felt it keenly. I too was dejected. I could not forget the little three-year-old boy who plays all day in his old grandfather's blacksmith shop, while his mother lies always sick and alone in the cabin beside it. I could not forget how joyously and competently that curly-haired elf used the tools in the shop where his grandfather's forge had burned

for over fifty years, to make his own playthings. The grandfather is
very old and the mother cannot last long. There is no one else. What
then, for that wonderful little creature? Buddie's father, so the grandfather told me, had kissed him and ridden away into the night.

"Hit war like this," he said. "We-all had allus made good corn
whiskey. The sheriff of this county, he owns all the stills now, and he
makes whiskey quick with this hyar red-devil lye. Lige, he wouldn't
jine 'em, so one night they come and burned his still, and whooped
him and putt him on his horse and driv him outen the country. I
couldn't holp none. I jest stayed on with Buddie. Whar you-all'll
camp to-night by the big spring is whar the sheriff is buildin' a big
pleasure place. But he don't live thar. He lives down in the valley, and
he's got fifty thousand dollars in the bank thar, made outen red-devil
lye."

We knew our hike through this particular country held an
element of danger. We had been repeatedly warned to turn back, and
we had often been stopped by half-drunken men in motor cars and
keenly questioned as to our business in these mountains. We had
always succeeded in making them believe we were not revenue
officers. But we were careful, at night, to set our little tent near a
human habitation. We camped that night by the big spring near the
sheriff's pleasure palace. The caretaker's wife brought us some milk.
Milk is buttermilk, in the mountains. Sweet milk is so called and is a
luxury. After supper I sat on the porch and talked with the caretaker's
wife. A mountain woman talks only of fundamental, basic things of
life. She tells me how her husband has pellagra; of her two sons, dead
of pellagra. How old am I? And how many children have I? And she
tells me if I look away beyond the cotton patch I can see the stone
that marks a little grave. "She war my only gal. She choked to death
of dipthery. We couldn't get no doctor." And I tell her of a little
green grave so far away I shall never see it again. We are silent then,
but not far apart in spirit, and watch the young moon shine from the
lilac west.

The next morning, as we leave, she tells me in her sad monotone,—a mountain woman does not whisper,—very softly, that even
Peter may not hear, that I must never leave the pushcart. "Hit won't
be safe even with the dog quiled under hit. They'll putt a bottle of
whiskey in hit. Then they'll catch your man and he'll have to work
out his fine on the road. The convicts air a-buildin' a road for the
automobiles to peddle whiskey on a right smart piece beyant hyar. I

reckon I orten to told you. But you-all don't look like you could pay no fine."

Now we were nearing the road the convicts were building. Beyond, on either side we could see the great iron cages—larger, but exactly like the animal cages of the circus—where the convicts lived.

Down the hot road between the iron cages walked a tall, gaunt mountain woman. She was neatly dressed, as are all mountain women outside their homes, and she carried a basket from the crossroads store at the top of the mountain. "Happy Top" it is called. God save the mark!

As the woman reached us, she fixed me with her great fierce eyes and asked, "Air you the woman as is walkin' fer comfort?"

I laughed. I couldn't help it. But Peter understood. He knew that *Comfort* is the name of the family paper which has the largest circulation of any paper in America, and that a Pearle someone was writing a hiking experience for this paper. If a mountain woman reads a paper, she reads *Comfort*. I was sorry I was not Pearle. The woman's world was small. She was disappointed. So I told her I had a fiddle in the cart, and would she wait, and did she think I might play for the convicts at noon?

"I'm scairt they won't want to hear no music when they belong to eat," she replied. "I reckon the gyard won't let you nohow. You might play to-night, after they're in their cages, ef thay all ain't dead then. Hit's a powerful hot day fer 'em. Yesterday a little city feller, he fell down a-diggin' in the sun, and I axed the gyard ef I couldn't carry him a gourd o' water. He wouldn't let me, and he kicked the feller up agin and he fell down agin and they throwed a bucket o' water on to him and let him lay. He war in a faint. You'll see him as you pass by. He wears big specs, and his hands air a-tremblin' so he can't wipe the sweat off'n 'em."

"What did he do? What was his crime?" Peter asks.

"He war a-walkin' down to Gadsden by hisself and they slipped a bottle o'moonshine in his bundle, and then ketched him to work out his fine. Thar's a ole man—you see him on the left side a-diggin'; hit's him with the long white whiskers—his wife's a-dyin' and he went over on tother mounting to shoot something—she war a-honin' for something more 'n hawg meat—and he couldn't find nothing but a chicken a-drinkin' at the crik, and he shot hit and carried hit home, kind o'brash like—he war miserable—and they ketched him, and he's workin' out his fine, an' the neighbors on tother mounting air a-holpin' his wife. She's a-dyin' o' pellagra. The ole man's allus been kind o' lackin'. He's powerful old, and him bein' lackin' he's kinda off 'n his haid. He hollers out loud and prays. The gyards hit him over the haid yesterday when he hollered to some folks a-passin'. You see the sun is so hot, an' the ole man's lackin' anyhow."

"There is a store beyond?" I ask faintly. "We want to buy some alcohol. My husband has ivy poison."

"Yes," she answered. "Hit's a right smart store. I don't know about alcohol. The storekeeper he owns a right smart chance of everything on this and tother mounting. Sence the boll weevil tuck us we all owe him duebills, and he owns all the land. They're about all renters but me. My son's a engineer in Birmingham. I own my place. He's a-movin' the mounting to get me out. Good-bye. I'd be proud if you-all'd write me a card. I kin read writin' too."

We put John on the chain, and trudged on up the hot road between the iron cages. Mules and scrapers; negroes and whites; guards with pistols; and over all a pall of silence. Dirt and toil and sweat and torture! The "city feller" with the "specs" turned away his pallid face; the old man who was "lackin' " cried out a prayer to us; the guard shook him roughly by the shoulder. The silent horror of the road, broken only by the old man's cry, crept into our blood and caught at our hearts.

The store was packed with silent, lank mountaineers, sitting on boxes, spitting tobacco with great accuracy and perfect regularity from the open windows. Each man took his turn. There was a small amount of denatured alcohol in the lamp. We might have it, but there was no bottle to be found, no can, no receptacle whatever. We were in despair. Peter, tortured with ivy poison, grew more dejected.

A tall, lean mountaineer unfolded himself in sections from his box.

"Stranger," he said, "my advice is to step behind thim flour sacks and putt hit on. Hit'll be yourn then."

Presently a stifled groan came from behind the flour sacks. The mountaineer spat through the window out of his turn—it was an unusual occasion—and remarked dryly, "All of which he done so."

We camped that night by a stream where I fished. John, barking at every fish I caught, forgot the kitten. Once more he was a gay dog. Peter, the pain of ivy poison allayed, was serene again. Nature healed us. But the old man who was lacking wept in his iron cage for his wife who was dying alone on "tother mounting." God send, the pallid city youth slept the sleep of exhaustion. The little boy who played all day by the forge lay beside his tubercular mother in the cabin near the shop. Perhaps the father who wouldn't join the sheriff in making red-devil whiskey thinks of them to-night. The caretaker's wife, whose husband has pellagra, rocks in the moonlight that shines on the grave of a child "that thar warn't no doctor to holp."

O America! Land of peace and plenty. Alabama! Here we rest.

The next morning we set out for Wildcat Dam, "the lonesomest place in the mountings, whar thar is two houses and the best fishin' in the world." We met no one, although there were moonshine caches along the way. We had learned to read the signs, like gypsy patrins, of fresh boughs where we could follow a dim path and, putting a quarter on a stump and turning our backs, find a good drink of corn liquor.

It was late afternoon when we came to a grassy cove hemmed in close by mountains. A ruined water mill added a sadness to the scene. Across a wide rushing river stood the old dam, and from its crenate wall dozens of vipers obtruded their flattened heads and forked tongues, their lidless eyes looking down on the foaming water below. Peter stopped to shoot at them, and I walked on by the river road to find a house. For the place oppressed me, and I craved a camp this night near friendly human beings. The river sang a haunting song. Old memories waked and cried, and conquered griefs woke to fight again. But when I came upon a white house with a long gallery where, on a rustic chair, lay an open book, I called myself names, and reflected that I was tired. For walking down a mountain is harder muscle-work than climbing.

Through an open screened door I saw a neat room where a scholarly-looking man, with jetty hair pushed back from a noble forehead, sat delicately leafing a book. I knocked and knocked again, but the man never looked up or ceased his careful leafing of his book. Concluding that the man was deaf, I called, for, through another room, I saw two women sitting on a porch before a little garden gay with hollyhocks and zinnias. A young woman, with the same intellectual beauty of the reading man, came and, in a beautifully modulated, full-throated voice, bade me enter. The reading man never looked up from his book. A woman of the type once called motherly sat stringing beans, and a curly-haired boy of six, perhaps, played with a kitten. I sat and helped string the beans and talked of ourselves. The place was neat, like a New England home. For the Southern home aims at beauty rather than order and convenience. After a while I said, "Though we are camping, I wonder if you would take us to board a few days, while I fish." And, fearing a recrudescence of sadness, I added, "I believe I could be happy here."

The woman called softly, "Father! Father!" and from another room appeared the most gigantic man I had ever seen. His fiery eyes were set in a finely modeled head utterly destitute of a single hair. "Father," said the woman, "here is a lady who wants to stop with us a few days. She says she thinks she might be happy here."

The old man offered me his mighty hand. He said, "If you think you can be happy here, stay a day or a year." I thanked him; and the young woman—sullenly, I thought—showed me a room with dainty curtains and hooked rugs and oh, bliss! an outside bathroom with a row of white towels! I hastened away with the joyful news.

But at the door the woman stopped me. "I must tell you," she said, "there is a reason why you may not like to stop with us. My son, here, is what they call an idiot. He is quite harmless, but people are afraid of him."

"You mean," I cried, "the scholarly gentleman reading?"

"He has leafed books like that for forty years. He never tears or soils a book, and he'll cry if we take them away. He is as helpless as a baby, and I've never left him day or night for forty-three years."

I leaned against the screen and looked at the man in his long clean Russian blouse, leafing his book with dainty care. And I, in my insolent egoism, had asked these people to take me in that *I* might be happy! Suddenly the man looked up and wailed in a long descending cadence the word "*F–l–y!*" "It's the only word he can say," said his mother, "and he'll say it till I catch the fly." And incessantly he sang the word until the fly was caught!

We stopped outside and a man rattled up in a wagon. He called, "I'll be pow'ful obleeged ef you'all'll jist ask Charlie to step outside and see ef hit's goin' ter rain. I've got ter cut hay, and don't wanter hev hit down in the rain." The woman led her son gently to the porch. He stood a moment like a sage in profound meditation. Then his body began to sway, and his arms waved like a tree in the distress of storm, and his voice rose like the sough of the wind until it was unbearable.

"Much obleeged!" said the man. "I won't cut hay till after the storm."

"He always knows when it will rain, and people come for miles

around to consult him," the mother said proudly. Astonished, I asked her what sign he made if it was to be clear. "He dances as light, and makes the prettiest sound—like bees murmuring."

Peter came up the road, and I beckoned him. It was curious to watch John's attitude toward the imbecile. He stared and cringed, and fixed his eyes on the man as though he saw forms invisible to us. During our three days' stay John haunted him, staring transfixed before the idiot, who never lifted his eyes. A youth of an inferior type came in and was introduced as the husband of Emma, the daughter. And I observed that the child feared and disliked him.

After supper,—and what white linen and what a dainty tea cozy!—while Peter admired the grandfather's clock, I looked curiously at the books, remarking on the many books of travel.

"Yes," said our host, "I am an Englishman. I was a sailor, and was wrecked on the coast of Africa. That's where I got this bald head. Three of us got to shore, but the other two died on the way. They picked me up crazy with fever. When I woke in a native hut there wasn't a hair on my head."

"But how," I asked, "did you find this remote place?"

"I shipped for America and found my wife here. I bought the finest wig in Boston to win her," he laughed. "I wear it now on our anniversary days."

"I am English too," said his wife, "but I came to America as a child. Father was always hankering for the sea, so we came here to be out of the sight and sound of the water."

And in my Pollyanna way I said, "But you have found peace and quiet here."

The old man smiled at me sadly. "A man's fate is written on his forehead. He can't sidestep his destiny. You are looking at those Correspondence Courses. I had to educate my children here, so I just learned along with them. Emma can read French as well as she can English."

"You have other children?" I asked.

"Yes, two sons," he said shortly.

That night there was a violent storm and a tree crashed down near our window. I thought of Charlie, and I marveled. I marvel still.

WILLIAM O. DOUGLAS

Why Not Go Home Tonight?

"I was chilled to the heart . . ."

Justice William O. Douglas of the United States Supreme Court has hiked all over the world, but his heart plainly belongs to the Cascades of Washington State. The son of a circuit-riding Presbyterian minister, Douglas grew up with his widowed mother in Yakima, Washington. As a boy he had infantile paralysis, and it was westward to the Cascades that he turned to test his recovery. In the account which follows, Justice Douglas recalls more than the discouragement of great distance, the fits and starts of a frying pan race, the agony of a four-hour breakfast, or that universal urge to break for home. He tells also of the triumph of weak legs made strong.

The following summer with less premeditation I gave my legs a more severe test. One day Brad Emery and I walked more than 40 miles in the Cascades with packs on our backs. It was early June just after high school was out and before the cherries were ready for picking. We took that opportunity to have a week together in the Cascades. We went by stage through Wiley City and past the Ahtanum Mission and the Narrows to Tampico. There we caught a ride to Soda Springs. Then we put the horseshoe packs over our shoulders, took to the trail up the North Fork of the Ahtanum, and headed for the Klickitat Meadows, 16 miles distant. We planned to camp there that night.

Not far up the North Fork the old trail divided, the left fork going over the southeastern shoulder of Darling Mountain and down to the Meadows, the right fork climbing to the very top of Darling. We were chatting as we walked along and overlooked the branching of the trail. We took the wrong fork, and did not realize it until the increased pitch of the trail in a quarter-mile or so told us of our error.

We then decided to abide by our mistake. Our contour map showed that the trail we were on went over the top of Darling, turned north onto Short and Dirty Ridge, and dropped to the South Fork of the Tieton not far from the Tieton Basin. The tops of both Darling Mountain and Short and Dirty Ridge were new territory for both of us. We decided to explore them. We pushed on. Darling Mountain stands at 6972 feet, which meant we had close to 3500 feet to climb before we reached its peak. The trail at once told us of its trials, for it climbed almost without respite.

Brad and I left most of the wild flowers behind us when we started up the steep trail. It was a late season. We had supposed that the soft chinook had melted the snow that powdered Darling Mountain in great drifts during the winter; but we soon discovered we were wrong. There was a lot of snow in the ravines and under the trees; the trail was still damp with its moisture; and the air was chill as if it were coming out of the open door of a cold-storage plant. It was like raw March and April weather. The warmth of the lava rock and sagebrush hills in the valley had not yet reached these slopes. Patches of snow soon appeared in the trail; and it was not long before our shoes were wet through. But it was good weather for exertion. We climbed the 3500 feet with our 30-pound packs with hardly a stop.

We were greatly discouraged because of the snow; and we grumbled about it as we climbed. It meant wet ground for camping, poor fishing, and restricted hiking. But it offered advantages too. This was the first time that I had seen the glorious avalanche lily. This day I saw its tender shoots coming up right on the edge of the snow, sometimes even through a thin layer of snow. And then within a few feet or even inches of a snowdrift would be the delicate flower itself.

It's an *Erythronium*, clear white with an orange center, the flowers two or three inches across. Alpine basins will produce whole acres of this dainty flower. I have seen great meadows on the shoulders of Rainier and Hood filled with it. That sight is breath-taking. But even small patches of it under high rock cliffs, on open slopes, or at the edge of great snowbanks, have the same effect on me. And they always bring me to a reverent halt. The size of the flower, the delicacy of its texture, the gracefulness of its stance, make it one of the most wondrous of all the creations of nature. It never ceases to be startling to find something so exquisitely beautiful and delicate growing in the raw, cold atmosphere of a snowdrift.

The avalanche lily has more than my adoration; it also commands a great respect. For this flower spurns the lowlands. It does not survive transplanting. Unlike its cousin of golden hue, the glacier lily that I have found in great abundance on American Ridge above Bumping Lake, the avalanche lily has an aversion to gardens. It grows in a rugged environment; there and there alone it thrives. Like man, it needs a challenge to reach its full fruition. Its stimulus is the raw wind, cold thin earth, chill nights, and icy waters of the Cascades.

Thus the snow which dampened our enthusiasm for this mountain trip brought rewards. It introduced me to this fragile but stout-hearted beauty of the high mountains.

There is a narrow, hogback saddle that connects the eastern end of Darling's top with the western end. The wind had cleared this saddle of all snow. But as we crossed it we saw ahead of us on the higher western end of the mountain great drifts that covered the trail. They were 15 to 20 feet deep. We worked our way around them and over and slowly came to the western edge of Darling's top. It was late afternoon on a clear day. There was not a cloud in the sky. Brad and I stopped near the spot where a State Forest Service lookout tower now stands, threw off our packs on an outcropping of lava rock, and drank in the view.

This is without doubt the most commanding view in the Cascades. To the east and the southeast were glimpses of the valleys around Yakima and Toppenish, gold and brown in the distance. Way to the south, deep in Oregon, the cold snowy shaft of Mount Jefferson loomed through a light haze. Then came Mount Hood—the one that Lewis and Clark called the falls mountain or Timm Mountain—touching the sky with its broad-bladed shoulder that ends in a sharp peak. Adams was next—high humped and rounded, friendly and intimate. Beyond it and to the right was St. Helens, a touch of fleecy cloud at the top of its white cone.

Running south between us and Adams was a rough gash in the earth, the deep, serpentine canyon through which the Big Klickitat finds its way to the Columbia at Lyle, Washington. North of Adams was the jagged, snow-capped line of the Goat Rocks running in a northwesterly direction for 15 or 20 miles. North of it was mighty Rainier, dominating every peak and ridge in the range. To our north stood the jagged Tatoosh Range, the high rounded American Ridge, and other ranges that seemed to go on endlessly as waves in a vast sea until they finally were absorbed in the thickening haze of the horizon.

Below us to the south, west and north was a tumbled mass of peaks, rocks, and pinnacles. Valleys and ridges ran every which way, as if they were built without design or relation to the whole; and yet they all fitted as huge blocks into the gargantuan pattern of this tremendous range.

When one stands on Darling Mountain, he is not remote and apart from the wilderness; he is an intimate part of it. The ridges run away at his feet and lead to friendly meadows. Every trail leads beyond the frontier. Every ridge, every valley, every peak offers a solitude deeper even than that of the sea. It offers the peace that comes only from solitude. It is in solitude that man can come to know both his heart and his mind.

Brad and I had no choice but to camp on the top of Darling Mountain all night. The western and northern slopes were covered with snow. The remaining hours of daylight did not leave time enough to make a descent to any of the valleys below us. We selected an open space between snowdrifts where there was a stand of whitebark pine, and there pitched our pup tent and built our fire.

We melted snow for cooking, finished supper before all the stars were out, and put beans to soak for tomorrow's breakfast. The wind came up. It was not the warm chinook that comes from the southwest. It came from the northwest with the chill of ice in its breath. We built a brisk fire to dry out our shoes and socks that had become soaked in the snow; and we tried to sit close to it to keep warm. But we finally gave up, put logs around the edges of the pup tent to impede the wind, and went to bed early.

It was a cold, cold night. I napped fitfully, chilled and uncomfortable on the mattress of whitebark pine boughs.

We rose by the break of day and put on the beans that had been soaking all night. They, along with pancake bread and coffee, were to be our breakfast. But before that breakfast was eaten we had learned that cooking at a high altitude could be a slow process. We were camped at about 7,000 feet. Boiling water is not very hot at that elevation. We had no pressure cooker. So all we could do was to keep the pot bubbling. This we did for over four hours, and still the beans were only half-done. The day was wasting; we were impatient to get off the mountain into the lowlands where we hoped to fish. So we started on the beans anyway. The outer part was done; but the inner core was as hard as plaster. Though we chewed and ate some of them, for the most part we spat them out as we would cherry pits. It was perhaps the most unsatisfactory mountain meal I ever had.

We broke camp then. Down the western slope of Darling Mountain was a snow field almost a mile long and dropping perhaps a thousand feet or more in elevation. It offered us an acceptable route, since it led to the South Fork of the Tieton where we wanted to go. The snow was what skiers call "corn" snow, hard and coarsely granulated. We had no skis, but we did have a frying pan apiece.

"Why not use them as toboggans?" asked Brad.

The idea was to sit in the frying pan, hold the feet up, lean slightly backwards, and, keeping the handle to the rear, use it as a steering rod. The problem of balance was complicated by the horseshoe packs around our necks, which became awkward and unwieldy when we were seated.

Brad started off. The frying pan which he used as a sled bit slightly into the crust of the snow. He was soon going like a flash, rocking crazily from side to side, the ends of his horseshoe pack bobbing along on the snow. He had only a short run of 100 feet or so when he turned sideways and then rolled over and over. He finally dug his foot in the snow and ended up half-buried in the mountainside. His blue eyes were laughing as he brushed snow out of his hair. I followed suit and repeated his performance. I tried again and landed head down with my pack buried with me and only my feet free. Thus we rolled and slid off Darling Mountain, yelling and laughing and shouting as we went. We were on and off the frying pans a dozen times or more. We had snow in our shoes and down our necks. Our hands were cold and raw from the rough snow; and our pants were wet. But the bottoms of our frying pans shone like new silver dollars.

We camped that night at the base of Darling, by a falls close to the confluence of Bear Creek and the South Fork of the Tieton. The latter was swollen from the snow and white with raging water, so we did not even attempt to fish it. We usually had good luck fishing the South Fork at Conrad Meadows, which was above us a few miles. We headed up there the next morning, hoping without much reason that the stream would be more moderate at that point.

Conrad Meadows is a good name and address in the Cascades. James H. Conrad, the man who homesteaded it and ran cattle in it for years, has a long-legged, clear eyed, friendly grandson, Norman Conrad, who runs cattle there today. Conrad Meadows is a mile or so long and perhaps a half-mile wide. It lies about 4000 feet above sea level. There are beautiful clumps of aspen in it and scatterings of black pine. We used to see knee-high grass there in early summer. The South Fork usually has a bit of the milk of glaciers in it, for a goodly portion of its supply comes off the Goat Rocks. But Conrad Creek, which joins the South Fork at the eastern edge of the Meadow, is always clear and cold. We would usually camp at that spot.

It was a friendly and hospitable camping place. Less than ten
miles to the west, standing way above an intervening ridge, is the
rugged nose of Gilbert Peak of the Goat Rocks, inlaid with a streak of
glacial ice and snow. There it stands alone, dominating the horizon.
Gilbert Peak, seen from the low-rimmed Conrad Basin, is an invitation for exploration. It has always drawn me like a magnet. It has
always lifted my heart. A peak that only nudges the sky with its nose,
leaving the rest concealed, has peculiar appeal. It suggests that what
lies beneath, hidden from view, may be valleys and lakes of unusual
mystery, basins and meadows of romance, glaciers agleam with breath-
taking thrills. Such is the special invitation that Gilbert Peak extends
from Conrad Meadows.

There was more than beauty in those meadows. The South Fork
was a good rainbow stream. Deep pools; long riffles; banks shaded by
pine, fir, and willow; fast, cold water; a stream 30 to 50 feet wide—
this was the South Fork. Here we developed our skills as fly-fisher-
men. Here we found a generous food supply of fat, fighting rainbow.

But the June day we arrived there the fishing was poor. Snow
water filled the river and we had little luck. We decided against
taking the trail through the steep draw on the south to the Klickitat
Meadows, which had been our original destination, for its stream too
would be full of snow water. So we watched the sun set over Gilbert
Peak, broke camp the next morning, and headed down the South
Fork to the Tieton Basin, some 12 to 14 miles to the northeast.

Along we went on the easy down trail lined with lupine, vanilla
leaf, huckleberry, cinquefoil, snowberry, and snowbrush not yet in
bloom. We never stopped once as Brad, in the lead, set a good pace of
three to four miles an hour. We crossed No Name Creek, Bear Creek,
and innumerable smaller streams that in midsummer are rivulets and
that now were freshets. We went through a grove of aspen and yellow
pine at Minnie Meadows, crossed Middle Creek and Grey's Creek,
and soon dropped into the Basin.

We camped that night at McAllister Meadows near the junction
of the North Fork and South Fork of the Tieton. To the north were
Westfall Rocks and Goose Egg Mountain. Between them Rimrock
Dam has since been erected to form the great reservoir that buried
McAllister Meadows forever under its waters. To the east were the
sheer cliffs of Kloochman, where once Doug Corpron and I almost
lost our lives. In the shadow of these mighty fortresses we had afternoon fishing in the North Fork. But it too was poor because of the
snow water. As a result we decided to head for Fish Lake, where we

were almost certain to get fish. It is a small, shallow lake whose waters are warm by early summer. Accordingly the next morning, shortly after sunrise, we started up the Indian Creek Trail.

One branch of this trail goes to the headwaters of Indian Creek just below Pear Lake, climbs to the Blankenship Meadows, passes Twin Sister Lakes and drops to Fish Lake—a good 18-mile hike. There is a fork in the trail about half-way to Pear Lake that leads west, passes near Dumbbell Lake, crosses Cowlitz Pass, skirts Frying-pan Lake, and, joining the trail out of the Twin Sisters, drops to Fish Lake. This was known as the Sand Ridge Trail. It was the one we decided to take.

We followed the North Fork of the Tieton through Russell Ranch, climbed out of the Basin on the right side of Indian Creek, passing Boot Jack Rock on our right. We were on the lower reaches of Russell Ridge until we came to the Sand Ridge Trail about seven miles from our starting point. Here the trail turns west, crosses Indian Creek, and climbs precipitously almost a thousand feet. At this point we struck snow. It was soft and slushy and it wet us through. We struggled in it for an hour or more, frequently losing the trail and expending energy far out of proportion to our progress.

We sat down on a ledge of rock for rest and consultation. Our decision was to turn back, to camp that night in McAllister Meadows, and the next day to go down the Tieton River to the Naches, then along the Naches to home.

We made an early camp in the Basin. It was not yet dark when we were eating our supper. Suddenly we said, almost in unison, "Why not go home tonight?"

Since then I have seen the same thing happen over and again. Men in the mountains, nearing the end of their trip, have an urge to cut it short by a day or two and bolt for home. For some reason the pull of home at once becomes overpowering and irresistible. And a man headed for home, like a horse headed for oats in his stable, is headstrong and unreasonable.

Once made, the decision to push on that night became irrevocable. We hurried to do the dishes and reassemble our packs before dark. They were already light, as we had been eating from them for about five days. We made them even lighter by leaving behind all the food except dried prunes and dried apples (which we put in our pockets and munched through the night) and some flour which we could use to bake bread if need be.

It was dark when we started. There was no moon; but the stars were out. We soon left Goose Egg Mountain as a great dark splotch against the western skyline, crossed Milk Creek, and keeping it on our left worked our way along the edge of a hillside until we descended to the Tieton River.

The trail crossed the river a mile or so later. The night was cold and the Tieton was filled with snow water. The water was frightfully cold as it swept above our knees in midstream, licking at the bottoms of the packs. We gained the other side with much splashing and muttering. My shoes were full of water, my teeth were chattering, I was chilled to the heart.

We stopped on the far bank to stomp and try to shake some water from our trousers. Then a chill cramp hit my leg muscles. Brad too was seized. If there had been any doubt whether we would push on, the cramps in our legs and our shivering and shaking settled it. It was plain that it would take hours for us to thaw and dry out in camp. The best way was to keep moving.

We covered thirty miles in those eight hours or more of darkness. It was the most drab and dreary hike I ever took. Many times I have come off a mountain in the dark or walked the high ridges in the blackness of night. Usually there is an exhilaration in it, for then most of the animals of the woods are on the move and all one's senses are quickened. But this night was oppressive.

All the way down we were in the narrow Tieton canyon whose walls rise a thousand feet or so on each side. The bottom of such a canyon is naturally dark. It was a Stygian pit the night we traveled it. Shortly after we started, clouds had blotted out the stars and I could not see a hand in front of me.

The trail along the Tieton was in truth a dirt road at the point where we crossed the river. It grew still wider as we moved down the canyon. Most of the time therefore we walked abreast, never speaking, stumbling occasionally over a loose rock. The Tieton was high, as I have said. Soon we came to a portion of the road that had been overflowed. There was no detour we could find in the darkness. So for the second time we waded the icy water. More cramps made walking still more painful. But we had to keep moving to prevent the cramps from getting worse.

How many inhabitants of the darkness may have seen us I never knew. I saw none of them. A screech owl protested our invasion of the canyon. There was an occasional slithering sound in the dry grasses beside the road. But though rattlers infest the lower reaches of the Tieton, I heard none that night—it was too cold perhaps for snakes as sensitive as rattlers to be abroad. A piercing wind at our backs whirled and howled through the funnels of the canyon. It whipped the willows that lined the road so that occasionally they touched our faces.

Several hours before daybreak, we began to see against the sky the vague outline of the hills that rose on either side. This was the first break in the darkness that had enveloped us the night long. The dimly lighted skyline at once became a guide. My eyes were more and more upon it. Over and again I said to myself, "Surely, the next turn must mark the end of the canyon." My hope increased as the skyline of hills brightened. But on each turn the hope vanished; ahead another few hundred yards was another twist in the ravine. The canyon appeared to go on without end—and so it seems even to this day when I drive this canyon or any other like it. Each bend was like the bend behind, each was only the forerunner of a bend ahead. We were on a treadmill, plodding on and on but standing still.

Brad was a stout hiker. There was a mark of determination on his sharp features, an impression verified by his deep and almost gruff voice and by his shock of unruly light-brown hair. He stood about five feet ten and was all muscle. He was short-legged and sturdy. He usually set the pace on our trips. He seemed to me to have endless energy, and I was always proud to be able to keep up with him. Brad was the pace-setter this night. It was a slow steady pace, the pace of a plodder, the pace of one who is distributing his energies over a 40- or 50-mile stretch. It was the pace of marching men, like the one I became acquainted with in 1918. It was steady, on and on, left, right, left, right, through the night.

I was proud of my legs. They were so tired they felt numb. But they never failed. They did not cry out in anguish nor did they ache. The plop, plop of my feet sounded far away, remote, impersonal. I went down the canyon in the darkness, shoulder to shoulder with Brad. I was an automaton that had been set for a course and never missed a beat.

The dawn came stealthily. As the gray of the sky increased, the wind died down. Rocks and bushes and trees for the first time became recognizable, not in detail but as identifiable blotches on a landscape. Then they emerged in daylight, stark naked in their poverty. For we had left the pines and fir and green hillsides far behind us. We had left the Tieton and were in the lower reaches of the Naches canyon.

Mount Cleman, sterile and dry, was on our left. Its deep ravines, washed out by thousands of rains, looked in the dim light like folds of flesh on the face of an old, old person. So far as the eye could tell, the hills on both sides of the canyon were bare except for cheatgrass, bunchgrass, and sage. But as the sun rose, a soft green tinge touched them—the light green of tender shoots and of the myriad wild flowers that were scattered in the sage and grass. There were cottonwoods and oak in the draw and sumac and elderberry bushes by the river which gave a sparse greenness to the bottom of the canyon. A magpie appeared; but no other bird or animal greeted the dawn with us. The raven usually comes at this hour as the scavenger who picks up the carcasses of rabbits killed by the traffic of the night, but none was on hand this June morning.

Now we could get our bearings. We were on familiar ground, and realized at once that we were only three or four miles from Naches. We paused briefly for a rest, taking off our packs and stretching out on the side of the road. We did not plan to go to sleep; but we did. We could not have slept long, for the sun was not yet up when we were awakened by the clattering of a truck. It was a truck en route to pick up cream from farms in the Naches canyon. We rose, startled and unsteady, when we saw it bearing down on us as we lay sprawled with our feet in the road itself.

Once aroused we pushed on; and knowing that our goal was near, we picked up our pace. It was not long before there was a song in my heart. The sun was above the rim of hills to the east when I saw the village of Naches. Acres and acres of green alfalfa fields and scattered apple orchards lay before us, a friendly oasis in the desert. Only one who, in his great suffering throughout the night, despaired that morning would come, could have welcomed this sunrise more than I. I was so relieved to have the dark ordeal behind me that I did not appreciate how great was my fatigue. Since it was Sunday, no lunch counter would open until 8 o'clock. It was now about 6:30. And the train—known as Sagebrush Annie—that would take us to Yakima, would not go down until 11 o'clock. After 8, when at last I had my fill of ham, eggs, potatoes, and toast, an overwhelming drowsiness claimed me. I fell asleep on the station platform and was awakened by the clatter of the train.

The next I knew the conductor was shaking me. I was home, saying good-by to Brad. In spite of my fatigue I put the horseshoe pack over my shoulder and walked the half dozen blocks to my home with a spring in my legs. I was happy at heart if not in the flesh. I had walked with a pack over 40 miles in one day. I had walked the whole night through. I was proud of my legs. I wanted to shout "Look at my legs! Hear what I have done!" Remember, I was a boy. I wanted to laugh at the guys that said I had puny legs. I wanted to take them to the hills for a contest—an endurance contest, if you please. Brad and I could outwalk anyone in the valley.

And then I went to bed and slept from that noon until the sun was high the next day.

When I awoke, the doubt was gone forever. The achievement of walking 40 miles with a pack in one day had banished it, just as the sun rising over Naches had absorbed the long fingers of mist that hung over the hayfields yesterday morning.

ROY BEDICHEK

The Cedar Chopper

"Defeat was closing in . . ."

Roy Bedichek was born on the Illinois prairie, in 1878, the son of one of Quantrill's Raiders—a circumstance which early set his course in life south by west. He anchored at the University of Texas as director of the Interscholastic League, an organization encouraging athletic and academic competition among the state's high schools. There he became a fixture, part of a Lone Star triumvirate which included J. Frank Dobie and Walter Prescott Webb. Less known than his cohorts, Bedichek brought to his work the same deliberate spirit which marked theirs. He was all of sixty-eight years old when he set himself up in an old stone house near Friday Mountain to write his first book and walk himself out of the "shallows and miseries of routine" along the Pedernales. There is something metaphysical about the state of Texas, and about the men who have walked its distances. So it is not unusual that Roy Bedichek should stop to speculate on shadows, or hear through the cedar the slow and measured ticking of an axe—as sure as time, or death, which overtook him in 1959.

I was camped for a few days under a live oak of enormous spread crowning a bluff which overlooked the Pedernales River with its little pocket bottoms wedged in between cliff and water, strung along its winding course.

Striking camp is a relief something like that the snake feels in sloughing off his old skin. It saves washing up and disposes of stains no washing will remedy. The soiled page gives place to a fresh one with no fingerprints on it, exhaling a wind-washed odor as of bedclothes just in from a thorough airing and with the cleanliness of sun-dried dew upon them. If gypsies have that supersense of smell with which they are credited, it's no wonder that they are always on the move.

A stationary camp is quickly cluttered up. Stay too long or return to the same camping place too often, and the inevitable encrustation appears. You fix up a cupboard, install a bench between two trees, improvise a table. These and other little conveniences may be nothing more than a few pimples, but they indicate that the disease of civilization is setting in. You had better be on your way again; otherwise, you may build a camp house, then a summer home, then neighbors, and eventually find yourself right back where you started.

Moving camp is a sloughing-off process to be undertaken before there are any adhesions. This is the wisdom of the serpent.

Ill luck had shadowed me on this particular trip. I had tramped the river's narrow bottoms and had explored tributary creeks for three days without finding a new bird or learning anything new about an old one. It was early spring, too—time of all times for new things to be turning up, but they didn't choose to turn.

Nature has spells of reserve like this, or else your own spirit is asleep or preoccupied with something lodged in subconsciousness and fermenting there like the yeast of a neglected duty.

I have a theory that one never goes to nature in proper mood, patient and receptive as an earnest student should be, without learning something treasurable, but on this particular occasion defeat was closing in.

On the morning of the fourth day, I was busy packing up when the sun burst over the rim of a hill across the river, sudden as a revelation. I paused, skillet in hand, to look about. Well, I thought, this is rather pleasant and there's no need to hurry so. Why not stay until noon anyway?

I fell to looking at a shadow cast by the live oak across a glade and up a smooth slope to westward. I tried to recall the name and details of a story I had read once on a time about a man who lost his shadow—a fanciful tale; and I seemed to remember that the man had sold his shadow, and that the purchaser, perhaps the devil himself, kneeled and began rolling it tight up to the point where it joined the man's feet. Then with a quick jerk the buyer disengaged it from where it was hinged to the heels and, carefully placing it in his poke, moved off, sardonically wishing the now shadowless vendor good day. The story was concerned from then on with the embarrassments of being without a shadow.

From this I drifted into a consideration of the shadow of the live oak. For how many hundreds of years had this shadow fallen upon that same slope at sunrise, gradually shortening until midday, and then moved out eastward to the edge of the bluff, leaping the river to the rugged declivities on the other side.

I thought of the oak's laboring not to lose its shadow which swayed with the seasons, a little north returning then to center, then a little south, and back again, a pendulum geared only one complete swing in the solar year—a slow clock, but harmonious with the age of this long-lived tree, which, some authorities say, stays green a thousand years. Before Columbus this shadow with its diurnal climb, descent, and leap across the river, and with its yearly swing from north to south and back again, had caricatured the tree on slope and glade in the mornings and resumed its fantastic prank on the irregular ledges across the river in the afternoon.

Daily, for ages, the same routine. The first beams of the sun spread it far up the slope, grotesquely diffused. As the morning advances, it is pulled in, sharpened, contracted, and the caricature gradually subdued until at midday a clear and faithful outline of the great tree appears upon the grass. But all this labor goes for naught, for after a short siesta the truant begins escaping eastward and presently leaps from the bluff, landing light as a feather across the river among the tumbled boulders on the other side. Now it is in for steep and laborious climbing, but it manages to edge farther and farther away, finally to make good its escape into the purple hills.

We say of this oak (*Quercus virginiana*) that it is evergreen, but the word "ever" here means only "a long time and continuously," for even to the live oak the spring will finally come when the browned and yellowed leaves it sheds will not be replaced. It becomes first naked, then fleshless; "only the man of bone remains." Its early-morning shadow becomes a wilder caricature, sprawling, thinned, and sketchy; but, drawn up at midday, it verifies the skeleton which casts it—a skeleton trying to dominate its ghost.

I lingered around the camp until after lunch and then struck out across the hills. Following an abandoned wood road over the cedar-thicketed slope, I soon heard the wooing note of a paisano and sat down to look and listen. I have never decided whether to call this bird's amorous noises a croak or a moan. It's not dreary enough to be called a moan, and too melodious for a croak. It is a wandering, uncertain sound, now near, now far away, and fading out until you doubt whether you are hearing anything at all. I have heard it, however, only in the wooded hills, never on plains or prairies where it may have a different quality. Perhaps in this rough and wooded area it comes to the ear modified by leafy interference and by bouncing over boulders and glancing off cliffs or ledges, leaving a fragment of itself with each obstruction. Apparently the call is not tempered for such

tough going. Maybe sound experts in their laboratories can take it to
pieces and tell exactly what happens and why; but until then, I can
only say of this love call that it seems to issue from nowhere in
particular and go wandering about, seeking, but without much hope
of finding, "the nothing it set out from."

On this occasion, I had only a few moments to wait before the
paisano appeared, as I was sure he would, crest flushed and tail near
perpendicular. He stood there in the field of my binoculars for full
five minutes, stock-still except for a slight rotary motion of the head,
as if he were turning his glance now to the ground, now to the sky,
giving each eye a look up and a look down. Then, lowering his tail
and stretching his long neck forward, he made off, sneaking through
low growths in the direction of his answering mate.

The authorities accuse this bird of being careless about whose
nests she lays her eggs in, and of occasional cuckolding not only her
own kind but individuals of other species as well. The practice is not
habitual, however, as with our cowbird and with the Old World
cuckoos.

Presently, hoping for another glimpse of the paisanos who were
still carrying on their amorous converse, I heard the sound of an axe,
slow and measured—very, very slow. I thought it must be some Mexi-
can chopping by the day rather than by the post, the strokes fell with
such a manana tempo.

Keeping my direction for a little while, I saw through an opening
in the cedars a sight I shall never forget. My glasses brought him up
close—an aged man cutting cedar. It was obviously the weight of
years upon the trim, streamlined axe which had slowed it down. After
a dozen strokes or so, he leaned heavily upon a tree, his chest heaving.
As soon as his breathing quieted a little, he resumed his chopping,
slow, steady, and accurate to a hair, like the "slow-motion" of a
woodchopper to show correct form.

His gigantic frame was stripped to the waist. He was at least six-
feet-two, broad-shouldered, tapering to the hips, with an almost wasp-
like waist accentuated by a belt drawn tightly above the bony hips. In
full flesh this frame could carry two hundred pounds without feeling
it. He now weighed certainly less than one hundred and fifty. I did
not know until then that so much skin could be hung upon the bony
framework of a man. As his emaciated arms went up with the rising
stroke, there was at least a three-inch movement of skin across the
washboard of his ribs. Up and down, the loose skin slipped over those

regular furrows enclosing the mighty chest, making a ripple like water running across corrugations.

I now realized what the physiology books mean when they talk of a cushion of flesh—that's exactly what our flesh is, a cushion enclosed in skin. Remove the cushion, and the envelope wrinkles and sags. This man's flesh was gone and he was almost literally skin and bone. When his arms dropped to his sides, long, flapping bags of skin hung down at the juncture of arms with shoulders. Aged obesity is grotesque, but better fat flesh than none at all.

Then, focusing my glasses a little better, I saw something along the arms that gave me an additional start. The veins were as big as lead pencils or whipcords, and in the swinging of the arms these hard, huge, purplish blood vessels stretched and slipped under the skin.

Alas, poor Yorick! The grave-diggers arrived too late. A mere skeleton is unimpressive.

Stooping my way through the brush, I came near him and spoke, but he continued chopping. I raised my voice a bit, and still he paid no attention. I spoke louder, then shouted, and he turned his face slowly toward me. There were two large, ulcerous-looking sores on his face, one near the right temple and one on the cheekbone just below it. They had been dusted over with some medicament through which a trickle of sweat had furrowed its way down toward the point of his chin.

As he laid his axe aside, I noticed his hands—immense, bony, enormously veined over the backs and interiorly curved to fit an axe handle. The fingers looked as though they could never be straightened at all, and were hard and horny enough to crack a seed tick.

His eyes were blue and smiling, with a little clouding around the edges of the iris. Unlike the hardened beachcomber whose face Thoreau describes as "too grave to smile, too tough for tears," this man's countenance radiated good will. The skin of the face, contrasting with that of the torso, was drawn tight as a drum over a massive, bony structure, allowing little mobility, one would think, for emotional expression of any kind. But unmistakably he was smiling.

He began apologizing at once for the pitiful little pile posts he had hewed out since dinner, saying that, although he was old and not able to do much, still he wanted to do *something* or, he was afraid, he might soon become bed-ridden like his neighbor.

His voice was firm but he could not control its volume, since he was nearly deaf and had long been accustomed to speaking in wind and weather. He shouted at me and I at him, and the conversation which ensued could have been heard at some distance without benefit of amplifiers.

He told me that he couldn't do anything but cut cedar, since that was all he had ever done except to farm a little. I found that he was eighty-six years old and that here in this locality his father had put him to cutting cedar when he was only ten.

Seventy-six years cutting cedar!

I later learned that this man is wealthy. It was not economic necessity that forced him to this dismal labor, but a grim, determined fight against the helplessness which he feared old age would force upon him.

He thought he might die soon anyway, and that it was better to keep doing something. His neighbor, eighty-nine, was now in the hospital, had been in there four months, didn't know if he would ever get out—alive.

There was a reproach in the way he told me that this man "stopped doing something" at eighty-eight, and a suggestion that he was now being punished for his dereliction by confinement in the hospital and loss of his voice. "He can't talk any more, you know," he said.

This is the pioneer philosophy of being up and doing, of marching on to the end of the row, of never quitting. It is the gospel of salvation by work.

But the old fellow finally shook his head sadly. "I 'low," he said, "when a man is old there ain't much pleasure left for him; and when he's young, he ain't got sense enough to take care of himself,"—which observation George Bernard Shaw polished up into an epigram. Or maybe Mark Twain said this before Shaw did.

I asked the old man for the time. Glancing at the sun, he said "It's about four: I'd say the sun is two hours high."

"Well," I objected, "if it's only two hours high it must be five, as the sun sets at seven or thereabouts."

"Oh," he grunted, showing irritation, "that's by that fast time."

I sensed here the resentment out-of-door people feel toward artificial time—as if all measuring of time were not artificial—*fast* time, they call it. Tampering with sun time seems to them a sacrilege. Perhaps there's a survival of sun worship hidden deep down from long ago; and this city-folk presumption of telling the sun when to come up and when to go down is a blasphemy. Roosevelt lost more rural votes by tampering with time than he did by trying to modernize the Supreme Court.

All the way through his long novel, *The Magic Mountain*, Thomas Mann is continually tampering with time. He insists on divisions of time into occasions, such as Christmas and Easter; into routine, or the regular daily grind; or into periodical discomforts, such as holding a thermometer in your mouth seven minutes. He emphasizes the essential emptiness of the time concept. It is content of time that matters—all else: illusion. An attempt to divide the flow of time into watertight compartments, irrespective of content, introduces artificiality into our lives. Clocks, calendars, gongs may be a convenience for running a factory or a train, but they are in opposition to the spirit of life. Poets occasionally enlarge upon this point of view. Slipping into a featureless routine, clock-and-calendar governed, is slipping into something really worse than death, because you still remain conscious.

Routine machines our lives to conform to industrialization. Life is its opposite: dawn, stars, storms, calm, the witchery of twilight, the whimsicality of the seasons, and the vast and ample variety of the natural day—all proclaim an antagonism to routine.

I doubt the truth of the oft-told tale of the calendar-governed migrations of the swallows of Capistrano, because the whole of nature leans the other way. I tried for a number of years to make the purple martin arrive in the Texas state capital on March 2, Texas Independence Day. And they did arrive at my box for four consecutive years exactly on that date. Then, not wanting to spoil a good story, I began to fudge a little by not looking very hard until March 2, on which date I looked my eyes out and even called my friends by phone to find out if their martins had arrived. I accumulated six "straights" in this way and was about to offer my research for publication, when a group of four noisy martins awakened me on the morning of February 15 and stayed around the box the whole day, uttering their cool hello calls until the neighbors were brought in to witness.

The swallow cannot proceed north without flying insects with which to fuel his flight. Warm weather is necessary for insects to penetrate the high martin-zone. So cause-linking-cause leads back to the weather. If the weather were identical by calendar dates year after year from the martin's point of departure in Brazil clear to my martin box in Austin, Texas, then I might have made a Texas Independence Day bird out of him. But the great storms which sweep across his migration route, destroying the high-flying insects for hundreds of miles, have no dependable schedule. Neither have the martins. Nature ignores the calendar; she approves approximations, however.

The so-called literature of escape with its growing popularity is in part a revolt against the tyranny of clocks. It is not labor that kills, but the small attritions of daily routine that wear us down. A month of days, a year of months, twenty years of months in the treadmill is the life that slays everything worthy the name of life.

A camping companion of mine insists on leaving watches at home when we go out for a week or two in the woods or by the seashore. If we forget, he gathers those instruments and locks them up. He maintains that the sun, moon, and stars are time guides, and makes quite an oration which I have listened to many times, about adjusting your life to the rhythm of nature.

Another philosophical person I know, finding his life bounded in the shallows and miseries of routine, broke away with the determination to do something quite irrational every so often. He has become, after a few years of this, not a mere classroom instructor, as he had been for thirty years before, but a man of affairs, with houses, lands, and other investments to look after, and has recovered, so he declares, a little of the old joy of living.

As I resumed my walk, the slow strokes of the axe began again. I was reminded of the huge clock that used to stand on our mantel shelf when I was a boy. If one noticed carefully, he could tell by the slowing up of the tick-tock when the clock needed rewinding. But no rewinding will accelerate the tick-tocking of these strokes I hear today in the quiet cedar brake.

With the lengthening of the span of human life, the problems of old age become increasingly difficult. There is more old age now than there ever was, and science promises in the immediate future an even greater supply. . . . One rarely finds an animal in feral state suffering from sickness or old age. Life and death are here so nicely balanced that a feather out of place, a rheumatic stiffness in a joint, a motor reaction slowed down by a fraction of a second, or a dimmed vision means instant extinction. In a state of nature, nearly every individual animal must be in full possession of all his powers, mental and physical, to survive at all. No drunkenness or eating to excess is permitted. The sapsucker, drunk on fermented sap, falls an easy prey to the ever-watchful hawk, if indeed he does not dash himself to death against a limb with the usual overconfidence of inebriety. So also the robin, staggering about your lawn from overindulgence in chinaberries, is snapped up quickly by the harmful and unnecessary cat.

A sharp, unsentimental surgery obtains throughout the animate world. Mother Nature wants to see her creatures healthy and happy or not see them at all. It is only in domestication that man's physical ailments are conferred upon the lower animals.

Lingering illnesses and old age appear among herding animals wherever an exceptionally favorable environment produces a surplus over and above the number taken by the herd's predatory enemies. Buffalo hunters found aging bulls, which had been driven out of the herd, still surviving. J. W. Abert's *Journal* records meeting with an old buffalo bull, "which appeared reluctant to move out of our road. He looked old and was so gaunt that his skin hung upon him like wet drapery upon a skeleton." I have heard that old age appears also among the rabbit hordes of Australia. But these are the exceptions.

I once followed a distressful call through the woods for half an hour before finally identifying it. It was a sick mockingbird. When I finally got sight of him, he was sitting on a limb, tail down, wings loose at his side, and head hung forward. The sound he made was nothing like anything I had ever heard come from a bird's throat before or since. I accounted for his persistence in that state by the fact that he is such a terrific fighter that his enemies want to be sure he is quite incapable of resistance before attacking him. I have heard also that lions in a natural state sometimes die of old age because of the fear in which they are held by other denizens of the forest.

Trees, on the other hand, as well as vegetable life generally, are subject to diseases which do not kill; they have warts, wens, cancerous growths, grotesque deformities, and come gradually to declining years with definite symptoms of senility, lingering on and on.

As I finally turned back toward my camp under the shadow-troubled live oak, the sound of the cedar cutter's axe became fainter and fainter, until it seemed to be an echo loose in the lonely cedar brake. *Chop-tick, chop-tock,* steady, slow, and then a brief silence. Again, a dozen strokes or so and pause; until finally I could hear it no more.

HENRY BESTON

An Inland Stroll

"There was a sense of old times dead, new times beginning."

Henry Beston was thirty-nine years old when he moved into a wind-swept, two-room shack off Eastham on Cape Cod and began the lonely, elemental residence which resulted in his classic account, The Outermost House. *"The world today is sick to its thin blood for lack of elemental things," he wrote, "for fire before the hands, for water welling from the earth, for air, for the dear earth itself underfoot." From the outermost house, Henry Beston watched and walked alone, always with a patient, studying eye. In the account which follows, he captured with practiced precision the experience of one man afoot at the turning of the season.*

I devoted the entire day yesterday to an adventure I have long had in mind, a walk across the Cape from outer ocean to Cape Cod Bay. As the crow flies, the distance from the Fo'castle to the west shore is about four and a half miles; afoot and by the road, it is nearer seven and a half, for one must follow roads lying north of the great lagoon. The day was pleasant; cool, easterly winds blew across the moors, and it was warm enough when I found both shelter and the sun.

I walked to Nauset Station close along the landward edge of the dunes, out of sight and sound of the sea. All up and down these western gradients of grass and sand the plant life of the region is pushing through the surface drifts and sandy overflowings which crept eastward during winter; green leaves of the beach pea are thrusting up; sand crumbs still lodged in their unfolded crevices; the dune goldenrod is shouldering the bright particles aside. Against the new olive colouring of the dunes, the compact thickets of beach plum are as charred-looking as ever, but when I stroll over to a thicket I find its buds tipped with a tiny show of green.

Arriving at Nauset, I found my coast guard neighbours airing their bedding and cleaning house. Andrew Wetherbee hailed me from the tower; we shouted pleasantries and passed the time of day. Then down Nauset road I went, turning my back on ocean and a rising tide.

The first mile of the road from Nauset to Eastham village winds through a singular country. It is a belt of wild, rolling, and treeless sand moorland which follows along the rim of the earth cliff for two thirds of its length and runs inland for something like a mile. Nauset Station, with its tiny floor of man-made greenery, lies at the frontier between my dune world and this sea-girt waste. Coast guard paths and the low, serried poles of the coast guard telephone are the only clues to the neighbourhood of man.

Desolate and half desert as it is, this borderland of the Cape has an extraordinary beauty, and for me the double attraction of mystery and wide horizons. Just to the north of the station, the grass turns starveling and thin, and the floor of the border waste becomes a thick carpet of poverty grass, *Hudsonia tomentosa*, variegated with channels and starry openings of whitish sand. All winter long this plant has been a kind of a rag grey; it has had a clothlike look and feel, but now it wears one of the rarest and loveliest greens in nature. I shall have to use the term "sage green" in telling of it, but the colour is not so simply ticketed; it is a sage green, yes, but of an unequalled richness and sable depth. All along the waste, the increasing light is transmuting the grey sand of winter to a mellowness of grey-white touched with silver; the moor blanches, the plant puts on the dark. To my mind this wild region is at its best in twilight, for its dun floor gathers the dark long before the sunset colour has faded from the flattened sky, and one may then walk there in the peace of the earth gloom and hear from far below the great reverberation of the sea.

West of this treeless waste the Nauset road mounts to the upland floor of the Cape and to the inhabited lands.

When Henry Thoreau walked through Eastham in 1849, warding off a drenching autumnal rain with his Concord umbrella, he found this region practically treeless, and the inhabitants gathering their firewood on the beach. Nowadays, people on the outer Cape have their wood lots as well as inlanders. The tree that has rooted itself into the wind-swept bar is the pitch pine, *Pinus rigida*, the familiar tree of the outer Long Island wastes and the Jersey barrens. *Rigida* has no particular interest or beauty—one writer on trees calls it "rough and scraggly"—yet let me say no harm of it, for it is of value here: it furnishes firewood, holds down the earth and sand, and shelters the ploughed fields. In favourable situations, the pine reaches a height of between forty and fifty feet; on these windy sands, trees of the oldest growth struggle to reach between twenty-five and thirty. The trunk of this pine is brownish, with an overtone of violet, and seldom grows straight to its top; its leaves occur in a cluster of three, and its dry cones have a way of adhering for years to its branches.

They are forever burning up, these pitch-pine woods. A recent great fire in Wellfleet burned four days, and at one time seemed about to descend upon the town. Coast guard crews were sent to help the villagers. Many deer, they tell me, were seen running about in the burning woods, terror-stricken by the smoke and the on-coming crackle of the crest of flame. Encircled by fire, one man jumped into a pond; scarce had he plunged when he heard a plunge close by and found a deer swimming by his side.

The thickets were rusty yesterday, for the tree thins out its winter-worn foliage in the spring. As I paused to study a group of particularly dead-looking trees, I scared up a large bird from the wood north of the road; it was a marsh hawk, *Circus Hudsonius*. Out of the withered tops flew this shape of warm, living brown, flapped, sailed on, and sank in the thickets by the marsh. I was glad to see this bird and to have some hint of its residence, because a female bird of this species makes a regular daily visit to the dunes. She comes from somewhere on the mainland north of the marsh, crosses the northeast corner of the flats, and on reaching the dune aligns her flight with the long five miles of the great wall. Down the wall she comes, this great brown bird, flying fifteen or twenty feet above the awakening green. Now she hovers a second as if about to swoop, now she sinks as if about to snatch a prey—and all the time advancing. I have seen her flutter by the west windows of the Fo'castle so near that I could have touched her with a stick. Apparently, she is on the watch for beach mice, though I have as yet seen no mouse tracks on the dunes. She arrives between ten and eleven o'clock on practically all fair weather mornings, and occasionally I see her search the dunes again late in the afternoon. *Circus Hudsonius* is a migrant, but some birds spend the winter in southern New England, and I have a notion that this female has wintered in Nauset woods.

Once Nauset road approaches Eastham village the thickets of pitch pines to the eastward fall behind, the fields south of the road widen into superb treeless moorlands rolling down to the shores of the great lagoon, orchard tops become visible in hollows, and a few houses sit upon the moors like stranded ships. Eastham village itself, however, is not treeless, for there are shade trees near many houses and trees along the road.

All trees on the outer Cape are of interest to me, for they are the outermost of trees—trees with the roar of breakers in their leaves— but I find one group of especial interest. As one goes south along the main highway, one encounters a straggle of authentic western cottonwoods, *Populus deltoides*. The tree is rare in the northeast; indeed, these trees are the only ones of their kind I have ever chanced to find in Massachusetts. They were planted long ago, the village declares, by Cape Codders who emigrated to Kansas, and then returned, homesick for the sea. The trees grow close by the roadside, and there is a particularly fine group at the turn of the road near Mr. Austin Cole's. In this part of the Cape, an aerial fungus paints the trunks of the deciduous trees an odd mustard-orange, and as I passed yesterday by the cottonwoods I saw that the group was particularly overspread with this picturesque stain. The growth seems to do no harm of any kind.

At a boulder commemorative of the men of Eastham who served in the Great War, I turned south on the main highway and presently reached the town hall and the western top of the moorland country. There I left the road and walked east into the moors to enjoy the incomparable view of the great Eastham marshes and the dunes. Viewed from the seaward scarp of the moors, the marsh takes form as the greener floor of a great encirclement of rolling, tawny, and treeless land. From a marsh just below, the vast flat islands and winding rivers of the marsh run level to the yellow bulwark of the dunes, and at the end of the vista the eye escapes through valleys in the wall to the cold April blue of the North Atlantic plain. The floor of the ocean there seems higher than the floor of the marsh, and sailing vessels often have an air of sailing past the dunes low along the sky. A faint green colours the skyline of the dunes, and on the wide flanks of the empty moorlands stains of springtime greenness well from the old tawniness of earth. Yesterday I heard no ocean sound.

So beautiful was the spacious and elemental scene that I lingered a while on the top of the moor cliff shelving to the marsh. The tide was rising in the creeks and channels, and the gulls remaining in the region had been floated off their banks and shoals. The great levels seemed, for the moment, empty of their winged and silvery life.

During the winter, one bird has made this moorland region all his own, and that bird the English starling. The birds apparently spend the winter on these hills. I have crossed the open country during a northeast gale just to watch them wheeling in the snow. Scarce had one flock settled ere another was up; I saw them here and there and far away. I find these Eastham birds of particular interest, for they are the first American starlings I have seen to recover their ancestral and European mode of life. In Europe, the bird is given to

congregating in vast flocks—there are river lowlands in England where such starling flocks gather in crowded thousands—and once this starling army has established itself in a region it is theirs completely and forever.

Are the flocks at Eastham the beginning of one of those European mobs? Will the various flocks now inhabiting the moors ultimately mingle to form one enormous and tyrannous confederacy? The separate winter swarms already consist of fifty to seventy-five birds, and I imagine that, if the stray members of each flock were to return to their congregations, these bands might be found to contain well over a hundred individuals. Such a mingling as I speak of may possibly take place; again, it may be that the resources of the region are already taxed to support the present birds; let us hope that this last is the truth. The presence of these rabble blackbirds disturbs the entire natural economy of the region, for they strip every autumnal bush and plant bare of its last seed and berry and leave nothing for our native birds to feed on when they return in the spring.

With spring, the birds desert the moors, pair off, and retire to the village barns and the chimneys of unopened summer cottages.

The hour of flood tide approaching, I left the moors behind and went to the west shore to see what I could of the strangest of all regional migrations.

Some five years ago, on a night in early April, I happened to be aboard a United States naval vessel bound coastwise from the southern drill grounds to New York. Our course lay well out of sight of land; the night was springlike, still and mild, the stars thick-sown in a faintly hazy sky. I remember that we saw the lights of a few ships standing in to Philadelphia. Once these had dimmed and disappeared behind, the sea was entirely our own, a vast, lonely, still, and starlit sea. Just after one o'clock I saw ahead of us on the sea a field, a shimmer of pale light, formless as the reflection of a cloud and mysteriously troubled by auroral undulations. We had overtaken a migration of fish moving north along the coast with the advance of spring. The skirts of the sun's robe, trailing over the ocean, stir the deep, and its mysterious peoples move North on the fringes of the light. I do not know what species of fish I chanced that night to see, for there is a definite and populous area of marine life lying between Hatteras and Cape Cod. They may possibly have been herring. As our vessel neared the living shoal, it seemed to move as one thing, there coursed through it a new vibration, and it turned east, grew vague, and vanished completely in the night.

Every spring even such a fish migration, moving through ocean as mysteriously as the force of a wave, breaks against our south New England shore. In colonial times the younger Winthrop wrote of it, telling of "the coming up of a fish called aloofes into the rivers. Where the ground is bad or worn out, the Indians used to put two or three of the forementioned fishes under or adjacent each corn hill. The English have learned like husbandry where these aloofes come up in great plenty." This "aloofe" of the colonists, better known as the "alewife," and often and incorrectly called a "herring," is really not a herring at all but a related fish, *Pomolobus pseudoharengus*. It is distinguishable from the true sea herring by its greater depth of body and by the serrations on the midline of its belly which are stronger and sharper than those of the true herring—so sharp, indeed, that the fish is sometimes called a "saw belly." In April they leave the sea and run up our brooks to spawn in freshwater ponds.

There is a famous brook in Weymouth, Massachusetts, which I try to visit every year. I remember the last warm April day. The "herring" brook—it is scarce more than ten or twelve feet wide and hardly more than a foot deep—was flowing freely, its clear brownish waters rippling almost noiselessly in the morning light. The fish were "in," moving up the brook as thickly massed as a battalion along a narrow road; there were no ranks—only an onward swarming. So numerous were the fish, and so regimented, that I stopped at the water's edge and easily caught two or three with my bare hand. Through the brownish stream the eye looked down to numberless long backs of a subdued dark lavender-grey and to a fleet of dorsal fins breaking water. The brook smelt of fish. Here and there were dead ones, aground on the edges of the stream or held by the current against a rock; dead things lying on their sides, with opaque, slime-coated eyes, and rock bruises on their sides—raw spots of fish blood red in a side of brown and golden scales. Sometimes the advance seemed stilled till the studying eye perceived the constant individual advance. A hundred thousand had come.

These alewives of Weymouth come up out of the sea, and from Heaven knows just where out of the sea. They run up Weymouth Brook, are stopped by a dam, are fished out in a net, dumped into barrels of water, and carted overland in a truck to Whitman's Pond. I have watched them follow currents in the pond, once they have been spilled out into it. Then comes, perhaps, a sense of arrival and intended time; each female lays from sixty thousand to a hundred thousand glutinous eggs, these drop to the bottom, drift along the

mud, and ooze and attach themselves as chance directs. The spawn-
ing females and the males then go over the dam and back to sea, the
herring born in the pond follow them ten months or a year later, and
then comes another spring and a great mystery. Somewhere in the
depths of ocean, each Weymouth-born fish remembers Whitman's
Pond, and comes to it through the directionless leagues of the sea.
What stirs in each cold brain? what call quivers as the new sun strikes
down into the river of ocean? how do the creatures find their way?
Birds have landscape and rivers and headlands of the coast, the fish
have—what? But presently the fish are "in" at Weymouth, breasting
the brook's spring overflow to the ancestral pond.

Some remember Whitman's Pond, others remember the ponds
of the Cape. There are "herring" ponds and "herring" brooks on the
map of Eastham.

The road to the bay leads off at the town hall, passing an old
windmill which still has its grinding machinery in place. I entered it
once, long ago, to see the dusty chutes, the empty bins, and the stones
in their cheese-box cases of ancient and mellow wood. Locust trees
inclose it, and song sparrows perch on the arms that have not turned
for years. I heard one as I trod the dusty floor, his mating song entering through a broken pane. Beyond the mill, the road passes a scatter
of houses, crosses the railroad track, winds between the ponds of
Eastham, and then comes to an open mile of sandy fields and pitch-
pine country extending to the bay.

The road descends, for the bay rim of the outer Cape is lower
than the ocean wall. North of the road, it is but a bank at the end of
fields. Accustomed to the roar of the ocean beach and to the salt wind
in my ears, the quiet of the bay fell strangely about me. There was no
surf, scarce a lakelike ripple; masses of weed, shaped in long undulations by water waves, lay heavy on the beach; forty miles across, earth-
blue beyond blue water, and mounded and separate as so many isles,
appeared the highlands of Plymouth woods and Sagamore. A few
ducks were feeding more than a mile offshore, and, as I watched, a
solitary drake rose from the broad marshes to my right and flew off to
join them.

The quiet of the bay, the subdued easterly blowing across the
fields, the belt of winter weed, the glint and warmth of the sun, the
solitary bird—there was a sense of old times dead and of new times
beginning—recurrence, life, the turn of the sun's wheel, always the
imperative, bright sun.

I walked along the beach to the mouth of the "herring" brook.

The stream is but a clogged gully of clean water running down to the sea through the sandy open meadows. Arriving at the shore, it spills out over the beach and trickles down to the bay. Low tides wash at the trickling rills and cover them; high tides climb the beach and enter a pool which has formed at the mouth behind a dam of weed. Yesterday, the low course tide had scarce touched the edge of the barrier and had begun to ebb an hour before my coming. Between the dam and the high-tide mark of the day lay a twenty-foot interval of beach traced by flat rillets seeping from the barrier. I looked into the pool. The "herring" had been in, for there was a dead one lying on the bottom of weed, a golden fish silted over with fine mud.

Suddenly, on chancing to look bay-ward, I saw a small school of "herring" just off the mouth of the brook and scarce more than fifteen feet from the motionless rim of the tide. There were, perhaps, fifty or a hundred fish in the school. Occasional fins chopped the quiet water. "Herrings" of Eastham brook unable to enter the pond in which they were born, barred from it by a dam of Nature's making. As I stood looking off to the baffled creatures, now huddled and seemingly still in deeper water, now huddled and all astir in the shallowest fringes of the tide, I began to reflect on Nature's eagerness to sow life everywhere, to fill the planet with it, to crowd with it the earth, the air, and the seas. Into every empty corner, into all forgotten things and nooks, Nature struggles to pour life, pouring life into the dead, life into life itself. That immense, overwhelming, relentless, burning ardency of Nature for the stir of life! And all these her creatures, even as these thwarted lives, what travail, what hunger and cold, what bruising and slow-killing struggle will they not endure to accomplish the earth's purpose? and what conscious resolution of men can equal their impersonal, their congregate will to yield self life to the will of life universal?

The tide ebbed, swiftly shallowing over the flats, the "herring" vanished from sight like a reflection from a glass; I could not tell when they were gone or the manner of their going.

Returning to the outer beach late in the afternoon, I found the ocean all a cold jade-green sown with whitecaps, the wind rising, and great broken clouds flowing over from the east. And in this northern current was a new warmth.

CHARLES F. LUMMIS

Shadows in the Sky

"One had then to earn his passage . . ."

Charles F. Lummis called himself a "man who got outside the fences of civilization and was glad of it." He liked mustard on his pie, and he took the longest walk in this collection: a thirty-five-hundred-mile tramp across the continent from Cincinnati to Los Angeles. A native of Massachusetts, Lummis could claim descent from John Paul Jones. He was educated at a female seminary (which his father administered), and dropped out of Harvard three days before commencement because of "brain fever." For a time, he managed a farm in Ohio. Then he turned to journalism. Two years of running the Scioto Gazette *convinced him that he needed a walk; so off he hiked to California, and a job as city editor of the Los Angeles* Times. *The West fenced Lummis in, and he blossomed as a writer, editor, librarian and evangelist of the Great Southwest. "God made California," he finally decided, "and He made it on Purpose." At the time of his cross-country walk, Lummis was twenty-five years old, full of swagger and brag. We follow him here—"knocking over an antelope now and then"—as far as Pike's Peak. Lummis died in 1928 of advanced cancer of the brain; in the end, he still preferred flint and steel to matches.*

This account is abridged from A Tramp Across the Continent, *by Charles F. Lummis, published in 1892.*

On the 11th of September, 1884, I left Chillicothe by rail for Cincinnati,—that ninety miles being already an old story,—and from the latter city began next day my long walk. I wore a close, but not tight, knickerbocker suit,—one who has not learned the science of walking doesn't dream what an aggregate hampering there is in that two feet of flapping trousers below the knee,—with flannel shirt, and low, light Curtis & Wheeler shoes. My rifle went by express to Wa Keeny, Kansas, where I was to shoulder it; and my small valise and light, but capacious duck knapsack made their daily marches on the broader shoulders of the express companies. In my pockets were writing-material, fishing-tackle, matches, and tobacco, and a small revolver, which was discarded for a forty-four-calibre later on. A strong hunting-knife, the most useful of all tools, hung at my belt, and in a money-belt next to my skin was buttoned $300 in $2.50 gold pieces, which would not suffer from perspiration as paper money would, and was of small denomination, as was necessary in a trip where the changing of a $20 piece would have cost my life in a hundred places.

It might be interesting to detail my experiences in trudging across the corner of Ohio, the whole length of Indiana and Illinois; but it would make this story too long, and it were better that the space be saved for the greater interest and excitement of the tramp in the farther West. The weather was hardly the best for walking. Across the first two States it was oppressively hot, and then I had several days of trudging in a pouring rain. However, it did not drench the spirits within, and it was welcome as an experience.

Crossing the noble bridge which wades, with giant legs of gran-ite, across the Father of Waters at St. Louis, I followed the general course of the Missouri Pacific Railroad across Missouri, having some funny experiences with back-country people; and at last a bit of adventure a little west of Warrensburg. From over the hedge of a cosy little farmhouse a huge and savage dog leaped in pursuit of me. He did not come to bark,—that was plain from the first,—but on busi-ness. He evidently liked strangers—and liked them *raw*. He did not pause to threaten or reconnoitre, but made a bee-line for me; and when close, made a savage leap straight at my throat. My hunting-knife chanced to be at my hand, and as he sprang I threw up a light switch in my left hand. He caught it in his big jaws; and in the same instant, with the instinct of a boxer, I gave a desperate "upper cut" with my hunting-knife. The strong, double-edged, eight-inch blade caught him squarely under the throat, and the point came out of his forehead, so fierce had been the blow. He never made a sound except a dying gurgle; and tugging out the bedded blade by a violent effort I hastened to depart, leaving him stretched in the road.

A couple of days later two cheap tramps of the ordinary sort "held me up" during one of my returns to the railroad. They were burly, greasy fellows, the first glance at whom assured me that they were cowards, and not worth serious treatment. They were both so much larger than I that they did not deem it worth while to take even a club to me, and one of them grabbed my coat with sublime confi-dence. My weapons were handy, but unneeded. The largest fellow stood just in front of the rail, so loose, so unbalanced, that it would have been a sinful waste of opportunity not to tumble him. Just as he

reached his left hand for my watch, biff! biff! with left and right—his
heels caught on the rail and down he went as only a big and clumsy
animal can fall. Then I whipped out the knife and started for the
amateur robbers, with a murderous face, but chuckling inwardly—a
chuckle which broke into open laughter as they fled incontinently
down the track, their tatters streaming behind upon the wind. It was
cheap fun and no danger, for I was armed and they were not; and the
laugh lasts whenever I recall their comical cowardice.

At Independence, Missouri, I heard a good deal of the notorious
train robbers and murderers, the James "boys," and had a long talk
with Frank James, who was the brains of the gang, as his unlamented
brother Jesse was its authority. He looked very little like the typical
desperado—a tallish, slender, angular, thin-chested, round-shoul-
dered, dull-eyed fellow, of cunning but not repulsive face, and an
interesting talker. The home nest of the outlaws was about Independence, and many of the citizens who were not their sympathizers had
participated in some of the exciting attempts to capture the criminals.
Frank was as free as you or I, a prominent figure at the county fairs,
and a rather influential personage,—all of which struck me as a trifle
odd. I found him in the post-office, reading his big bundle of mail—
most of which, as the chirography betrayed, was from the "softer"
sex. His hands were long, taper, and flexible; his feet particularly
"well-bred." He talked unreservedly of his trials, and was very sar-
castic about the then fashionable habit of attributing to his "gang"
most of the crimes in the United States. I also ran across several of
the self-appointed heroes who had sought and conscientiously failed
to catch the miscreants after their various robberies and murders, and
heard of their blood-curdling adventures.

For several days after leaving Kansas City my course lay along
the pretty valley of the Kansas River, properly named the Kaweily,
but in common parlance the Kaw; and very pleasant days they were. I
made quick work of "stepping off" Kansas; and, after the Kaw Valley
had fallen behind me, with daily growing interest. A couple of hundred miles from Kansas City it began to feel as if I were getting
"really out West." In one day I stepped upon a young rattlesnake—
which was luckily too cold and sluggish to strike me before I could
jump off—and saw my first "dog town," with its chattering rodents
and stolid owls, my first sage-brush and cactus and cattle rancho. And
the Plains impressed me greatly. They seemed lonelier and more
hopeless than mid-ocean. Such an infinity of nothing—such a weight

of silence! The outlook was endless; it seemed as if one could fairly see the day after to-morrow crawling up that infinite horizon!

Trudging up the long, smooth acclivity, pausing now and then for a shot at the flocks of sandhill cranes that purred far overhead, I stepped across the imaginary line into Colorado—my fifth State—and in the cool, enchanted dusk of an October evening swung into First View. The "town" consisted of a section house, where a supper of rancid bacon, half-raw potatoes, leaden bread flounced with sorghum, and coffee which looked exactly like some alkaline pools I wot of and tasted as cheerful, encouraged my lonely belt to reassert itself. There was no temptation to sleep in the infested house, and after supper I found a luxurious little gully in the grassy plain, gathered a little resin-weed for a pillow, spread my sleeping-bag on the soft sand, and turned in. Just as I was dozing off a tiny patter roused me, and, opening my eyes, I saw the sharp, inquisitive face of a coyote looking down at me from the bank not five feet above. I slid my hand softly to my forty-four, but he was off like a shot, carrying with him the pretty pelt for which I was so anxious.

Next morning, before the sun had climbed above the bare, brown divides of Kansas, I rolled out of "bed," danced about a few moments in the cold morning air to unlimber my joints, and then hastened to introduce my chattering teeth to a breakfast which would have swamped any less burglar-proof stomach. Its only merit was that it was warming. As the day burst into bloom, the section people pointed out the faint patch of white upon the far-off western sky from which First View takes its name—the noble head of Pike's Peak, which half a century ago was one of the saddest and most romantic goals toward which man ever struggled. It is nearly one hundred and fifty miles from First View.

Then, filling the long magazine of my Winchester and stowing a quart bottle of water in one of the capacious pockets of my coat, I struck out at a rapid gait northwestwardly, desiring to hunt well out into the plain and still get back to Kit Carson, fifteen miles ahead, before night. It is no easy walking upon the plains at this season of the year. The short, brown buffalo grass soon polishes one's soles till they shine like glass, and directly the feet slip, so that it is rather hard to tell whether the step carries one farther forward or the slide farther back.

Ten slippery miles must have been traversed in this dubious and aggravating locomotion before my eyes rested on the object of their search. Three or four miles off, in a low divide, were four tiny gray dots. They had no apparent shape, nor did they seem to move; but the hunter's eye—even when it has been abused by years in chasing the alphabet across a white page—is not easily fooled. They were antelope—and the next thing was to get them.

The theories of antelope-hunting were sufficiently familiar to me by reading, but when put into practice they did not fully bear out the books. A big red bandanna, tied to the end of my bamboo staff, was soon flapping to the wind, and I lay fully an hour behind a handy rosette of the Spanish dagger, innocently expecting my game to come straight up to me—as they should have done according to all precedent in the stories. Their attention soon grasped my signal, and they did sidle toward me by degrees, demurely nibbling the dry grass as they advanced. But they had probably seen auction flags before, and after perhaps a mile of their herbivorous advance they stopped, and even began grazing away from me. It was plain that any further advances toward an acquaintance must come from me.

Leaving the banner snapping in the wind, I crawled backward on my stomach some hundred yards to the foot of my low ridge, and then, behind its shelter, started on a dog-trot up the ravine. For half a mile or so this shelter lasted, and thence I had to crawl flat on my face from sage-brush to cactus and from cactus to sage-brush, for fully a mile, dragging the rifle along the ground, and frequently stabbed by inhospitable cactus needles. At last, only three hundred yards away, I pushed the Winchester over a little tuft of blue-stem; but before my eye could run along the sight, the buck gave a quick stamp, and off went the four like the wind. It was a very sore hunter that clambered stiffly to his feet and shook an impotent fist at those vanishing specks, already half a mile away, and limped back to where the flag and coat were lying.

But ill-luck can never outweary perseverance; and a couple of hours later came my revenge. Just as my head came level with the top of an unusually high swell a sight caught my eye which made me drop as if shot. There in the hollow, not over two hundred and fifty yards away, were three antelope grazing from me—an old buck with two-inch prongs on his antlers, a young buck, and a sleek doe. By good luck they did not suspect my presence, and it must have been minutes that I watched the pretty creatures through a tuft of grass before I pulled the trigger. As the smoke blew back past me I saw the old buck spring high in the air, run a few rods, and pitch forward upon the earth. His companions stood bewildered for a second, unknowing which way to run, and that hesitation was fatal to the young buck. He started north, but before he had run a hundred feet another bullet broke his spine. Before another cartridge could jump from magazine to barrel the doe was out of sight.

Beautiful animals are these shy rovers of the plains, graceful and slender as a greyhound, and fleeter of foot. I can think of nothing else so agile. They seem, when scared, not to run, but rather to fly upon the wind like exaggerated thistle-downs. They stand about three feet high, and weigh from forty to sixty pounds, but the smallest seemed to me much nearer six tons by the time I had "packed" him twenty miles. It took an hour's work, and the scouring of several acres to get together enough sage-brush, blue-stem and the bulbous root of the soapweed to build a fire which would roast a few pounds of steaks, and despite the bitter ashes with which it was covered, meat never tasted better.

The later afternoon brought another experience—different, but no less exciting. A lucky shot brought down a large hawk at very long range, and I went over to get him. Coming back through a patch of thick, tall, gumbo grass to where my antelope and blanket lay, I was wading carelessly along when a sharp sk-r-r-r! under my very feet, sent me about a yard into the air. There were my tracks in the broken stems on each side of a big rattler. I had stepped right across him! Now he had thrown himself into a coil and was in unmistakably bad humor, with angry head and the dry whir of his tail, which moved so fast as to look like a yellow sheet. From boyhood I have had a curious affection for snakes—an attraction which invariably prompts me to play with them awhile before killing them when the one-sided romp is over. Even the scare of a rattlesnake bite on my forefinger, and the memory of its torture, have not taught me better.

Now I poked out the muzzle of my rifle to his angry snakeship, and no eye could follow the swift flash in which he smote it, his fangs striking the barrel with a little tick, as though a needle had been stabbed at a pane of glass. I know of nothing more dreamily delicious than to tease a rattler with some stick or other object just long enough to keep those grim fangs from one's own flesh. I have stood for hours thus, thoughtless of discomfort, carried away by the indescribable charm of that grisly presence. Perhaps the consciousness of playing with death and as his master contributes something of that charm. Be that as it may, no one who has ever played with a rattle-snake can fully disbelieve the superstition that it fascinates its prey. I have felt it often—a sweet dreaminess which has tempted me to drop the stick and reach out my arms to that beautiful death.

When our play was over, and it was time to hasten toward Kit Carson, I pinned the neck of the snake to the ground with the broad muzzle of the rifle, and reached around for my hunting-knife to chop off that unsafe head. Just as I was stooping thus above him he writhed loose, and quicker than thought made a lunge at my face. That hideous open mouth, which in that instant seemed larger than my hand, came within three or four inches of my nose; but luckily he struck short—for my wild jump backward was not a tithe swift enough to have escaped. But I must have made a considerable dent in the atmosphere. At last I got him pinned down again and finished him.

Kit Carson, which I reached that night, was a sad example of the "floating towns" of early Colorado. When it was the terminal of the track, it was a rough, bustling place of 6000 people. But soon the railroad poked a few miles further through the brown plains; the houses of Kit Carson were torn down and moved to the new terminus, and so it went; and the cities of a day had soon left only a station and dugout or two, up to which the coyotes sneaked impudently as of yore.

Saturday night brought me to Bo-ye-ro—a little water tank thirty miles west of Kit Carson—after a long, vain hunt for antelopes. The only game I saw was one "cotton-tail" (the small, ordinary rabbit), and he was in such a sorry pickle that I made no offer to shoot him. A huge, dark eagle, with swooping wings that must have spread over six feet, had his big, sharp talons fixed in the poor little fellow's wool, and flopped along over him as he ran. How the rabbit yelled! In that still, open air you might have heard him a mile, and his screams were almost human in their agony. Before the great bird had flown away with his quarry, however, he spied me and scared off, while poor cotton-tail limped to his hole to die—for a rabbit never survives even a trifling scratch.

My stomach is never likely to forget those days across the Colorado plains. Meals were procurable only at the far-apart section-houses—and such meals! Had it not been for the rifle I should probably have been starved out. Tough and ancient corned beef; bread the color and consistency of Illinois mud; coffee suggestive of the Ohio "on a raise"; fermented molasses; butter which needs no testimonial from me, being old enough to speak for itself; and potatoes with all the water the rivers lack—that was the range of the bill of unfair. A fifty-verse song, which one of the section-men at White Horse sang, touched a responsive chord of my abused within:—

> *"His bread was nothin' but corndodger,*
> *His beef you couldn't chaw,*
> *But he charged us fifty cents a meal*
> *In the State of Arkansaw!"*

As for the sleeping, the softest beds to be found—and the only clean ones—were the sand and the grass; and upon them I stretched my sleeping-bag nightly, writing till late by the wavering fire of grass and little roots, and then turning over for so sweet a sleep as beds of down seldom know. My feet, too, shared the adversity, though now so tough. In hunting I was continually stepping—when my eyes were busy—into patches of the prickly pear, and more than once the maddening needles pierced shoes and feet.

But for these drawbacks there were equal atonements. That high, dry air was an exhilarating joy to the swelling lungs; and the eyes, sharpened daily to their long-forgotten keenness, feasted full on a sight whose memory will never dim. The snowy range of the Rockies, shutting the whole western sky from north to south, far as sight could reach—dazzling white by day, melting to indescribable purples at dawn and dusk, distant, severe, and cold—they are the pictures of a lifetime.

Near Magnolia a hard, mean-faced, foul-mouthed fellow met me, and before I fairly noticed him, had a cocked revolver under my nose with a demand to "give up my stuff." I was considerably worried, but a look into his eyes convinced me that he lacked what is called, in the expressive idiom of the plains, "sand." "Well," I drawled, "I haven't very much, but what there is you are welcome to," and unbuttoning my coat deliberately, as if for a pocketbook, I jerked out the big, hidden forty-four, knocked the pistol from his fist with the heavy barrel in the same motion, and gave him a turn at looking down a muzzle. Now he was as craven as he had been abusive, and begged and knelt and blubbered like the cowardly cur he was. I pocketed the pistol, which is still among my relics, gave him a few hearty kicks and cuffs for the horrible names he had called me when he was "in power," and left him grovelling there.

So, striding across the bare, dry plateaus, over the alkali-frosted sands of waterless rivers, glad in the glorious air and the glorious view, knocking over an antelope now and then, companioned by squeaky prairie dogs and sung to sleep by the vociferous coyotes, I came, on the 23d of October, to handsome, wide-awake Denver, the Queen City of the plains.

Here I met my family, who had come by the swifter but less interesting Pullman, and we had four happy days together before they started for San Francisco by the Central Pacific, and I donned my knapsack again and turned my tough feet southward. And what a glorious revenge those four days in civilization gave my stomach upon its weeks of adversity! The waiters at the Windsor used to stand along the wall in respectful awe to see that wilderness of dishes before me explored, conquered, and finally overwhelmed!

With an increased and decidedly irksome load I walked south from Denver, planning to reach Colorado Springs as speedily as possible, and thence make numerous side trips; but we spin not the thread of Clotho. At Acequia (a town named after the Spanish irrigating ditch, and popularly pronounced Saky) an accidental chat with the section foreman threw me a fortnight out of my course. He said there were "trout over behind yan hogbacks"—pointing to a long, rocky wall at the foot of the range, some twenty miles away. Trout? *Trout!* Why, for three years I had been fairly starving for a bout with those beauties—a hunger which the catfish and "lamplighters" of Ohio had utterly failed to satisfy. Hardly pausing to thank the herald of joyful tidings, I took a bee-line across the rough plain at a five-mile gait, forgetful of dinner, my load—and indeed of everything save my polka-dotted idols over younder. The range looked but two or three miles away at the outset; but when I had walked rapidly for three solid hours and the dusk was closing in, it seemed farther away than ever, and the wolf began to knaw at my belt. Just in the edge of night I found a shabby little cabin on Plum Creek, whose kindly, inquisitive folk found a good supper and a good bed for me. But my heart sank when they declared with great positiveness that there were no trout within two days' march, and they "reckoned they mout know, bein's they'd lived in them mount'ns goin' on twenty year." So to-morrow I was to have no trout, but only that pretty tramp back to the railroad. I dreamt that night a monster trout was swallowing the section foreman; and I heartily wished the dream might come true.

But with the morning came better thoughts. I would see for myself—and sunrise found me scrambling over the steep, rocky foothills toward Turk's Head. At two in the afternoon a sandy side ravine brought me suddenly out into the bottom of the Platte Cañon, beside the shouting river. A glorious little stream it is—clear and confident and headstrong as youth, cold as ice, swift as an arrow, rollicking noisily along the tortuous, boulder-strewn channel it has chiselled, down through a thousand feet of granite.

Two minutes later I was trimming the branches from a long, heavy young cottonwood, and attaching a line. Grasshoppers were plenty in the cañon—and soon plenty in the case of my harmonica. Just where a huge ledge jutted twenty feet into a deep pool of delicious green I made the first cast. As the 'hopper fell within a foot of the water, whizz! came a flash from the depths high into the air, smote the bait with dexterous tail, and drove it straight into an open mouth. Splash! Swish! Off went the line, sawing through the deep water, while that twenty-pound mollusk of a pole bent fairly double. What a glorious electricity it is that tingles through your fingers at that first strike of a trout. It took me full five minutes to land my game, though he weighed but three-quarters of a pound; and when he flopped beside me on the bank I threw up my hat and whooped and danced as wildly as twenty years before. During the afternoon I caught twenty more, and in that whole noble string one could not tell "t'other from which," so exactly were they of a size.

I finally got back to the little rancho on Plum Creek, where my pack awaited me. As I attacked a late and lonely supper, the gawky son of the family sat up to the table and leisurely dressed my fish under my very nose—but a hunter's stomach does not mind these little things.

My writing kept me busy till within two hours of sunset next day, and then there was a rough seventeen miles between me and the necessary post-office. Over hills and valleys, gullies, irrigating ditches, and cactus I stumbled on through the dark, steering by the stars; and at last reached Sedalia, just in time for the mail, but wet, lame, and ravenous. A pair of scales showed me that my load—the heavy rifle and six-shooter, cartridge-belt, knapsack, blanket, change of shirt and stockings, etc., weighed thirty-seven pounds; and that at once struck me as "riding a free horse to death." Thenceforth all that could possibly be spared went ahead from station to station on the broader shoulders of the express company; and many a night I nearly froze for want of the blanket which was sure to be ahead of or behind me.

Lightened by twelve grateful pounds I resumed the march next day, zigzagging for a week from road to mountains and back again, as the whim seized me, finding enough game to be interesting, and enjoying every moment as keenly as only trained muscles and careless mind can enjoy. The full moon was high overhead as I wound through the lonely cañon of Plum Creek; and midway of that bare defile my ears pricked up at an old familiar sound, for years unheard and almost forgotten—the long, weird howl of the gray wolf. It is a cry to make the blood curdle; but there was no answering yell, and after the first startled grab at the butt of my forty-four I plodded on.

At Larkspur that night there awaited me a cold welcome. It was bitter weather. Under the watertank the ice was three inches thick, and the savage wind roared down the cañon in icy gusts. There was no place to sleep save in the "bunk-house." That had one occupant, and he had one blanket. My own was in Colorado Springs, and not even a gunny-sack was to be found to mitigate the night. The old track-walker shivered under his one tattered cover, and would have no fire in the battered stove; he said it "would make the boogs too wa-ake-ful." I froze on the bare planks till midnight and then in desperation took the law and the stove into my own hands and built a roaring fire, which made the night endurable, though I had to sally forth several times before morning to "rustle" fuel.

From Larkspur to the top of the divide, 8000 feet above sea level, was a steady uphill pull, growing cooler at every step and in the teeth of the very worst wind I ever encountered. By afternoon it was a perfect gale, against which I could make scant two miles an hour by the most violent exertion. At the door of one lonely house I knocked, and politely asked if they could lend me an auger. "What d'ye want of a auger?" snapped the hard-faced woman who answered my rap. "Why, I thought, madam, that it might help me bore through this wind"—but she slammed the door in the face of this ill-timed witticism, and I went without dinner to pay for being "funny."

The temperature kept falling and the gale rising as the day wore on. It was already generously below zero. Near the aptly named side track of Greenland, I was crossing a trestle which spans Carpenter's Creek when a sudden gust, resistless as a wall, swept me off bodily and flung me upon the ice and frozen sand a score of feet below. The ice—thanks to the wind—had but lately formed, and through I went into a shallow pool. It was better than falling on the slag rip-rap at the ends of the bridge; but the eight miles to shelter, walking with clothing frozen stiff as a plank and nearly every bone in my body aching, were anything but hilarious.

From the top of the divide there were no temptations from a straight road to Colorado Springs, the lovely little city in the edge of the plain under the very shadow of Pike's Peak.

Sallying forth from pretty little Manitou at 10 A.M. on November 4 I strode up the steep trail to Engleman's Cañon, bound for Pike's Peak. This was before the skyward railroad had been built or even planned, and to get to the top of that giant mountain one had then to earn his passage. But mountain-climbing was an old story, and for several miles I found little difficulty. The old trail was very rough and steep along the dashing brook, whose fringe of bushes bent with pear-shaped icicles. It seemed odd to see icicles with the big end down; but these came from the spray, which, of course, was thickest near the brook.

After getting up out of the cañon, and upon a southerly spur of the peak, I began to find trouble with the snow, which had drifted a couple of feet deep in the trough-like trail. There was no dodging it, however, for outside the one path all was loose, sharp rocks. At the wild, desolate timberline, where the last scrubby dwarf of a tree clung sadly amid the rocks, matters grew worse; for as soon as I rounded Windy Point, a savage, icy blast from the snow peaks of the Sangre de Cristo fairly stabbed me through and through. My perspiration-soaked clothing turned stiff as a board in five minutes, and the very marrow in my bones seemed frozen despite the violent exercise of climbing. Worst of all, it was almost impossible to breathe in the face of that icy gale, though otherwise I have never felt any of the unpleasant symptoms, either in heart, lungs, or nerves, experienced by many at that altitude.

It was 3:30 P.M. when I stood panting at the door of the signal service station on the very crest of Pike's Peak—then, and perhaps still, the highest inhabited building on earth. There are many curious things about an altitude of two miles and a half above the sea. The nerves are always affected seriously in time, and often very unpleasantly at once. Few people can sleep at first at such an elevation. The rare air seems to evaporate on one's skin, and leaves a delicious coolness like that from an alcohol bath. The great lessening of the atmospheric pressure gives a strange and delightful sense of buoyancy.

The view from Pike's Peak is of the noblest and strangest. Such a vista could only be where the greatest mountains elbow the infinite plains. At their edge are the cameos of Manitou and Colorado Springs; the Garden of the Gods, now a toy; the dark thread of the Ute Pass, through which, in Leadville's palmy days, streamed the motley human tide. Seventy miles north is the cloud that is Denver. Fifty miles to the south, the smoke of Pueblo curls up from the prairie, falls back and trails along the plain in a misty belt, that reaches farther eastward than the eye can follow. A little pond-like broadening in this smoke-river shows the location of La Junta, one hundred miles away. West of south, in long and serried ranks, stand the Culebra and Sangre de Cristo ranges, while nearer, tower the southern walls of the Grand Cañon of the Arkansas. Off to the west are the far giants of the Rockies in incomparable phalanx—for Pike stands in regal isolation a hundred miles from any peer.

With the setting of the sun came a sight even more memorable. As the red disk sank behind the west, the gigantic shadow of the peak crept up on the foothills, leapt across the plains, and climbed at last the far horizon and stood high in the paling heavens, a vast, shadowy pyramid. It is a startling thing to see a shadow in the sky. For a few moments it lingers and then fades in the slow twilight.

A perpendicular mile below my feet that night the soft, fleecy clouds went drifting along the scarred flanks of the grim, unmindful giant, while the full moon poured down on them her cold, white glory. Dimmer than the clouds, I traced the white wraiths of Pike's brother titans, as they tossed back the snow-hair from their furrowed brows, and stared solemnly at the round-faced moon. The icy wind howled against the low building, or dashed off to drive his cloud-flocks scurrying hither and yon down the deepest passes of the range. Time seems hardly to exist up there. Alive, one is yet out of the world. The impression could hardly be stronger if one stood upon a planet sole in all space.

DAVID DOUGLAS

Tough Trip Through Paradise

"The most courageous mind feels weakened and
  unhinged . . ."

Never was there a walking party more picturesque than that which set out on the island of Hawaii in January of 1834—an asthmatic guide who cowered under an umbrella rain or shine; a one-eyed porter too weak to carry a quire of paper; a bird catcher who caught no birds. Leading this motley crew was David Douglas, the Scottish-born botanist who proved to be one of the greatest plant collectors for the Royal Horticultural Society (the Douglas fir is named for him). One day thousands of Americans would follow his steps to their newest state. David Douglas died six months after the journey described here; he fell into a pit containing a wild bull, and was gored to death.

This account is from the Journal Kept by David Douglas During His Travels in North America, *edited by W. Wilks and published under the direction of the Royal Horticultural Society by William Wesley & Son, London, 1914. A few meteorological notes and incidental observations have been omitted.*

On the 22nd of January, the air being pleasant, and the sun occasionally visible, I had all my packages assorted by nine A.M., and engaged my old guide, Honori, and nine men to accompany me to the volcano and to Mouna Roa. As usual, there was a formidable display of luggage, consisting of *Tapas, Calabashes, Poe, Taro*, &c., while each individual provided himself with the solace of a staff of sugar-cane, which shortens with the distance, for the pedestrian, when tired and thirsty, sits down and bites off an inch or two from the end of his staff. A friend accompanied me as far as his house on the road, where there is a large church, his kind intention being to give me some provision for the excursion, but as he was a stout person, I soon outstripped him.

On leaving the bay, we passed through a fertile spot, consisting of Taro patches in ponds, where the ground is purposely overflowed, and afterwards covered with a deep layer of Fern-leaves to keep it damp. Here were fine groves of *Bread-fruit* and ponds of Mullet and Ava-fish; the scenery is beautiful, being studded with dwellings and little plantations of vegetables and of *Morus papyrifera*, of which there are two kinds, one much whiter than the other. The most striking feature in the vegetation consists in the Tree-fern, some smaller species of the same tribe, and a curious kind of *Compositae*, like an *Eupatorium*. At about four miles and a half from the bay, we entered the wood, through which there is a tolerably cleared path, the muddy spots being rendered passable by the stems or trunks of Tree-ferns, laid close together crosswise.

About an hour's walk brought us through the wood, and we then crossed another open plain of three miles and a half, at the upper end of which, in a most beautiful situation, stands the church, and close to it the chief's house. Some heavy showers had drenched us through; still, as soon as our friend arrived, and the needful arrangements were made, I started and continued the ascent over a very gently rising ground, in a southerly direction, passing through some delightful country, interspersed with low timber.

At night we halted at a house, of which the owner was a very civil person, though remarkably talkative. Four old women were inmates of the same dwelling, one of whom, eighty years of age, with hair white as snow, was engaged in feeding two favourite cats with fish. My little terrier disputed the fare with them, to the no small annoyance of their mistress. A well-looking young female amused me with singing, while she was engaged in the process of cooking a dog on heated stones. I also observed a handsome young man, whose very strong stiff black hair was allowed to grow to a great length on the top of his head, while it was cut close over the ears, and falling down on the back of his head and neck, had all the appearance of a Roman helmet.

January the 23rd. This morning the old lady was engaged in feeding a dog with fox-like ears, instead of her cats. She compelled the poor animal to swallow *Poe*, by cramming it into his mouth, and what he put out at the sides, she took up and ate herself; this she did, as she informed me, by way of fattening the dog for food. A little while before daylight my host went to the door of the lodge, and after calling over some extraordinary words which would seem to set orthography at defiance, a loud grunt in response from under the thick shade of some adjoining Tree-ferns, was followed by the appearance of a fine large black pig, which coming at his master's call, was forthwith caught and killed for the use of myself and my attendants. The meat was cooked on heated stones, and three men were kindly sent to carry it to the volcano, a distance of twenty-three miles, tied up in the large leaves of Banana and Ti-tree.

The morning was deliciously cool and clear, with a light breeze. Immediately on passing through a narrow belt of wood, where the timber was large, and its trunks matted with parasitic Ferns, I arrived at a tract of ground, over which there was but a scanty covering of soil above the lava, interspersed with low bushes and Ferns. Here I beheld one of the grandest scenes imaginable;—Mouna Roa reared his bold front, covered with snow, far above the region of verdure, while Mouna Kuah was similarly clothed, to the timber region on the South side, while the summit was cleared of the snow that had fallen on the nights of the 12th and two following days. The district of Hido, 'Byron's Bay,' which I had quitted the previous day, presented, from its great moisture, a truly lovely appearance, contrasting in a striking manner with the country where I then stood, and which extended to the sea, whose surface bore evident signs of having been repeatedly ravaged by volcanic fires.

In the distance, to the South-West, the dense black cloud which overhangs the great volcano, attests, amid the otherwise unsullied purity of the sky, the mighty operations at present going on in that immense laboratory. The lava, throughout the whole district, appeared to be of every colour and shape, compact, bluish and black, porous or vesicular, heavy and light. In some places it lies in regular lines and masses, resembling narrow horizontal basaltic columns; in others, in tortuous forms, or gathered into rugged humps of small elevation; while, scattered over the whole plain, are numerous extinct, abrupt, generally circular craters, varying in height from one hundred to three hundred feet, and with about an equal diameter at their tops.

The steam that now arose from the cracks bespoke our near approach to the summit, and at two P.M., I arrived at its northern extremity, where finding it nearly level, and observing that water was not far distant, I chose that spot for my encampment. As, however, the people were not likely to arrive before the evening, I took a walk round the West side, now the most active part of the volcano, and sat down there, not correctly speaking, to enjoy, but to gaze with wonder and amazement on this terrific sight, which inspired the beholder with a fearful pleasure.

From the description of former visitors, I judge that Mouna Roa must now be in a state of comparative tranquillity. A lake of liquid fire, in extent about a thirteenth part of the whole crater, was boiling with furious agitation; not constantly, however, for at one time it appeared calm and level, the numerous fiery red streaks on its surface alone attesting its state of ebullition, when again, the red hot lava would dart upwards and boil with a terrific grandeur, spouting to a height which, from the distance at which I stood, I calculated to be from forty to seventy feet, when it would dash violently against the black ledge, and then subside again for a few moments.

Close by the fire was a chimney, about forty feet high, which occasionally discharges its steam, as if all the steam-engines in the world were concentrated in it. This preceded the tranquil state of the lake, which is situated near the South-West, or smaller end of the crater. In the centre of the Great Crater, a second lake of fire, of circular form, but smaller dimensions, was boiling with equal intensity: the noise was dreadful beyond all description.

The people having arrived, Honori last, my tent was pitched twenty yards back from the perpendicular wall of the crater; and as there was an old hut of Ti-leaves on the intermediate bank, only six feet from the extreme verge, my people soon repaired it for their own use. As the sun sunk behind the western flank of Mouna Roa, the splendour of the scene increased; but when the nearly full moon rose in a cloudless sky, and shed her silvery brightness on the fiery lake, roaring and boiling in fearful majesty, the spectacle became so commanding, that I lost a fine night for making astronomical observations, by gazing on the volcano, the illumination of which was but little diminished by a thick haze that set in at midnight.

On Friday, January the 24th, the air was delightfully clear, and I was enabled to take the bearings of the volcano and adjoining objects with great exactness. I had furnished shoes for those persons who should descend into the crater with me, but none of them could walk when so equipped, preferring a mat sole, made of tough leaves, and fastened round the heel and between the toes, which seemed indeed to answer the purpose entirely well. Accompanied by three individuals, I proceeded at one P.M. along the North side, and descended the first ledge over such rugged ground as bespoke a long state of repose, the fissures and flanks being clothed with verdure of considerable size: thence we ascended two hundred feet to the level platform that divides the great and small volcanoes.

On the left, a perpendicular rock, three hundred feet above the level, shows the extent of the volcano to have been originally much greater than it is at present. The small crater appears to have enjoyed a long period of tranquillity, for down to the very edge of the crust of the lava, particularly on the East side, there are trees of considerable size, on which I counted from sixty to one hundred and twenty-four annual rings or concentric layers. The lava at the bottom flowed from a spot, nearly equidistant from the great and small craters, both uniting into a river, from forty to seventy yards in breadth, and which appears comparatively recent. A little South of this stream, over a dreadfully rugged bank, I descended the first ledge of the crater, and proceeded for three hundred yards over a level space, composed of ashes, scoriae, and large stones that have been ejected from the mouth of the volcano. The stream formerly described is the only fluid lava here.

A most uncomfortable feeling is experienced when the traveller becomes aware that the lava is hollow and faithless beneath his tread. Of all sensations in nature, that produced by earthquakes or volcanic agency is the most alarming: the strongest nerves are unstrung and the most courageous mind feels weakened and unhinged, when exposed to either.

I remained for upwards of two hours in the crater, suffering all the time an intense headache, with my pulse strong and irregular, and my tongue parched, together with other symptoms of fever. The intense heat and sulphurous nature of the ground had corroded my shoes so much, that they barely protected my feet from the hot lava. I ascended out of the crater at the South-West, and returned by the West side to my tent, having thus walked quite round this mighty crater. The evening was foggy; I took some cooling medicine, and lay down early to rest.

Saturday, January the 25th. I slept profoundly till two A.M., when, as not a speck could be seen on the horizon, and the moon was unusually bright, I rose with the intention of making some lunar observations, but though the thermometer stood at 41°, still the keen mountain-breeze affected me so much, of course mainly owing to the fatigue and heat I had suffered the day before, that I was reluctantly obliged to relinquish the attempt, and being unable to settle again to sleep, I replenished my blazing stock of fuel, and sat gazing on the roaring and agitated state of the crater, where three new fires had burst out since ten o'clock the preceding evening. Poor Honori, my guide, who is a martyr to asthma, was so much affected by their exhalations (for they were on the North bank, just below my tent), that he coughed incessantly the whole night, and complained of cold, though he was wrapped in my best blanket, besides his own tapas and some other articles which he had borrowed from my Woahu man. The latter slept with his head toward the fire, coiled up most luxuriously, and neither cold, heat, nor the roaring of the volcano at all disturbed his repose.

Leaving the charge of my papers and collections under the special care of one individual, and giving plenty of provision for twelve days to the rest, consisting of one quarter of pork, with *poe* and *taro*, I started for Kapupala soon after eight A.M. The path struck off for two miles in a North-West direction, to avoid the rugged lava and ashes on the West flank of Mouna Roa, still it was indescribably difficult in many places, as the lava rose in great masses, some perpendicular, others lying horizontal, in fact with every variation of form and situation. In other parts the walking was pretty good, over grassy undulating plains, clothed with a healthy sward, and studded here and there with *Maurarii* Trees in full blossom, a beautifull tree, much resembling the English Laburnum. Arrived at Kapupala, at three P.M., I found that the chief or head man had prepared a house for me, a nice and clean dwelling, with abundance of fine mats, &c., but as near it there stood several large canoes filled with water, containing Mulberry Bark in a state of fermentation, and highly offensive, as also a large pig-fold, surrounded by a lava-wall, and shaded with large bushes of *Ricinus communis*, altogether forming an unsuitable situation for making observations, to say nothing of the din and bustle constantly going on when strangers are present, besides the annoyance from fleas, I caused my tent to be pitched one hundred yards behind the house.

The chief would have been better pleased if I had occupied his dwelling, but through Honori, I had this matter explained to his satisfaction. He sent me a fowl, cooked on heated stones underground, some baked Taro, and Sweet Potatoes, together with a calabash full of delicious goat's-milk, poured through the husk of a Cocoa-nut in lieu of a sieve.

Tuesday, January the 28th. I hired two guides, the elder of whom a short stout man, was particularly recommended to me by the chief, for his knowledge of the mountain. By profession he is a birdcatcher, going in quest of that particular kind of bird which furnishes the feathers of which the ancient cloaks, used by the natives of these islands, are made. The other guide was a young man. Three volunteers offered to accompany me; one a very stout, fat dame, apparently about thirty, another not much more than half that age, a really well-looking girl, tall and athletic: but to the first, the bird-catcher gave such an awful account of the perils to be undergone, that both the females finally declined the attempt, and only the third person, a young man, went with me.

My original party of ten, besides Honori and the two guides, set out at eight, with, as usual, a terrible array of Taro, calabashes full of Poe, Sweet Potatoes, dry Poe tied up in Ti-leaves, and goat's flesh, each bearing a pole on his shoulder with a bundle at either end. Of their vegetable food, a Sandwich Islander cannot carry more than a week's consumption, besides what he may pick up on the way.

One, whose office it was to convey five quires of paper for me, was so strangely attired, in a double-milled grey great coat, with a spencer of still thicker materials above it, that he lamented to his companions that his load was too great, and begged their help to lift it on his back. I had to show the fellow, who was blind of one eye, the unreasonableness of his grumbling by hanging the parcel, by the cord, on my little finger. He said, "Ah! the stranger is strong," and walked off. Among my attendants was one singular-looking personage, a stripling, who carried a small packet of instruments, and trotted away, arrayed in "a Cutty-Sark," of most "scanty longitude," the upper portion of which had been once of white, and the lower of red flannel. Honori brought up the rear, with a small telescope slung over his shoulder, and an umbrella, which, owing perhaps to his asthmatic complaint, he never fails to carry with him, both in fair and foul weather.

We returned for about a mile and a half along the road that led to the Great Volcano, and then struck off to the left in a small path that wound in a northerly direction up the green grassy flank of Mouna Roa. I soon found that Honori's cough would not allow him to keep up with the rest of the party, so leaving one guide with him, and making the bird-catcher take the lead, I proceeded at a quicker rate. This part of the island is very beautiful; the ground, though hilly, is covered with a tolerably thick coating of soil, which supports a fine sward of Grass, Ferns, climbing plants, and in some places, timber of considerable size, Coa, Tutui, and Mamme trees. Though fallen trees and brushwood occasionally intercepted the path, still it was by no means so difficult as that by which I had ascended Mouna Kuah.

To avoid a woody point of steep ascent, we turned a little east-

ward, after having travelled about five miles and a half, and passed
several deserted dwellings, apparently only intended as the temporary
abodes of bird-catchers and sandal-wood-cutters. Calabashes and
Pumpkins, with Tobacco, were the only plants that I observed growing near them. At eleven A.M. we came to a small pool of fresh
water, collected in the lava; here my people halted for a few minutes
to smoke. The wind was from the South, with a gentle fanning breeze
and a clear sky.

Hence the path turns North-West, for a mile and half, becoming
a little steeper, till it leads to a beautiful circular well, three feet deep,
flowing in the lava, its banks fringed with Strawberry Vines, and
shaded by an Acacia Tree grove. Here we again rested for half an
hour. I would recommend to any Naturalists who may in future visit
this mountain, to have their canteens filled at the well just mentioned, for my guide, trusting to one which existed in a cave further
up, and which he was unable to find, declined to provide himself with
this indispensable article at the lower well, and we were consequently
put to the greatest inconvenience.

At four P.M. we arrived at a place where the lava suddenly
became very rugged, and the brushwood low, where we rested and
chewed sugar-cane, of which we carried a large supply, and where the
guides were anxious to remain all night. As this was not very desir-
able, since we had no water, I proceeded for an hour longer, to what
might be called the Line of Shrubs, and at two miles and a half
further on, encamped for the night. We collected some small stems
of a heath-like plant, which, with the dried stalks of the same species
of *Compositae* which I observed on Mouna Kuah, afforded a tolerably
good fire. The man who carried the provisions did not make his
appearance—indeed it is very difficult, except by literally driving them
before you, to make the natives keep up with an active traveller. Thus
I had to sup upon Taro-roots. Honori, as I expected, did not come
up.

I had no view of the surrounding country, for the region below,
especially over the land, was covered with a thick layer of fleecy mist,
and the cloud which always hovers above the great volcano, overhung
the horizon and rose into the air, like a great tower. Sunset gave a
totally different aspect to the whole, the fleecy clouds changed their
hue to a vapoury tint, and the volume of mist above the volcano,
which is silvery bright during the prevalence of sunshine, assumed a
fiery aspect, and illumined the sky for many miles around. A strong

North-West mountain-breeze sprung up, and the stars, especially Canopus and Sirius, shone with unusual brilliancy. Never, even under a tropical sky, did I behold so many stars. Sheltered by a little brush-wood, I lay down on the lava beside the fire, and enjoyed a good night's rest, while my attendants swarmed together in a small cave, which they literally converted into an oven by the immense fire they kindled in it.

Wednesday, January the 29th. The morning rose bright and clear, but cold, from the influence of a keen mountain-breeze. As the man who carried the provisions was still missing, the preparation of breakfast occupied but little time, so that, accompanied by the bird-catcher and Cutty-Sark, I started at half-past six for the summit of the mountain, leaving the others to collect fuel and to look for water. Shortly before daybreak the sky was exceedingly clear and beautiful, especially that part of the horizon where the sun rose, and above which the upper limb of his disc was visible like a thread of gold, soon to be quenched in a thick haze, which was extended over the horizon. It were difficult, nay, almost impossible, to describe the beauty of the sky and the glorious scenes of this day.

The lava is terrible beyond description, and our track lay over ledges of the roughest kind, in some places glassy and smooth like slag from the furnace, compact and heavy like basalt; in others, tumbled into enormous mounds, or sunk in deep valleys, or rent into fissures, ridges, and clefts. This was at the verge of the snow—not twenty yards of the whole space could be called level or even. In every direction vast holes or mouths are seen, varying in size, form, and colour, from ten to seventy feet high. The lava that has been vomited forth from these openings presents a truly novel spectacle. From some, and occasionally indeed from the same mouth, the streams may be seen, pressed forward transversely, or in curved segments, while other channels present a floating appearance; occasionally the circular tortu-ous masses resemble gigantic cables, or are drawn into cords, or even capillary threads, finer than any silken thread, and carried to a great distance by the wind.

Walking was rendered dangerous by the multitude of fissures, many of which are but slightly covered with a thin crust, and every-where our progress was exceedingly laborious and fatiguing. As we continued to ascend, the cold and fatigue disheartened the Islanders, who required all the encouragement I could give to induce them to proceed. As I took the lead, it was needful for me to look behind me continually, for when once out of sight, they would pop themselves down, and neither rise nor answer my call.

After resting a few moments at the last station, I proceeded about seven miles further, over a similar kind of formation, till I came to a sort of low ridge, the top of which I gained soon after eleven. This part was of gradual ascent, and its summit might be considered the southern part of the dome. The snow became very deep, and the influence of the sun melting its crust, which concealed the sharp points of the lava, was very unfavourable to my progress. From this place to the North towards the centre of the dome, the hill is more flattened. Rested a short time, and a few moments before noon, halted near the highest black shaggy chimney to observe the sun's passage. The summit of this extraordinary mountain is so flat, that from this point no part of the island can be seen, not even the high peaks of Mouna Kuah, nor the distant horizon of the sea, though the sky was remarkably clear. It is a horizon of itself, and about seven miles in diameter.

I ought, ere now, to have said that the bird-catcher's knowledge of the volcano did not rise above the woody region, and now he and my two other followers were unable to proceed further. Leaving these three behind, and accompanied by only Calipio, I went on about two miles and a half, when the Great Terminal Volcano or Cone of Mouna Roa burst on my view: all my attempts to scale the black ledge here were ineffectual, as the fissures in the lava were so much concealed, though not protected by the snow, that the undertaking was accompanied with great danger. Most reluctantly was I obliged to return, without being able to measure accurately its extraordinary depth.

From this point I walked along upon the brink of the high ledge, along the East side, to the hump, so to speak, of the mountain, the point which, as seen from Mouna Kuah, appears the highest.

As I stood on the brink of the ledge, the wind whirled up from the cavity with such furious violence that I could hardly keep my footing within twenty paces of it. The ancient crater has an extent of about twenty-four miles. Terrible chasms exist at the bottom, appearing, in some places, as if the mountain had been rent to its very roots: no termination can be seen to their depth, even when the eye is aided with a good glass, and the sky is clear of smoke, and the sun shining brightly. Fearful indeed must the spectacle have been, when this volcano was in a state of activity. Near the top I saw one small bird, about the size of a common sparrow, of a light mixed grey colour, with a faintly yellow beak—no other living creature met my view above the woody region. This little creature, which was perched on a block of lava, was so tame as to permit me to catch it with my hand, when I instantly restored it its liberty. I also saw a dead hawk in one of the caves.

At four P.M. I returned to the centre of the dome, where I found the three men whom I had left huddling together to keep themselves warm. After collecting a few specimens of lava, no time was to be lost in quitting this dreary and terrific scene. The descent was even more fatiguing, dangerous, and distressing than the ascent had proved, and required great caution in us to escape unhurt; for the natives, benumbed with cold, could not walk fast. Darkness came on all too quickly, and though the twilight is of considerable duration, I was obliged to halt, as I feared, for the night, in a small cave. Here, though sheltered from the North-West breeze, which set in more and more strongly as the sun sunk below the horizon, the thermometer fell to 19°, and as I was yet far above the line of vegetation, unable to obtain any materials for a fire, and destitute of clothing except the thin garments soaked in perspiration in which I had travelled all day, and which rendered the cold most intense to my feelings, I ventured, between ten and eleven P.M. to make an effort to proceed to the camp.

Never shall I forget the joy I felt when the welcome moon, for whose appearance I had long been watching, first showed herself above the volcano. Her pale face actually threw a glow of warmth into my whole frame, and I joyfully and thankfully rose to scramble over the rough way, in the solitude of the night, rather than await the approach of day in this comfortless place. Not so thought my followers. The bird-catcher and his two companions would not stir; so with my trusty man Calipio, who follows me like a shadow, I proceeded in the descent.

Of necessity we walked slowly, stepping cautiously from ledge to ledge, but still having exercise enough to excite a genial heat. The splendid constellation of Orion, which had so often attracted my admiring gaze in my own native land, and which had shortly passed the meridian, was my guide. I continued in a South-East direction till two o'clock, when all at once I came to a low place, full of stunted shrubs, of more robust habit, however, than those at the camp. No response was given to our repeated calls—it was evident that no human being was near, so by the help of the moon's light, we shortly collected plenty of fuel, and kindled a fine fire. No sooner did its warmth and light begin to diffuse themselves over my frame, than I found myself instantly seized with violent pain and inflammation in my eyes, which had been rather painful on the mountain, from the effect of the sun's rays shining on the snow; a slight discharge of blood from both eyes followed, which gave me some relief, and which proved that the attack was as much attributable to violent fatigue as any other cause.

Having tasted neither food nor water since an early hour in the morning, I suffered severely from thirst; still I slept for a few hours, dreaming the while of gurgling cascades, overhung with sparkling rainbows, of which the dewy spray moistened my whole body, while my lips were all the time glued together with thirst, and my parched tongue almost rattled in my mouth. My poor man, Calipio, was also attacked with inflammation in his eyes, and gladly did we hail the approach of day.

The sun rose brightly on the morning of Thursday, January 30th, and gilding the snow over which we had passed, showed our way to have been infinitely more rugged and precarious than it had appeared by moon-light. I discovered that by keeping about a mile and a half too much to the East, we had left camp nearly five hundred feet above our present situation; and returning thither over the rocks, we found Honori engaged in preparing breakfast. He had himself reached the camp about noon on the second day. He gave me a Calabash full of water, with a large piece of ice in it, which refreshed me greatly. A few drops of opium in the eyes afforded instant relief both to Calipio and myself. The man with the provision was here also, so we shortly made a comfortable meal, and immediately after, leaving one man behind with some food for the bird-catcher and his two companions, we prepared to descend, and started at nine A.M. to retrace the path by which we had come.

Gratified though one may be at witnessing the wonderful works of God in such a place as the summit of a mountain presents, still it is with thankfulness that we again approach a climate more congenial to our natures, and welcome the habitations of our fellow-men, where we are refreshed with the scent of vegetation, and soothed by the melody of birds. When about three miles below the camp, my three companions of yesterday appeared like mawkins, on the craggy lava, just at the very spot where I had come down. A signal was made them to proceed to the camp, which was seen and obeyed, and we proceeded onwards, collecting a good many plants by the way. Arriving at Strawberry Well, we made a short halt to dine. We arrived at Kapupala at four P.M. The three other men came up at seven, much fatigued, like myself.

HENRY DAVID THOREAU

A Winter Walk

"The tracks of men and beasts are lost . . ."

We begin and end with Thoreau. This clean and bracing account of a winter walk, taken in "happy resistance to the cold," is less well-known than his classic essay on "Walking." Yet one Thoreau scholar considers this Thoreau at his best, while another judges it "the most evocative and lyrical short prose work Thoreau ever wrote." Evocative and lyrical it is—and more. Here Thoreau captures the ultimate in walking: the mind and body are in step, the eye is clear, the ear alert and the skin alive, and the walker himself is indispensably a part of the path he walks.

This account is taken from the Excursions *volume of* The Writings of Thoreau, *Riverside Edition, published by Houghton, Mifflin and Company,* 1893.

The wind has gently murmured through the blinds, or puffed with feathery softness against the windows, and occasionally sighed like a summer zephyr lifting the leaves along, the livelong night. The meadow-mouse has slept in his snug gallery in the sod, the owl has sat in a hollow tree in the depth of the swamp, the rabbit, the squirrel, and the fox have all been housed. The watch-dog has lain quiet on the hearth, and the cattle have stood silent in their stalls. The earth itself has slept, as it were its first, not its last sleep, save when some street-sign or wood-house door has faintly creaked upon its hinge, cheering forlorn nature at her midnight work,—the only sound awake 'twixt Venus and Mars,—advertising us of a remote inward warmth, a divine cheer and fellowship, where gods are met together, but where it is very bleak for man to stand. But while the earth has slumbered, all the air has been alive with feathery flakes descending, as if some northern Ceres reigned, showering her silvery grain over all the fields.

We sleep, and at length awake to the still reality of a winter morning. The snow lies warm as cotton or down upon the window-sill; the broadened sash and frosted panes admit a dim and private light, which enhances the snug cheer within. The stillness of the morning is impressive. The floor creaks under our feet as we move toward the window to look abroad through some clear space over the fields. We see the roofs stand under their snow burden. From the eaves and fences hang stalactites of snow, and in the yard stand stalagmites covering some concealed core. The trees and shrubs rear white arms to the sky on every side; and where were walls and fences, we see fantastic forms stretching in frolic gambols across the dusky landscape, as if nature had strewn her fresh designs over the fields by night as models for man's art.

Silently we unlatch the door, letting the drift fall in, and step abroad to face the cutting air. Already the stars have lost some of their sparkle, and a dull, leaden mist skirts the horizon. A lurid brazen light in the east proclaims the approach of day, while the western landscape is dim and spectral still, and clothed in a sombre Tartarian light, like the shadowy realms. They are Infernal sounds only that you hear; the crowing of cocks, the barking of dogs, the chopping of wood, the lowing of kine, all seem to come from Pluto's barn-yard and beyond the Styx,—not for any melancholy they suggest, but their twilight bustle is too solemn and mysterious for earth. The recent tracks of the fox or otter, in the yard, remind us that each hour of the night is crowded with events, and the primeval nature is still working and making tracks in the snow. Opening the gate, we tread briskly along the lone country road, crunching the dry and crisped snow under our feet, or aroused by the sharp clear creak of the wood sled, just starting for the distant market, from the early farmer's door, where it has lain the summer long, dreaming amid the chips and stubble; while far through the drifts and powdered windows we see the farmer's early candle, like a paled star, emitting a lonely beam, as if some severe virtue were at its matins there. And one by one the smokes begin to ascend from the chimneys amid the trees and snows.

We hear the sound of wood-chopping at the farmers' doors, far over the frozen earth, the baying of the house-dog, and the distant clarion of the cock,—though the thin and frosty air conveys only the finer particles of sound to our ears, with short and sweet vibrations, as the waves subside soonest on the purest and lightest liquids, in which gross substances sink to the bottom. They come clear and bell-like, and from a greater distance in the horizon, as if there were fewer impediments than in summer to make them faint and ragged. The ground is sonorous, like seasoned wood, and even the ordinary rural sounds are melodious, and the jingling of the ice on the trees is sweet and liquid. There is the least possible moisture in the atmosphere, all being dried up, or congealed, and it is of such extreme tenuity and elasticity that it becomes a source of delight. The withdrawn and tense sky seems groined like the aisles of a cathedral, and the polished air sparkles as if there were crystals of ice floating in it. . . .

The sun at length rises through the distant woods, as if with the faint clashing swinging sound of cymbals, melting the air with his beams, and with such rapid steps the morning travels, that already his rays are gilding the distant western mountains. Meanwhile we step hastily along through the powdery snow, warmed by an inward heat, enjoying an Indian summer still, in the increased glow of thought and feeling. Probably if our lives were more conformed to nature, we should not need to defend ourselves against her heats and colds, but find her our constant nurse and friend, as do plants and quadrupeds. If our bodies were fed with pure and simple elements, and not with a stimulating and heating diet, they would afford no more pasture for cold than a leafless twig, but thrive like the trees, which find even winter genial to their expansion.

The wonderful purity of nature at this season is a most pleasing fact. Every decayed stump and moss-grown stone and rail, and the dead leaves of autumn, are concealed by a clean napkin of snow. In the bare fields and tinkling woods, see what virtue survives. In the coldest and bleakest places, the warmest charities still maintain a foothold. A cold and searching wind drives away all contagion, and nothing can withstand it but what has a virtue in it, and accordingly, whatever we meet with in cold and bleak places, as the tops of mountains, we respect for a sort of sturdy innocence, a Puritan toughness. All things beside seem to be called in for shelter, and what stays out must be part of the original frame of the universe, and of such valor as God himself. It is invigorating to breathe the cleansed air. Its greater fineness and purity are visible to the eye, and we would fain stay out long and late, that the gales may sigh through us, too, as through the leafless trees, and fit us for the winter,—as if we hoped to borrow some pure and steadfast virtue, which will stead us in all seasons.

There is a slumbering subterranean fire in nature which never goes out, and which no cold can chill. It finally melts the great snow, and in January or July is only buried under a thicker or thinner covering. In the coldest day it flows somewhere, and the snow melts around every tree. This field of winter rye, which sprouted late in the fall, and now speedily dissolves the snow, is where the fire is very thinly covered. We feel warmed by it. In the winter, warmth stands for all virtue, and we resort in thought to a trickling rill, with its bare stones shining in the sun, and to warm springs in the woods, with so much eagerness as rabbits and robins. The steam which rises from swamps and pools is as dear and domestic as that of our own kettle. What fire could ever equal the sunshine of a winter's day, when the meadow mice come out by the wall-sides, and the chickadee lisps in the defiles of the wood? The warmth comes directly from the sun, and is not radiated from the earth, as in summer; and when we feel his beams on our backs as we are treading some snowy dell, we are grateful as for a special kindness, and bless the sun which has followed us into that by-place.

This subterranean fire has its altar in each man's breast; for in the coldest day, and on the bleakest hill, the traveler cherishes a warmer fire within the folds of his cloak than is kindled on any hearth. A healthy man, indeed, is the complement of the seasons, and in winter, summer is in his heart. There is the south. Thither have all birds and insects migrated, and around the warm springs in his breast are gathered the robin and the lark.

At length, having reached the edge of the woods, and shut out the gadding town, we enter within their covert as we go under the roof of a cottage, and cross its threshold, all ceiled and banked up with snow. They are glad and warm still, and as genial and cheery in winter as in summer. As we stand in the midst of the pines in the flickering and checkered light which straggles but little way into their maze, we wonder if the towns have ever heard their simple story. It seems to us that no traveler has ever explored them, and notwithstanding the wonders which science is elsewhere revealing every day, who would not like to hear their annals? Our humble villages in the plain are their contribution. We borrow from the forest the boards which shelter and the sticks which warm us. How important is their evergreen to winter, that portion of the summer which does not fade, the permanent year, the unwithered grass. Thus simply, and with little expense of altitude, is the surface of the earth diversified. What would human life be without forests, those natural cities? From the tops of mountains they appear like smooth-shaven lawns, yet whither shall we walk but in this taller grass?

In this glade covered with bushes of a year's growth, see how the silvery dust lies on every seared leaf and twig, deposited in such infinite and luxurious forms as by their very variety atone for the absence of color. Observe the tiny tracks of mice around every stem, and the triangular tracks of the rabbit. A pure elastic heaven hangs over all, as if the impurities of the summer air, refined and shrunk by the chaste winter's cold, had been winnowed from the heavens upon the earth.

Nature confounds her summer distinctions at this season. The heavens seem to be nearer the earth. The elements are less reserved and distinct. Water turns to ice, rain to snow. The day is but a Scandinavian night. The winter is an arctic summer.

How much more living is the life that is in nature, the furred life which still survives the stinging nights, and, from amidst fields and woods covered with frost and snow, sees the sun rise. The gray squirrel and rabbit are brisk and playful in the remote glens, even on the morning of the cold Friday. Here is our Lapland and Labrador, and for our Esquimaux and Knistenaux, Dog-ribbed Indians, Novazemnlaites, and Spitzbergeners, are there not the ice-cutter and wood-chopper, the fox, musk-rat, and mink?

Still, in the midst of the arctic day, we may trace the summer to its retreats, and sympathize with some contemporary life. Stretched over the brooks, in the midst of the frost-bound meadows, we may observe the submarine cottages of the caddice-worms, the larvae of the Plicipennes; their small cylindrical cases built around themselves, composed of flags, sticks, grass, and withered leaves, shells, and pebbles, in form and color like the wrecks which strew the bottom,— now drifting along over the pebbly bottom, now whirling in tiny eddies and dashing down steep falls, or sweeping rapidly along with the current, or else swaying to and fro at the end of some grass-blade or root. Anon they will leave their sunken habitations, and, crawling up the stems of plants, or to the surface, like gnats, as perfect insects henceforth, flutter over the surface of the water, or sacrifice their short lives in the flame of our candles at evening. Down yonder little glen the shrubs are drooping under their burden, and the red alder-berries contrast with the white ground. Here are the marks of myriad feet which have already been abroad. The sun rises as proudly over such a glen as over the valley of the Seine or the Tiber, and it seems the residence of a pure and self-subsistent valor, such as they never witnessed; which never knew defeat or fear. Here reign the simplicity and purity of a primitive age, and a health and hope far remote from towns and cities. Standing quite alone, far in the forest, while the wind is shaking down snow from the trees, and leaving only the human tracks behind us, we find our reflection of a richer variety than the life of cities. The chickadee and nuthatch are more inspiring society than statesmen and philosophers, and we shall return to these last as to more vulgar companions. In this lonely glen, with its brook draining the slopes, its creased ice and crystals of all hues, where the spruces and hemlocks stand up on either side, and the rush and sere wild oats in the rivulet itself, our lives are more serene and worthy to contemplate. . . .

Now our path begins to ascend gradually to the top of this high hill, from whose precipitous south side we can look over the broad country of forest and field and river, to the distant snowy mountains. See yonder thin column of smoke curling up through the woods from some invisible farmhouse; the standard raised over some rural home-stead. There must be a warmer and more genial spot there below, as where we detect the vapor from a spring forming a cloud above the trees. What fine relations are established between the traveler who discovers this airy column from some eminence in the forest and him who sits below. Up goes the smoke so silently and naturally as the vapor exhales from the leaves, and as busy disposing itself in wreaths as the housewife on the hearth below. It is a hieroglyphic of man's life, and suggests more intimate and important things than the boiling of a pot. Where its fine column rises above the forest, like an ensign, some human life has planted itself,—and such is the begin-ning of Rome, the establishment of the arts, and the foundation of empires, whether on the prairies of America or the steppes of Asia.

And now we descend again, to the brink of this woodland lake, which lies in a hollow of the hills, as if it were their expressed juice, and that of the leaves which are annually steeped in it. Without outlet or inlet to the eye, it has still its history, in the lapse of its waves, in the rounded pebbles on its shore, and in the pines which grow down to its brink. It has not been idle, though sedentary, but, like Abu Musa, teaches that "sitting still at home is the heavenly way; the going out is the way of the world." Yet in its evaporation it travels as far as any. In summer it is the earth's liquid eye; a mirror in the breast of nature. The sins of the wood are washed out in it. See how the woods form an amphitheatre about it, and it is an arena for all the genialness of nature. All trees direct the traveler to its brink, all paths seek it out, birds fly to it, quadrupeds flee to it, and the very ground inclines toward it. It is nature's saloon, where she has sat down to her toilet. Consider her silent economy and tidiness; how the sun comes with his evaporation to sweep the dust from its surface each morning, and a fresh surface is constantly welling up; and annually, after what-ever impurities have accumulated herein, its liquid transparency ap-

pears again in the spring. In summer a hushed music seems to sweep across its surface. But now a plain sheet of snow conceals it from our eyes, except where the wind has swept the ice bare, and the sere leaves are gliding from side to side, tacking and veering on their tiny voyages. Here is one just keeled up against a pebble on shore, a dry beech-leaf, rocking still, as if it would start again. A skillful engineer, methinks, might project its course since it fell from the parent stem. Here are all the elements for such a calculation. Its present position, the direction of the wind, the level of the pond, and how much more is given. In its scarred edges and veins is its log rolled up. . . .

But now, while we have loitered, the clouds have gathered again, and a few straggling snowflakes are beginning to descend. Faster and faster they fall, shutting out the distant objects from sight. The snow falls on every wood and field, and no crevice is forgotten; by the river and the pond, on the hill and in the valley. Quadrupeds are confined to their coverts and the birds sit upon their perches this peaceful hour. There is not so much sound as in fair weather, but silently and gradually every slope, and the gray walls and fences, and the polished ice, and the sere leaves, which were not buried before, are concealed, and the tracks of men and beasts are lost. With so little effort does nature reassert her rule and blot out the traces of men. Hear how Homer has described the same: "The snow-flakes fell thick and fast on a winter's day. The winds are lulled, and the snow falls incessant, covering the tops of the mountains, and the hills, and the plains where the lotus-tree grows, and the cultivated fields, and they are falling by the inlets and shores of the foaming sea, but are silently dissolved by the waves." The snow levels all things, and infolds them deeper in the bosom of nature, as, in the slow summer, vegetation creeps up to the entablature of the temple, and the turrets of the castle, and helps her to prevail over art.

The surly night-wind rustles through the wood, and warns us to retrace our steps, while the sun goes down behind the thickening storm, and birds seek their roosts, and cattle their stalls.

Though winter is represented in the almanac as an old man, facing the wind and sleet, and drawing his cloak about him, we rather think of him as a merry wood-chopper, and warm-blooded youth, as blithe as summer. The unexplored grandeur of the storm keeps up the spirits of the traveler. In winter we lead a more inward life. Our hearts are warm and cheery, like cottages under drifts, whose windows and doors are half concealed, but from whose chimneys the smoke

cheerfully ascends. The imprisoning drifts increase the sense of comfort to sit over the hearth and see the sky through the chimney top,
enjoying the quiet and serene life that may be had in a warm corner
by the chimney side, or feeling our pulse by listening to the low of
cattle in the street, or the sound of the flail in distant barns all the
long afternoon. No doubt a skillful physician could determine our
health by observing how these simple and natural sounds affected us.
We enjoy now, not an oriental, but a boreal leisure, around warm
stoves and fireplaces, and watch the shadow of motes in the sunbeams.

Sometimes our fate grows too homely and familiarly serious ever
to be cruel. Consider how for three months the human destiny is
wrapped in furs. The good Hebrew Revelation takes no cognizance of
all this cheerful snow. Is there no religion for the temperate and frigid
zones? We know of no scripture which records the pure benignity of
the gods on a New England winter night. Their praises have never been
sung, only their wrath deprecated. The best scripture, after all, records
but a meagre faith. Its saints live reserved and austere. Let a brave,
devout man spend the year in the woods of Maine or Labrador, and see
if the Hebrew Scriptures speak adequately to his condition and experience, from the setting in of winter to the breaking up of the ice.

Now commences the long winter evening around the farmer's
hearth, when the thoughts of the indwellers travel far abroad, and
men are by nature and necessity charitable and liberal to all creatures.
Now is the happy resistance to cold, when the farmer reaps his
reward, and thinks of his preparedness for winter, and, through the
glittering panes, sees with equanimity "the mansion of the northern
bear," for now the storm is over.

A Note on the Type

The text of this book was set in Electra, a type face designed by William Addison Dwiggins for the Mergenthaler Linotype Company and first made available in 1935. Electra cannot be classified as either "modern" or "old-style." It is not based on any historical model, and hence does not echo any particular period or style of type design. It avoids the extreme contrast between thick and thin elements that marks most modern faces, and is without eccentricities that catch the eye and interfere with reading. In general, Electra is a simple, readable typeface that attempts to give a feeling of fluidity, power, and speed.

W. A. Dwiggins (1880–1956) began an association with the Mergenthaler Linotype Company in 1929 and over the next twenty-seven years designed a number of book types which include the Metro series, Electra, Caledonia, Eldorado, and Falcon.

The book was composed, printed, and bound by American Book–Stratford Press, Inc., Saddlebrook, New Jersey.

The book was designed by Earl Tidwell.